THE LIBRARY OF HOLOCAUST TESTIMONIES

Life Strictly Forbidden

Life Strictly Forbidden

ANTONI MARIANOWICZ

Translated by
ALICIA NITECKI

VALLENTINE MITCHELL
LONDON • PORTLAND, OR

First published in 2004 in Great Britain by
VALLENTINE MITCHELL
Crown House, 47 Chase Side
Southgate, London N14 5BP

and in the United States of America by
VALLENTINE MITCHELL
c/o ISBS, 920 NE 58th Avenue, 300
Portland, OR, 97213-3786

Website: http://www.vmbooks.com

British Library Cataloguing in Publication Data

Marianowicz, Antoni
    Life Strictly Forbidden. – (Library of Holocaust Testimonies)
    1. Marianowicz, Antoni – Childhood and youth 2. Marianowicz, Antoni –
    Family 3. Holocaust, Jewish (1939–1945) – Poland – Personal narratives
    4. Jewish children – Poland – Biography 5. Protestants – Poland – Biography
    6. Poland – History – Occupation, 1939–1945
    I. Title
    940.5'318'092

ISBN 0-85303-502-4 (paper)

ISSN 1363-3759

Library of Congress Cataloging-in-Publication Data

Marianowicz, Antoni
    Life strictly forbidden/Antoni Marianowicz; translated by Alicia Nitecki.
        p. cm. – (The library of Holocaust testimonies)
    ISBN 0-85303-502-4 (pbk)
        1. Marianowicz, Antoni – Interviews. 2. Jewish Christians – Poland –
    Interviews. 3. Holocaust, Jewish – Poland – Warsaw – Personal narratives.
    4. Marianowicz, Antoni – Family. 5. Marianowicz family – Anecdotes.
    6. Poland – History – Occupation, 1939–1945 – Anecdotes. I. Title. II.
    Series.

    DS135.P63M36973 2004
    940.53'1853841– dc22   2003065118

Typeset in 11/13pt Palatino by FiSH Books, London WC1.
Printed in Great Britain by MPG Books Ltd, Victoria Square, Bodmin,
Cornwall.

For my daughter

Contents

Illustrations

The Library of Holocaust Testimonies

It is greatly to the credit of Frank Cass that this series of survivors' testimonies is being published in Britain. The need for such a series has long been apparent here, where many survivors made their homes.

Since the end of the war in 1945, the terrible events of the Nazi destruction of European Jewry have cast a pall over our time. Six million Jews were murdered within a short period; the few survivors have had to carry in their memories whatever remains of the knowledge of Jewish life in more than a dozen countries, in several thousand towns, in tens of thousands of villages and in innumerable families. The precious gift of recollection has been the sole memorial for millions of people whose lives were suddenly and brutally cut off.

For many years, individual survivors have published their testimonies. But many more have been reluctant to do so, often because they could not believe that they would find a publisher for their efforts.

In my own work over the past two decades, I have been approached by many survivors who had set down their memories in writing, but who did not know how to have them published. I realized what a considerable emotional strain the writing down of such hellish memories had been. I also realized, as I read many dozens of such accounts, how important each account was, in its own way, in recounting aspects of the story that had not been told before, and adding to our understanding of the wide range of human suffering, struggle and aspiration.

With so many people and so many places involved,

including many hundreds of camps, it was inevitable that the historians and students of the Holocaust would find it difficult at times to grasp the scale and range of these events. The publication of memoirs is therefore an indispensable part of the extension of knowledge, and of public awareness of the crimes that had been committed against a whole people.

Sir Martin Gilbert
Merton College, Oxford

Foreword

Whoever decides after many years to confront his youth inevitably exposes himself to the vagaries of his own memory.

He becomes overwhelmed with doubts – how was it really, and where does the truth lie? Jesting Pilate posed this question and did not wait for an answer. The author of a memoir should, however, wait a little.

Everything is relatively easy when you have materials at your disposal which allow you to verify your own version of the experiences of half a century ago. This is the case, for example, with the Warsaw ghetto, which has been the subject of many detailed though incomplete accounts. But where does one begin with the Occupation history of places outside Warsaw, such as Wołomin? It helps if you have someone with whom to check your memories. It is difficult when all you have at your disposal is your own memory.

I hope that my story will neither hurt nor offend anyone. If I am wrong in my facts, I am ready to admit my errors. In case this is so, the names of some of the people appearing here have been changed, or replaced with initials.

Almost all photographs and documents pertaining to my family were destroyed. For those which survived, I owe thanks to relations and friends, in particular the ones who survived the war abroad. None of them are any longer alive, and so I thank their children and grandchildren.

Two fragments of this story – part of Chapter 31 about Antoni and Janina Słonimski and a short excerpt from Chapter 40, Konstancin, come from my book *Pchli Targ* [Flea-market].

Certain other fragments were published in the press.

Although the cut-off date of these memoirs is basically 1945, there are numerous exceptions to this, and I hope that the reader will bear with me.

Finally, as to the division into two parts of this book and the use of a casual conversational form in the first, I did this because going back to Occupation experiences put me under a great deal of psychological strain and I wanted to get this work done quickly. Therefore, I relinquished literary ambition in favour of giving the reader, and in particular my nearest and dearest, an efficient and relatively painless account of the most difficult and most amazing period of my life which took place during my youth. The simple fact of my existence placed me then under sentence of death. Despite this, however, I lived, and I talk about it as honestly as I know how, without political or any other distortion.

The person with whom I am speaking, Hanna Baltyn, has a background in theatre. Not being a historian, she asks questions which any intelligent young person would ask. I prefer this to conversations with an expert who might intimidate me. And perhaps Hanna Baltyn sees in this story something of the conventions of theatre, where tragedy is intertwined with comedy and the *deus ex machina* is survival itself.

Part 1
My Wartime Experiences:
Conversations with
Hanna Baltyn

ONE

First Conversation

Over the past few years, you published fragments of your memoirs about the Occupation. I read them — you said that you wanted to write a book for the 50th anniversary of the ghetto uprising. It didn't work out, even though there was a lot of material. You suggested to me then an informal series of conversations, which together with the finished literary texts would comprise a book: Life Strictly Forbidden. *Tell me why it took you so long to decide to publish your memoirs, and what you see as unique about them.*

I intended to write a book in the 1960s, but I don't need to tell you what the atmosphere in this country was like then. The situation has recently changed in a fundamental way: I can write honestly now, without concealing things which would previously have been censored. That's the answer to the first question.

Let's turn now to the question of the uniqueness of my recollections. They're unique only in the sense that I didn't live through those years of Occupation under inhuman conditions. Quite the contrary; looking back, I can say that I survived them almost in the lap of luxury. I once read that the dictator of the Łódź ghetto, Chaim Rumkowski, had jurisdiction for a while over a boarding-house in Marysin, near Łódź. Of course, it wasn't a particularly comfortable place, but it provided its guests with clean beds and enough food to eat, not to mention the greenery surrounding the house. Rumkowski treated a fortnight's stay in the boarding-house as a reward for services for the most ardent workers in ghetto institutions. Whoever distinguished himself, or managed to find favour with the all-powerful 'Emperor', would receive a priceless gift in the shape of a vacation from the hell of hunger, epidemics and debasement. When I think about my life during the years of war and Occupation, I feel as though, by the will of some higher power – higher even than Rumkowski's – I had the opportunity to stay in just such an establishment at a safe distance from the most terrible dangers of those years.

I owe my survival not to any personal qualities, but to my ancestors, chance and luck. I did not spend a single minute in a concentration camp. No one shot at me and, no less fortunately, I shot at no one. My memoirs are not memoirs of horror. I want to tell my own truth about the Occupation, to describe that period from my own point of view. I walked through the Warsaw ghetto, looking with horror at what was going on there, and yet I always maintained a certain distance.

Many people are unaware that you are a Jew. Neither your surname nor your appearance point to that. You weren't maligned by the press, you didn't leave after 1968. Tell me why you want to talk about all that. What drives you to do so?

If I couldn't tell everything about myself today, I wouldn't know why I had survived the war. Someone might think I was ashamed of my roots, and that would be to misjudge me. I come from a Jewish family and I think that not a single drop of Aryan blood flows through my veins. An absurd thing to say, perhaps, just as all racism is absurd; nonetheless, given that I have faith in the marital fidelity of my female ancestors, I have to conclude that I am most probably racially pure. When asked about my background, I usually say that I'm the product of a mixed marriage: a Jew to an Israelite. At the same time, I've never been a Jew in the religious sense. My family left the faith of Moses dozens of years ago, and I was baptized immediately after birth by Fr Władysław Semadeni, Superintendent of the Evangelical Reformed Church. I'm not a convert since I've never changed religions. I'm simply a Pole. Not a Polish Catholic, which some rank highest, but a Polish Protestant, and, what's worse, of Jewish descent. I'm not religious, but I'm pleased to belong to the Reformed Evangelical community, because I've been the recipient of many acts of Christian mercy from them. And I consider myself a Christian because Christian ethics speak to me more strongly than any other ideology. It's simply a matter of choice. I consider myself a Christian not because I was baptized, but simply because it suits me.

The fact that I'm a Pole, on the other hand, isn't out of choice, and I don't necessarily like it. I'm a Pole because I am. This land is my land, this language, my language. My relationship to Poland is like the relationship one has with one's family. Sometimes I love it, sometimes I can hardly stand it, but I don't think that anyone, regardless of position or title, has the right to teach me patriotism.

Do you have any complexes?

Can one talk about complexes in a person from a wealthy and cultured family whose position, at the time when complexes are formed, might be the subject of envy rather than of contempt or scorn? And yet... Antoni Słonimski wrote of himself with pride, 'Son of a race much older than the Porta Romana.' He certainly had no reason to have complexes about his heritage. His father, grandfather and great-grandfather were celebrities. He himself surpassed the fame of his forefathers. He was every inch a patrician. And yet he delighted in quoting old lady Kossak: 'Le petit Słonimski, il est très bien.'

You ask why I'm coming out with revelations about my background? Such matters, I'm sometimes told by friends, are of concern to no one but lunatics who cling to their phobias in a land where there are practically no Jews anymore. Why doesn't Mr X insist on his French background, or Mr Y on his Swiss? They quite simply regard themselves as Poles, and no one gets excited or turned off by the question of their genealogy. True. But I don't recall there ever existing anti-French or anti-Swiss sentiment in Poland.

It seems anti-Semitic conditions are different...

Anti-Semitism in Poland does not depend at all on the existence of Jews. Before the war, Paweł Hulka-Laskowski described the patently absurd phenomenon of anti-Semitism without Jews. In *Wiadomosci Literackie* [Literary News] (pp.25–37), he put it this way:

> Let us imagine that the last Jewish tradeswoman and the last Jewish water-carrier crossed the Polish border

and there isn't a single Jew left in Poland. Will aggressive anti-Semitism finally end? By no means. The absence of Jews for him means unemployment, hunger and poverty. He'd have to start looking for Jews. Who else is a Jew? Who's got a drop of Jewish blood in his veins? Who's got a Jewish mentality? Jews, even were they to disappear off the face of the earth, will live on in anti-Semitism, scaring and worrying the world.

One has to admit that he wrote prophetically. And apart from that, neither Mr X nor Mr Y lived near Świętokrzyska Street, where the fascist student groups strutted their stuff before the war. They didn't constantly hear the scream, 'It's a disgrace for you to buy from a Jew.' During the war, they didn't qualify as raw material for the manufacture of soap, after the war, however...

I'm curious as to whether you were personally affected by any instances of Polish anti-Semitism?

I don't think so. I experienced no unpleasantness at home, at school, nor later, after the war, at my place of work or in public places. It might have been tempting to defect, but either out of stubborness, or out of a sense of loyalty, I was never able to cut myself off from the trunk from which I, willy-nilly, drew succour. Some people cut themselves off deliberately and made fools of themselves. A certain character actor, whose father was known to all of Warsaw — and not for being a bishop, at that — reacted with a stony face to even the friendliest allusions. A professor, whom before the war I called by his first name, Iziu (from Israel), asked me never, under any circumstances, to reveal his origins to his Polish children.

There are two reactions which constitute a response to anti-Semitism. The one I mentioned earlier, which seems absurd to me because you'll always find someone who will ferret out that someone is racially 'impure.' The second one is the opposite. I came across it, for example, in March of 1968, particularly among young women. A lot of young people suddenly learned, as a result of the anti-Semitic campaign, their parents' backgrounds. Did they hide the fact at all costs? No, quite the opposite. They reacted with pride, ostentation and fanaticism, even though, only the day before, they hadn't known of their Jewish origins.

And what lay between these two extremes?

Another kind of reaction which I know by heart and which irritates me a bit – a specifically Polish kind of reaction which exists nowhere else on earth. Let's say that I approach someone I don't know about something. We have a very friendly conversation. My host tells me that he's of the nobility; he tells me about his family's former estates, even though I haven't asked about that. And taking it for granted that I'm from the landed gentry as well, he turns to me and says, 'And where is your family from?' So then I say, 'I'm sorry, but my family is of Jewish background.' Consternation! It's as though I've farted in polite company. This gentleman, however, does not turn around and spit. On the contrary. He becomes excessively polite, as though he's heard that I am terminally ill. He searches desperately through his memory for examples of positive attitudes to Jews. He tells me that his Lord-of-the-manor father had a friend called Rabinowicz, or that his brother was very fond of some Rapoport or other. In doing so, he tries to prove that neither he nor his family were ever anti-Semites. It's particularly irritating because, actually, I don't care. Throughout my life, I've maintained that if someone wants to continue relations with me he'll do so. And that's good. But if, on the other hand, he doesn't want to, then that's his loss.

At what point did you start taking a deeper interest in this? How long did it take to get back to your roots?

Hundreds of other nations exist as well as the Jews. I don't consider Jews the epicentre of the universe, nor the most phenomenal of nations. No, it's just that I can't let go of the subject. I never knew much about Jewish culture because my family broke away from it. I didn't know the language because no one among us had spoken it for three generations. I didn't know the basis of Jewish holidays, of the faith or its customs. My ignorance in these matters was greater than that of solidly Polish boys who grew up in Jewish neighbourhoods. I lived in the very heart of Warsaw, where only the assimilated Jews lived. I knew nothing.

I once went to a Jewish neighbourhood with my father because he wanted to show me how poor Jews lived. I remember that, either on Gesia Street or Mila Street, my father tore a button off his coat. We walked into a stinking little shop belonging to a tailor with a mass of kids. Filth, stench, extreme poverty. Father asks, 'Could you sew this button on for me?' 'Why not?' He sews the button, and father asks, 'How much do I owe you? Twenty groszy.' Father left two złoty and walked out, which made a tremendous impression.

I can imagine it was a truly different world, above all because of that insurmountable economic barrier.

Financial, religious and cultural — however you want to put it. I know this ignorance speaks ill of me. A knowledge of one's own roots, after all, should come out of a simple human curiosity. But I have to admit that I lacked that curiosity for many years. I probably would have gone on underscoring my background without any real knowledge of it, had it not been for 1968.

The unprecedented campaign against so-called Zionists, a campaign which cost our country more than any other 'happy' move by the rulers of the Polish People's Republic, was decisive in changing my attitude to that whole legacy. Mr Gomułka, my favourite father of our nation, called for unilateral elections. You couldn't consider yourself both a Jew and a Pole. A Pole was a Pole: an entity in itself. As a Pole, you were not to have any Jewish leanings or interests. We were exhorted to a unilateral servile declaration. The Jews *en masse* were ordered to thank the anti-Semites for the Poles who had helped them survive the Occupation. One had to declare publicly, almost on one's knees, thanks to people who would have done anything to make that survival impossible.

How did it happen that you didn't leave? That you stuck it out?

I have to say that I found it hard to live through that period, but I truly didn't want to leave Poland. At that time, I was living in the country with my wife and very young child, and avoided contact with Warsaw at all costs. Had I gone to meetings and even once opposed official ideology, I would have found myself abroad. This way I stuck it out. Certain new Scandinavians still hold it against me to this day that I did not leave my own country. Those Jews who left thought that my staying proved that I was an opportunist. I think, however, that it is proof of something quite different.

That period left in me, apart from a feeling of shame, an interest in Jewish culture. I began collecting Judaica after that. I was most interested in Polish anti-Semitic texts. I took an almost masochistic pleasure in collecting the most disgusting materials, which I often bought for big money. One day I shall put them into the right hands. The unrivalled stupidity and crudeness of these materials is, in its own way, a hopeful sign.

I did this a bit out of spite, because after 1968, the Jewish subject was taboo in Poland. There was a justifiable fear about bringing up this problematic subject,. There was something inexplicable and disgusting about it. The Jews left Poland *en masse* in 1968 and 1969, but I don't recall any exodus of anti-Semites. They didn't emigrate. They're still here.

For a good few years, the Jewish subject hasn't vanished from newspaper columns. A lot of books are coming out — stories, memoirs, analyses. An overload, perhaps. What were the beginnings of this change like?

If the situation in Poland changed at all, I am partly responsible. I was a member of the first committee for the protection of Jewish cemeteries and cultural monuments in Poland, which was supported, in part, by money from *Fiddler on the Roof*, translated by me and brought, with enormous difficulty, to the Polish musical stage.

After *Fiddler*, whose Polish première took place years ago, there arose, especially among the young, an interest in Jewish matters. Who were the people who had lived with us on this earth for hundreds of years? What were their faith and customs like? Once, a few weeks after the splendid première in Gdynia, the director and stage-manager, Jerzy Gruza, telephoned me. I heard the typical round of applause. The ovation went on and on; they didn't want to let the actors leave the stage. Gruza said to me at the time, 'You know, this isn't the usual applause after a successful performance, this is a big political demonstration.' And he was right.

You can't hide the fact that, in spite of everything, there's anti-Semitism among us, and not just the kind where one old woman says to another old woman, 'You know, my dear, they murdered Our Lord'. Are you disappointed?

I never deluded myself into thinking that certain levels of our society would turn into pro-Semites overnight. I'd have to be a whole lot more na ve than I am. But since we're on the subject, do you know that Jews in the Warsaw ghetto, starved, murdered and abused by the Nazis, took comfort in this absurd vision of the future: 'If we survive, they'll carry us in their arms after the war.' I heard such utterances, but didn't know who would be doing the carrying. In April 1944, the great poet Julian Tuwim, from his exile in America, wrote in his piece, 'We, the Polish Jews':

> The Star of David was painted on the armbands which you wore in the ghetto. I believe in a future Poland in which that star, the one from the armbands, will become one of the highest honours given to the most valiant Polish soldiers and officers. They are going to wear it with pride on their breasts next to the old Virtuti Militari. There will also be the Ghetto Cross, a deeply symbolic name. And an Order of the Yellow Patch, more meritorious than any other current trinket. In Warsaw and in every other Polish town, some fragment of the ghetto will remain, preserved and conserved, in its unchanged state. The Church will acquire another national relic. We will take our children there and tell them about the worst murder of people in the history of the world. In the centre of this memorial, whose tragic nature will be enhanced by the surrounding new glass houses of the rebuilt city, an eternal flame will burn. Passers-by will doff their hats before it. And those who are Christians will make the sign of the cross.

I don't want to go on about this nobly intentioned text, but it's as unrealistic as the talk of those wretched souls in the ghetto of being carried. The issue isn't celebrating the Jews who survived, but rather not allowing anti-Semites to set the tone for contemporary Poland. I think we've talked enough about the subject for today . . .

You got me going with your question about the reason for the late publication of this book.

All right. But don't you think that it's time to go back at least 50 years?

I do.

TWO

Second Conversation

When you were telling me about the Occupation, before we began recording our conversations, I noticed that you attributed your survival specifically to your family's wealth. Tell me where they came from and how they acquired their fortune.

My family is of German-Jewish descent. I became interested in it rather late. I managed to get a few details from members of the previous generation: Janina ('Janka') Konarska-Słonimska (died in 1975), Jerzy Pański (died in 1979), and, in particular, from Wacław Solski, whose real surname was also Pański (died in 1990). Once, in his apartment in New York, I badgered him with questions about our ancestors who were the founders and owners of a large textile factory in Zawiercie. I couldn't for the life of me remember their surnames! In desperation, Wacław telephoned Professor Victor Weintraub in Boston, who came from Zawiercie and knew all about that town. I had a long conversation with him. It transpired that my ancestors were called Gincberg. It also turned out that, at the turn of the century, the Professor's father had been cashier at the factory – a position held much earlier by my great-grandfather, Adolf Seideman. You'll learn about the family fortune in the story 'Grandparents'.

What's the story behind your present surname?

It's a name from the Occupation.

Not the only one, surely?

When I was leaving the ghetto, all my documents were in the name Mieczysław Chiemelewski – a good name because it was ordinary. Jews felt good with popular surnames like that.

But on the Aryan side, it turned out that I was missing some documents I needed for the *Kennkarte*. I was very worried, because the *Kennkarte* was the essential personal identification card. So, in a panic, I started the process of creating documents in a different name. It was then that Antoni Marianowicz appeared. Only for me, however, mother had to assume the name Natalia Godlewska, daughter of — and this greatly appealed to me — a horse-drawn trolley conductor; she automatically became my aunt because it was hard as hell to get authentic documents for a mother and son.

All right, but what were you really called? Everyone calls you Kazio.

I was baptized Kazimierz Jerzy, so that's where the nickname 'Kazio' comes from. My grandfather, whose presence was the result of my grandmother's marriage – a marriage which did not enrapture the family (they felt similarly about my mother later) – was called Berman. My father was called Gustav Berman; my uncle, Stefan Berman. We didn't have any other relations by that name. I say this so no one gets it into their head that I am in any way related to...

Jakub?

Yes. Although the said Jakub, Stalin's representative and head of the Polish secret police, did play a certain part in my life. When I emerged from the anonymity of Occupation, I started to work at Polpress in Łódź. I was already publishing: was somebody. The question then arose what to do about the documents. At that time, nearly all the Poles, not just those of Jewish descent, had very odd papers. For example, I was officially three years older than I actually was. When I considered the question of a surname, I had a strong desire to return to my real name. But in the political circumstances of the time, I, and those nearest to me, came to the conclusion that each sign of my success would be put down to the fact that my name was Berman: one of the two most powerful people in Poland who, by a stroke of bad luck, had precisely that name.

So you kept your nom de guerre...

Yes, but I endowed Antoni Marianowicz with the authentic facts — age, father's name, other dates – everything else is real. It also seemed to me relevant that, by contrast with Chiemelewski, the name Marianowicz is fairly uncommon. There are practically no Marianowiczes. So, for someone in public life, it's good in so far as one isn't confused with someone else.

Once, some woman from the provinces called me, intent on discovering a relationship between us. I had to give her my most solemn word of honour — and did so with a clear conscience— that it was an impossibility. Only then did she believe me.

Why do you think some people kept their Occupation names?

Jews? Probably for individual reasons, and a large number did. The basic reason was fear. You have to remember that the survival of each Jew bordered on the miraculous and resulted in numerous traumas. The Kielce pogrom was one of the first events in the history of postwar Polish–Jewish relations. A terror reigned about reverting to Jewish names, as well as a desire to blend in, to melt into a fundamentally Polish background. Apart from this, there was a whole category of Jews who had come here from Russia; if they were party members and wanted to build a wonderful socialist system in Poland, they could hardly do so under their own Jewish names. They often assumed names which were grotesque in light of their appearance and way of speaking, and that, of course, contributed to the rise of anti-Semitism. For example, a typical Jew suddenly became Lech Fronczak or Ziemowit Nowak. That upset people—even me.

But it was generally easier to do that in those days. A man called Goldberg, for example, didn't immediately inspire the reaction 'Oh, a Pole of Jewish descent', he inspired vicious thoughts, repugnance. It's interesting that although German names didn't give rise to prejudice, Jewish names did...No matter, there were many true patriots of German descent, but still it's paradoxical.

Among the Jews there were also those who had real reasons for retaining their Jewish surnames, because they were attached to them in some special way. I wasn't particularly attached to the name Berman: it was as good as any other name and didn't invite attention. Actually, there were many well-known Bermans in the world, but they were not my relations: the outstanding American dramatist, S.N. Behrman; the comedian Shelley Berman; the scenographer Pancho Berman; the German publisher Gottfried

Bermann-Fischer; the Soviet pianist Lazar Berman. Despite all these super-Bermans, the name is fairly common and certainly doesn't belong in the ranks of the great Jewish surnames. Had I, for example, been called Bergson, Słonimski or Kronenberg, and changed to Marianowicz, then I could be considered a simple renegade. The fact that my grandfather happened to be called Berman held no particular significance for me.

Let's go back to the repugnance. Was such marked anti-Semitism felt before the war as well in relation to well-placed and culturally polonized people?

Of course, but I was always beyond the reach, or out of range, of anti-Semitism. I went to school at the Mikolai Rej Gimnazjum, which was blameless on that score. A truly liberal atmosphere reigned there: there were no, shall we say, nationalistic or fascistic tendencies. The professors were responsible for that. Oscar Bartel taught me history; Leon Rygier, Polish. The school was famous for tolerance; each faith had its own teacher. I didn't go to church, but attended a class for all levels on the Evangelical Reformed religion.

That means there weren't many of you.

Barely a handful, but I remember the religious instruction lessons with affection. We were taught by priests: Stefan Skierski, Jerzy Jelen and Ludwik Zaunar. I liked Jelen's classes best. He was still a young man and had a nice manner. He wore dark glasses and had a perverse sense of humour, which you don't expect in a clergyman. When he'd finished the 'required' material and had some time left, he'd tell us crime stories. Once, either out of curiosity or stupidity, I asked what the story he'd told us had to do with our religion lesson. With a glint of his spectacles, the priest retorted that it was quite obvious — all the heroes in that story were Reformed Evangelicals!

My classmates were probably aware of my background, or at least the more intelligent ones were.

Were there many Jews at Rej's?

It was probably 10–15 per cent Jewish. I want to mention one boy, because he was truly somebody – very promising. Marian Muszkat was his name: he perished in one of the first artillery raids in September 1939. As soon as the raid was over, I ran to

22 Sienna Street, where he lived. I saw the janitor at the door of the badly damaged building, and asked him about Attorney Muszkat and his family. 'You don't know, sir?' he asked with surprise. I realized at once that something terrible had happened. It turned out that Marian was dead. He was hiding in the cellar with his parents, and his father sent him upstairs for a shawl for his mother. It was then that the shell landed.

What was exceptional about your friend?

He stood out by his superior individuality, independence of thought, strength of will and physical strength. He was coura-geous, downright brazen at times, and he had an answer in every situation. Our friendship evolved in two ways. We were linked by a mutual love of the theatre and a liking for wandering around Warsaw. I owe a great deal to him because he taught me to hold independent opinions (even when they were at odds with the pronouncements of the two highest authorities: Boy-Żeleński and Słonimski), and to search out beautiful spots in my family town – Marienstat, for example, whose charms he discovered to our mutual advantage. It's thanks to him that I cured myself of thinking too well of my own importance because of my father's position.

Was it really a very high position?

Not really, because we didn't belong to the very wealthy bourgeoisie. The English term 'upper-middle-class' best describes my background. Above us were the greater factory owners, owners of banks, mines, and so on. There were perhaps a few hundred of them — the really big financiers.

Into which group would you place your family?

Somewhere between the middle-class and the so-called Jewish aristocracy.

What would you have been, were it not for the war?

I would have been wealthy. I would have gone into law. In fact, I had already arranged an apprenticeship with Wacław Brokman, an excellent lawyer.

Would you have had problems at the university with the seating ghetto?

There would have been problems, in the sense that I couldn't have sat on the right side of the lecture hall while my Jewish colleagues were sitting on the left. That's why I was set to study abroad, probably in France. And for the time being, I was attending Rej's.

Oh, yes, I interrupted your story about Marian Muszkat. Did you have any contact with his family later on?

I visited them regularly in the ghetto. I also made friends with Marian's beautiful girlfriend, Lilka Lipes. None of them survived the war. I don't even know whether Marian's grave remained standing in that jungle of smashed and overgrown stones in the Jewish cemetery. Nothing has survived of that unusual boy who perished in the 17th year of his life. Nothing but these few words.

I feel the same way about my friends Wojtek Roniewicz and Krzysztof Zborowski who perished in the Warsaw uprising, and Zdzisław Handelsman who was murdered by the Nazis. But in their case, families who remember them survived. Fortunately, my closest friends, Tadeusz Górowski and Gabriel Grasberg, survived.

Were there also Germans in your class?

Of course. The Rej school was private and very expensive. However, the Evangelical Augsburg Lutheran community gave numerous stipends to students from less wealthy families. It was not only to their benefit but also to those of us from plutocratic families, because thanks to it we weren't confined to our own narrow circle. Their behaviour after the outbreak of war in 1939, when *Volkslists* were created for people of German background, was interesting. Almost without exception, the offspring of the Warsaw patricians ignored the lists, while the sons of minor office workers, postmen and janitors, on the other hand, often renounced their Polish background. This was due, I think, not only to economic but also psychological reasons. The 1920s had brought them neither prosperity nor satisfaction; the Nazis promised them both.

Can you give any examples?

I think that a typical case was one Zdzisław Kohler – a small, not particularly intelligent boy who was always tidy and submissive. Already in September, young Kohler started to show up with a swastika on his lapel. He grew self-important and proud, and ignored — thank God! — his former friends. I think I heard that he died during the war.

I have a somewhat fonder memory of Fredek Gitz, an unremarkable boy from a not very well-to-do background, whom I remember as a protégé of General Górecki's wife. I should explain here that Romek, the son of Roman Górecki, a Piłsudski dignitary, was in our class for a few years. He was frail and lacked initiative, so his mother did what she could to ensure that he had friends. Every now and then, there would be great parties at the Góreckis. I normally didn't go to them because Mrs General-President-Minister cultivated a sweet, democratically philanthropic atmosphere for herself which made me sick. One of her successes was that she found a constant companion for Romek in the shape of Gitz. Even though, like Kohler, he'd become a *Volksdeutsch*,* he made nothing of it. Once, at a highly inopportune moment, I met up with him, face to face, on the street. I nearly died of fright. But Gitz behaved as though our meeting had taken place under normal circumstances. He was friendly and asked no questions. After we'd parted, I turned around several times and breathed a sigh of relief to see no policeman following me – not so much as a lame dog. I don't know what happened to Gitz, but I would be pleased to know that he had survived.

It's not surprising that it was hard to find a trace of the Volksdeutsch *after the war: they had nothing to brag about.*

You know, I did hear something specific about one of my colleagues who'd turned German. Leon Frey was a mediocre student, but he didn't give an impression of being a boy from the lower classes. He lost control of himself very easily and blushed like a girl over the least thing. Some of his behaviour made one uneasy. For instance, if someone had seriously misbehaved and the teacher threatened consequences for the entire class if the culprit didn't own up, Frey would stand up, turn crimson, and declare that he was the guilty one. We all knew that the real criminal was laughing his head off, but Frey had to have his five minutes of glory. He'd stand there happy,

---

* Person of German nationality, but without official German citizenship.

feverish, ready to make the sacrifice. Maybe it was touching, but finally it was disturbing. When I read in the *Warschauer Zeitung* [The Warsaw Gazette] an obituary for Lieutenant Leon Frey, Luftwaffe pilot, who, decorated with the Iron Cross, together with shields, diamonds and many other honourable emblems, had died heroically for Führer and *Vaterland*, I took it as the natural conclusion of his weird behaviour at school. He'd taken his suicidal tendencies to the very end.

Was your connection with the school severed in September 1939?

No. Thanks to clandestine classes it continued until October 1940: in other words, until the moment we were deported to the ghetto. But even then it was made possible for me to take my final diploma exams, which were useful after the war. The organization of underground education was an outstanding achievement under Occupation conditions.

THREE

Third Conversation

I'd like to know some more about your father. What kind of education did he have?

In 1903, he graduated from the Wojciech Górski Gimnazjum. He wasn't a particularly industrious student. Then he went with his brother to study in Germany, but he devoted this period to experiences of a romantically adventurous nature rather than to studies, which doesn't alter the fact that, during the First World War, he was a high-ranking bank official in Russia and by the end of it, the head of a department in what later became the Bank of Poland. In the early 1920s, he went into business on his own account.

Was he an industrialist?

Definitely not. It's true that he built some factories, but they never went into production before the war. My father was a businessman.

That term wasn't used in Poland before the war.

It's true it wasn't. An accurate description of father's profession is that he was involved with international trade.

With whom did he do business? Mainly with Jews?

You must be joking. In business, background is irrelevant. He traded mainly with tobacco-growers.

South America?

No. Europe – Turkey and other Balkan countries. Father bought tobacco and sold his consignments to monopolies and tobacco factories in Western Europe. They were huge transactions. Not very frequent, but even so, they brought in sizeable profits.

Another of my father's business enterprises was the Presto Company at 10 Fredro Street. In the early 1930s, it was involved with sending packages to Russia. In the period of the great hunger in the Soviet Union, international aid was set up. Many Polish and Jewish families had relations there. My father was the only person who, thanks to his contacts, was able to guarantee that the packages would arrive at their destination. During the First World War and the Russian Revolution, he had close contact with many revolutionaries. One of his friends was Commissar Unszlicht, later a high-ranking dignitary in the Soviet Union. Perhaps it was he who guaranteed the safe delivery of the packages.

Were the packages made up by the company, or were they brought there by the senders?

Exclusively by the company. They could be ordered in several versions, as was the case later at the Polish Guardian Bank. They consisted of food, which was unbelievably expensive because the price included bribes to the Soviet customs men. Before the war, the average wage for a maid was 30 złoty. A not very large package from Presto cost 120 złoty — a fortune, but they were sent out in quantities. My father made a lot of money out of it.

What did he do with his capital, what kind of real estate did he buy before the war?

Father was a bit of a spendthrift. He maintained a lavish lifestyle. He travelled, and had mistresses in the major centres of Europe who sometimes travelled around with him.

He didn't stint on outer show, either. His wardrobe was a veritable wonderland. His suits came from the Zaremba shop – the one on Wierzbowa Street. (There were four Zarembas, better ones and worse ones.) A few suits were made for him by a Jewish tailor, Weinappel, a celebrity in the trade, but in father's words, 'nothing special'. His shoes and silk shirts came from the better Warsaw establishments, and his ties from all over the world. I inherited them whenever the slightest stain appeared on any of them. I remember the most important thing — a leather box of men's jewellery, filled with collar-studs, cufflinks, pearls, tie-pins and other marvels, which I would spread out on the carpet when I was a child and look at by the hour. Today, you can only dream of such things.

When the fighting ended in 1939, we were left without

anything. It had all gone up in smoke. So father and I went to a Jewish ready-to-wear shop on Swiętokrzyska Street, near Szkolna Street, and got ourselves a suit and light overcoat each. It was very odd to see my father in a ready-made, not very well-fitting suit, discussing alterations with a bearded tailor: 'Director, you look superb in this suit ... What do you mean like a scarecrow? ... Take my word for it, it will look made-to-measure.' I realized then, for the first time, that the wonderland was over. We were entering the new era clad in ready-made.

How could your father, a businessman, allow himself such a free-wheeling lifestyle?

I don't think my father's business interests took up much of his time because he used to sit around at the Ziemiańska Café. The office where he worked, Presto, employed a number of people full-time to send out the packages. His tobacco business, on the other hand, depended on connections, a typewriter, telephone and secretary. Father was well known; everyone knew that he had connections in world monopolies and that he was the one to turn to if you wanted to sell part of such and such a tobacco.

What languages did he speak?

Other than Polish, he spoke three languages extremely well. His generation had a good knowledge of Russian. He had studied in Germany and went frequently to France. He could make himself understood in Italian – he had business interests there, too. He knew no English at all. He didn't trade with England.

At that time, every Polish intellectual knew German and French. You couldn't get by without them. Poland wasn't the centre of the universe before the war, as it now sometimes seems to us. When, in March 1939, England guaranteed Poland's safety, the famous British politician Alfred Duff Cooper conveyed this particularly forcefully: 'Never before in its history had England given a second-rate country a say in its decision to enter a war.'

But to get back to the subject of language: anyone who wanted to do business on a larger scale had to know German, and French was the language of the *haut monde*.

But you were also taught English.

My teacher was Hugh A. Mackenzie, the author of an international English handbook. I wrote about him in *Pchli Targ* [Flea-market]. He was the head of the British School in Warsaw and other European capitals. He went from country to country establishing these schools, and my father won him over with the help of the British Consul. He was a wonderful teacher; by the time the war broke out, I knew English. The first English sentence I learned came from one of Oscar Wilde's fairy-tales: 'Every afternoon, the children used to go and play in the giant's garden.' During the war, my teacher became one of the heroes of the writer Dygat's *The Bodensee*, and it turned out after the war that he was a high-ranking intelligence service agent.

I learned German from a *Fräulein*, employed when I was still in nappies. I learned it along with Polish. French came when I was about 4. Various old-maids and strange *demoiselles* taught it to me.

To go back to money, into what kind of property did your father put his profits?

He had an apartment building in the Praga district of Warsaw, and, as I say in the second half of this book, a villa in Konstancin – a nice house, a typically Polish estate, the apple of my father's eye. He also owned other real estate.

And the flat in Warsaw?

There were five rooms at 9 Swiętokrzyska Street. Nothing special; there was always talk about much-needed alterations. But father was very attached to that flat. It was well laid-out and spacious, with two balconies...

Did your father have a car?

He couldn't have one because in prewar Poland, the tax offices were vigilant and inquisitive. Owning a car without owning a business was ill-advised. Presto closed down around 1935 when the post office took over the parcel concession. Father didn't own a business establishment, only a secretary (an unattractive one, so as to avoid nasty repercussions) who worked in his study at our home. It might have damaging to him to have owned a car. So we had an arrangement with the Warsaw representative of Citroën, and whenever we wanted one, a car and driver would duly appear.

Tell me, how exactly was your home different, if at all, from other Polish homes of the wealthy middle class?

On the face of it, not at all. We didn't know the Jewish language or culture and we spoke normal Polish (a Polish which was sometimes too good, coming from the lips of people of Jewish descent). How were we different? Only in that our 'household' (the people who performed services for us) was almost exclusively Jewish.

Perhaps there's some truth in the saying that like attracts like.

I think we're dealing with two possibilities here. The first is the most normal one under the sun: using the services of neighbours from the same building, street, or neighbourhood. Why should a Jew in a *kapota* give up his *kapota*, or mend shoes for a Polish tradesman living outside the Jewish neighbourhood? Language, customs, in fact everything, divided them.

And the other possibility?

Our home was an example of it. Supporting Jews — from teachers all the way through to pedlars going from house to house — was a natural reaction to the relentless anti-Semitic propaganda. Even if it wasn't done on principle it was still deliberate.

Which contributed to the increasing anti-Semitism.

That's right. These reactions create a vicious circle: a situation with no way out. We're seeing this more and more in relationships between people who are geographically or ethnically close to each other.

You said a moment ago that a Jew from Gęsia Street had no reason to go to a shoe-mender in a Polish neighbourhood. How did passersby react to the presence of Jews dressed in traditional attire outside of Jewish areas? Before the First War, the rules of the Saxon Garden prohibited them, together with women in headscarves and men wearing caps, from entering.

Until the late 1930s, the sight of a Jew in a gabardine provoked no reaction; later, however, you couldn't rule out the possibility of random incidents.

For my generation, a Jew in gabardine and Jarmulke* *brings to mind the souvenir industry, satire, or Jewish jokes. A figure talking with its hands and saying things like 'Oy, vey'.*

---

* Small black peaked cap worn by Jews in prewar times.

It's commonplace for people to find something funny about otherness. Someone who doesn't talk, behave or dress as we do is an oddity, a deviant. In the Polish tradition, that isn't just limited to Jews but also to Germans and to Chinese people.

And what do you think of Jewish jokes? Are they examples of anti-Semitism?

It depends. There were vulgar and offensive jokes, but also ones which were civilized, clever, and full of wit. For example, Hemar and Tuwim's cabaret turns as performed by Krukowski and Lawinski. The first type of joke makes Jews odious; the second, however, makes them sympathetic.

So the attitude of Poles to Jews wasn't always disparaging?

Quite so. Our literature, as you know, tended to be pro-Semitic.

Mickiewicz, Norwid, Orzeszkowa, Konopnicka, Prus, Zapolska, and scores of other first-rate writers.

And not just those eminent writers, but several third-rate authors like Gawalewicz, plus a few decaying, once-talented weirdos like Tetmajer or Weysenhoff. However, it's not just a question of literature, but also of journalism, information pieces and commentaries in newspapers, and of the specific tone in the gutter press which was revived in the not-to-be-forgotten year of 1968.

Where, in our national writings, do you find the source of anti-Semitism?

There's no lack of it in old Polish literature, even that written in Latin. Already in Dantyszek (1485–1548), in Polish translation, of course, we read that the Jews are 'a nation which sets traps to catch others...bestial, cruel, envious and savage', while in Klonowic (1545–1602): 'You ask: why let the wolf enter the sheepfold? What is that cunning nation of serpents doing here? It greedily garners unlawful gains, and with cruel usury oppresses the poor.'

It doesn't sound particularly pro-Jewish.

I said that our literature *tended* to be pro-Jewish, which doesn't mean that it didn't spawn veritable pearls of anti-Semitism.

I see that you have a whole tasteful collection of such documents!

Assiduously collected since 1968. There exists, for example, an anonymous debate from the first half of the seventeenth century, *Robak zlego sumienia* [The Worm of the Bad Conscience], the author of which, according to experts, is Szyman Starowolski. In Chapter 11 we read:

> Who is the lease-holder of estates? The Jew. Who is a successful doctor? The Jew. Who is the most famous and the most competent merchant? The Jew. Who owns mills and inns? The Jew. Who is the toll-keeper and customs-man? The Jew. Who is the most faithful servant? The Jew. Who has the easiest access to the master? The Jew. Who has the best private and public protection? The Jew.

I'll skip over the rest of this itemizing in order to get to the conclusion: 'But how did this accursed nation unlock the gates to such paradise? Easy answer: they have a golden key and gain everything more easily because of it.'

You have to show me that key. Tell me, does the author say where the Jews got it?

The author knows exactly where. The Jews 'draw people to themselves by no other means but magic charms'. As you see, at least the polemic isn't easy.

If at all possible. Let's leave the subject. Tell me, which members of that prewar 'household' do you still remember?

The seamstress, Salcia Ganew, for example, whose nickname means thief, but despite it was a very decent woman who came 'to hem us up' every few months. Barber-surgeon Leipziger was an interesting figure. A tiny, rotund little man who would come to perform wet-cupping. Every single cold was treated in this fashion, so I would rather have choked to death than cough. Mr Leipziger, holding his burning brand, looked like Beelzebub to me. He'd often tell us about his son – the only Jew to have a souvenir business in Krupowki Street in Zakopane, and not badly off. After the treatment, father normally asked how much he owed him. Leipziger would name, for example, a price of eight złoty. Father would cover his face with his hands and moan that such prices were unheard of. Leipziger would swear that it was unbelievably cheap. Father would bargain and then give him ten złoty anyway. Both were happy with this performance.

I also remember a red-haired, bearded Jew in a *kapota* who came every few days to brush and press father's suits. About 30 of them hung in the wardrobe. Father never wore the same suit two days in a row, and this Jew's sole task was to freshen up the wardrobe.

Our doctor was Marcel Landsberg, who later became a professor. He'd start every visit with a lengthy litany of his physical woes. He'd listen to the medical advice we gave him and only then start to attend to us. He was an attractive man; I always associated him with Dr Szuman in Prus's *Lalka* [The Doll], whose prototype was, as is well known, Dr Stanisław Słonimski, Antoni's father.

As to shopping, in Konstancin we bought from Mrs Moczydlowska. She had competition later on from a young Jewish couple who brought us everything we needed on their bicycles. This was at the time of a strict economic boycott of Jews, so we did a lot to help them. Their produce was fresh, of excellent quality, and cheaper than in the Konstancin shops. Later, they rode around with a little child in their basket – it was very touching. They were brave; they deserved to survive the war, but, of course, they didn't. How could they have?

The subject of the war has come up. I understand that your father was a very sensible, well-organized man. Didn't he have any bad feelings regarding the war? After all, his own brother had suggested buying a house in Zaleszczyki and moving there, but he didn't do so. You write about this in your memoir about your Uncle Stefek. Why was this? Why did so many people not see what was happening?

The mood was other than you might imagine. You probably think that everybody predicted the apocalypse: the arrival of hoards of Huns, the mass murders. It was not like that. People had illusions. First, that it wouldn't come to war and second, that if it did, we wouldn't give up so much as a button off the Glorious Republic's cloak.

And the third illusion might have been that Germany, after all, was a civilized nation.

Exactly. No one took seriously the programme of the total

annihilation of Jews and the oppression of Poland which was outlined with startling sincerity in *Mein Kampf*. It never entered into anyone's head that millions of people would be murdered in cold blood. My father had studied in Germany and he had friends there, so he couldn't understand that Germany was, in a moral sense, a new place, something which the world hadn't seen until then. People believed that they would be helped by things such as having a doctorate *honoris causa* from Heidelberg, or being the representative of some German company. For a while, actually, that worked. Later on, they were just worthless bits of paper.

I remember an acquaintance who had close ties with Sweden. He was the head of the Polish–Swedish Trading Company. In the ghetto, he hung the proper certificate on his door, and during the liquidation, gave his documents to the Germans. They ripped the papers up and deported him with the others. It made no sense to count on consideration for such reasons. It was best to run as far away as possible.

I only once dared to show my documents, and completely unnecessarily at that. It was 9 August 1944, at the time of the Warsaw uprising. We were being herded from Filtrowa Street to the so-called Zieleniak camp. There was a long line of people waiting to enter the camp, and I noticed a high-ranking officer standing all by himself, watching. Walking through the crowd, I summoned the courage to go up to him. He moved back a pace and asked what I wanted. I showed him the document which said I was a worker at a factory under Waffen-SS command. 'Address yourself to the camp command', he said, without so much as a glance. Later, I found out that I had turned to Brigadeführer Mieczysław Kamiński, head of the predatory brigade of Soviet prisoners-of-war. Later on, the Germans shot him for plundering and infringements of military discipline. Contact with his vodka-besotted brutes is one of my most frightening memories.

You've gone ahead of yourself. You're speaking about the Warsaw uprising and the 1939 war hasn't started yet.

I'm sorry, but there is a reason for this. My mother carried a notebook out of the uprising which included, among other things, my notes on September 1939. This is one of them:

For a very long time, they said there wouldn't be war; very convincing arguments were raised. And then, on the radio, I heard President Moscicki's voice saying something about 'God and history'. I was very nervous, but not very scared. I was 15 at the time.

We went to Konstancin immediately because it is safer in the country. Father ordered a beautiful shelter to be dug in the middle of the garden, where we were going to hide from bombs. But then it turned out it was safer in the city, so we went back to our apartment in a two-storey house on Świętokrzyska Street in Warsaw. We arrived in the evening. They kept announcing and then calling off air raid alarms. Everybody was upset because we weren't going to let them poach on our preserves: the cavalry would finish them off and England and France would make mincemeat of Hitler.

But I got hysterical with fear. Father tried to understand—was I afraid in general, or here, on Swiętokrzyska Street, in particular. I was afraid to be in Swiętokrzyska Street, so we moved in immediately with my uncle, who lived opposite in a large, multi-storeyed apartment building. Then we arranged shelters for ourselves in the cellars and rushed around for gas-masks, because you never knew with those Germans, even though they were such weaklings. Colonel Umiastowski called the men into the army, but we refused. My uncle, who is a doctor, went into the army somewhere in Stanisławow, but they took one look at his galoshes and umbrella and quickly sent him back again. The staff headquarters of some division took up premises in our apartment on Swiętokrzyska Street. During one of the first air raids, nothing was left of the house or the staff headquarters. We saw the remains of our possessions hanging from various floors, and then we began to rescue what we could. The treasures we took from the rubble were put in my uncle's apartment.

And then we sat in the cellar, listening to a neighbour speculating on a speedy Allied victory. All of a
sudden, a young lady rushed by, screaming that we
were burning. We escaped in what we were wearing,
except for my mother, who lugged an enormous
suitcase with her, making herself the butt of jokes.
Everything was in flames, we moved across broken
beams and heaps of glass, across walls of fire. In this
way, we came to Professor and Mrs Sterling's, who
lived in the area. He wasn't home yet, only she, a
hysteric. The Professor arrived shortly afterwards and
fell into an armchair breathing heavily, like a beached
whale. Time after time came the sound of detonations.
Mrs Sterling screamed at her husband: 'See!...See!'
He had had it with her: 'What is it I am supposed to
see, you idiot, what is it?' he growled, and dug himself
deeper into the armchair.

Then it got even worse, and we went down to the
vestibule. Uncle pushed the maid into an alcove and
sheltered her with his back. My mother was furious
because she thought I should be the one to be pushed
into the alcove, not Uncle's girlfriend. The bombs kept
falling and the house moved in all directions. Some
woman from upstairs started screaming, 'The
chamber-pot, the chamber-pot, has anyone seen the
chamber-pot?' To this, Uncle replied that he had not
seen anything, but there was something dripping on
his head.

To what extent is this sarcastic account in keeping with the facts?
One hundred per cent. In fact, after we returned from
Konstancin to 9 Swiętokrzyska Street, I had such a severe panic
attack that my father arranged our move to Uncle Jermułowicz
at Number 16 that very same evening. Our cook, Mrs Boryńska,
stayed at Number 9 and miraculously survived when a heavy
bomb fell on the house. She sustained only superficial head
wounds. A few people, mainly military, died in the apartment.
The next stop, after Swiętokrzyska was in flames, was the house

at 1 Boduen Street. Friends of ours, Henryk and Roma Linde, lived there, as did Władisław and Róża Sterling, one floor down. The first night, that of 25/26 September, was particularly dramatic. It was then that I first saw people mutilated and bleeding.

When the bombs stopped falling and the artillery fire died down, we sat in a daze in the Linde armchairs. Uncle Jermułowicz, who had lost all his worldly possessions, was wiping his eyes, and my aunt was sobbing out loud. Father was being brave and doing what he could to comfort his sister and brother-in-law: 'Don't worry, Stefan. As soon as all this ends, I'll build you an even more beautiful study with the most modern equipment!' Unfortunately, all this was not going to end for another five years, when not one of the people present, apart from my mother and me, would be alive.

The following day, we learned that there was an empty apartment at 1 Boduen Street, belonging to the actress Irena Horwath who was in Lwów. The apartment was being looked after by the maid, who had instructions to rent it out. We moved in there after it had been disinfected. (I had never seen such a quantity of bed-bugs in such a relatively small area.) After we had taken down hundreds of pictures and photographs, and removed tons of clutter, the place became habitable. I was up to my ears in souvenirs left behind by Irene Horwath. She had once been an actress well known for her statuesque beauty. Her real surname was Kurzyjamska. In any event, she married Baron von Groer, a lawyer, and her son was a famous paediatrician, Professor Groer, also a photographer, and for a while, director of the Lwów Opera.

Was this your last apartment before you went into the ghetto?

Yes. We lived there for a year, and the next stop in our wanderings was Chłodna Street.

FOUR

Fourth Conversation

What did you do in the months after war broke out?

The Evangelical Reformed community, in the shape of Father Zaunar, helped us a great deal then. He offered me a job in the community's head offices, saying I was his relation. So I started working as a writer, penning copperplate entries into the church register. The work was rather monotonous, but not without its philosophical side. Death records were interwoven with birth records, the beginning of life with its end...The friendliness of the priests and office workers compensated for the tedium. I could have stayed there for the duration of the war.

It's 1940. You decided, however, to go into the ghetto. What were the reasons for and against?

We could have afforded to have gone into hiding. We had, for example, a 'good' appearance which, in Occupation language, meant no distinctively Jewish features. I would rate my mother's appearance excellent, my own very good, but my father's just good. We spoke impeccable Polish, didn't talk with our hands, and, as Christians, we were thoroughly grounded in the customs of Polish society. On top of that, we had many friends of whom at least half would quite willingly have helped us.

On the other hand, the basic problem was Father's illness, *angina pectoris*, which required quiet, and constant medical care. Father was known in Warsaw. If we'd remained on the Aryan side, he wouldn't have been able to go out on the streets, which would have been unthinkable to someone of his disposition, as would have been the daily pretending: the false *curriculum vitae* and the whole impossible pantomime of Occupation existence. In any case, being separated from my father at such a time would have been unthinkable.

Our illusions about the Germans, about which I spoke earlier, also played a part in the decision. And in actual fact, going into the ghetto was a legal course of action. The Germans, as is known, are legalistic. We reckoned that it was better to obey their orders.

Which German orders caused you to find yourselves inside the ghetto walls?

There was a succession of acts of dispossession. Armbands, prohibitions, contributions — we were coming ever nearer to the *Endlösung der Judenfrage*, in other words, to the final solution of the Jewish question. One day, the announcement came that by 15 October 1940, all Jews must be inside the confines of the ghetto, which was to be closed off on 15 November. Everything had to be arranged by then. Fortunately, there was total freedom in regard to exchanging housing. The Germans weren't concerned about it.

Our situation was not a happy one. Our flat at 9 Swiętokrzyska Street had been bombed, so we had nothing to swap. We looked at flats inside the ghetto area – a Jewish neighbourhood which we didn't know very well. The places were dreadful. We couldn't make up our minds.

You were, however, in an extreme situation. You had to find accommodation, if only a sub-let.

I remember one incident during the course of searching. I came to an apartment, 14 Nowolipki Street, occupied by one Izaak Lejpuner. This Lejpuner, a doctor by profession, was, unbeknown to me, an activist in a Jewish nationalist splinter group. When I asked about a room, he looked at me fiercely and said, 'Polish isn't spoken here! This is our home, and we talk in our own language.' I left without even looking at the room.

Mother had no success, either. We had to take up Aunt Róża Pańska's offer to take care of things. She had an attractive flat to exchange on Krasiński Street in the Warsaw suburb of Żoliborz. She was in a very difficult financial situation because none of her sons were around, and, anyway, she'd been supported all her life by my father, because her sons never had a penny to their names. So she offered to arrange everything, and we would finance the transaction. Father agreed. There was one drawback, however, and that was Aunt Róża's incessant chatter. But what did that matter compared to living under the same roof as the inhospitable Dr Lejpuner?

So where did you end up?

At 39 Chłodna Street.

A good address. Ringelblum* writes that the Warsaw ghetto consisted of three social strata: the aristocracy on Leszno, Elektoralna and Chłodna Streets; the middle class on Leszno Street; and the lower class everywhere else.

The house was, indeed, respectable: a three-roomed flat with kitchen and bathroom, luxurious by ghetto standards. It didn't have what the prewar aesthetes called '*Armeleutegeruch*' (the smell of human poverty). I lived in one room with my mother; my father had another room; while in the third room was the official occupant: my aunt. Mrs Boryńska, our prewar cook, and my father's trusted personal help, had the kitchen. We had to get special permission for that. We lived there until my father's death on 4 October 1941. A very short time after that, the borders of the ghetto were changed, as a result of which 39 Chłodna Street was relocated to the Aryan side, and we landed up in a new, collective and very comfortable flat at 16 Chłodna Street, right on its 'aristocratic' stretch where the ghetto rulers lived.

What was it like living in the ghetto; what was the atmosphere?

Not good. The circumstances were conducive to a revival of Jewish fanaticism and nationalism. People known to be converts didn't get a good press in the ghetto. And even though the Jewish Council wasn't made up of lunatics like Lejpuner, it was out of the question for a convert to perform any official function in the ghetto. This resulted in my father's enforced inactivity: he was limited to social work.

Would you like to recreate the first days in the ghetto, that feverish atmosphere of the movement of an enormous mass of people?

The first days were indeed ones of confusion and turmoil. There was never-ending coming and going: the Aryans were mov-

---

*   Dr Emanuel Ringelblum: well-known Jewish historian and chronicler of the Warsaw ghetto (Archiwum Ringelbaum-Ghetto Warszawskie lipiec 1942-sierpien 1943, PWN 1980).

ing out of flats and shops, and the Jews were moving in with all their belongings. Hitler's extermination plans hadn't yet become apparent. People knew about the impending closure of the Jewish area (the use of the term 'ghetto' was still prohibited at that point), but they deluded themselves into thinking that it wouldn't come to pass. 'You can do that in Africa, but not in a city of millions of people in the centre of Europe', they'd say. Not even the fact that walls were being erected worried people, because, as they said, 'Walls exist so that people can squeeze through the cracks.'

Where exactly was your building?

The house was centrally situated on the border between the small and large ghetto, but, at the same time, to the side, not in the eye of the storm. The wall with its entrance on Kercelak Square was close enough so that we could make some use of that location, but far enough away so as to protect the residents from contact with the gendarmes on guard.

What did you do? Did the move depress you, or did it rouse you to action?

At first, I took a good look around the area, visiting family and friends. All of them had established themselves quite well. The atmosphere was relaxed. The optimists triumphed. Even when the ghetto was closed, we weren't particularly worried. On the other hand, being cut off from the world created the illusion that we were away from German threat. There was no shortage of voices saying that here, inside the walls, we'd be able to survive the war in peace.

What about your education?

There were no schools, just courses. For example, there were courses for nursing personnel which fulfilled the role of secret medical studies. Professor Ludwik Hirszfeld, the renowned serologist, lectured in the ghetto. His were fascinating lectures – people fought just to get into the room. You needed to know somebody in order to get into that line of study, but I never felt the calling.

Could you pass the secondary school graduating exam only on the Aryan side?

Not necessarily, but someone from the Aryan side had to be charged with giving exams in the ghetto. Dr Zdzisław Libin from the Rej school was charged with giving exams in all the humanities subjects. An acquaintance of my father, a Mr Różycki, gave the science subjects. I didn't have a clue about mathematics, physics or chemistry. I think I passed the exam thanks to 'knowing' somebody. For Libin, on the other hand, I did well, and so got a good grade on the certificate handed to me after the war.

You were interested in law; you'd settled on that before the war already.

I heard that an acquaintance of ours, the lawyer Mieczysław Ettinger, was organizing law courses along university lines. These courses were illegal, the instructors of a very high level. Ettinger had managed to get an outstanding scholar of international law, legal adviser to the Ministry of Foreign Affairs, Dr Szymon Rundstein, and Counsellor Stanisław Adler. At the first meeting, we decided when and in whose house the lectures would take place. It was there that I met Olek Oszerowski, whose fate would be so closely tied to mine that we would leave the ghetto together. We became instant friends because our situations were similar. We'd both lost our fathers, we were both responsible for our mothers, and we came from similar backgrounds. (Olek's father had owned a very successful hosiery factory before the war.)

Did you work, other than attending the course? I know that work was required of Jews in the ghetto aged between 14 and 60.

Of course, in order to have your papers in order you had to find some kind of work; it was also tied in with owning an *Ausweis* [identity card]. As chance would have it, Father met his former acquaintance Colonel Szeryński (Szynkman), who organized the Ordnungsdienst [the Jewish Police], in the ghetto. Szeryński suggested that he would give me an office job, not involving police duties, which would provide me with the best of all possible identity papers.

Knowing you, I can't quite imagine you taking up such an offer.

I think my intense hatred for all kinds of discipline was more important than principles in this case. I adamantly rejected the very idea of 'serving' anywhere, and most particularly in the police. The very thought of parading around in uniform seemed terrifying to me. And anyway, Father didn't insist.

What acquaintances did you draw on? As I understand it, had you gone into offices straight off the street then nothing would have come of it.

The brothers Eugene and Gabriel Grasberg, with whom I'm still friendly today, were my friends at Rej. Their father, the great miller, Henryk Grasberg, was a millionaire. He had a good head for business. In the ghetto, he was asked to become vice-president of the *Versorgungsanstalt* [Provisioning Authority]: the distribution of food had to be organized somehow. And Grasberg was not just any expert. I remember an interesting conversation with him when he was old and already ill — he was barely 56 years old, but he seemed ancient to me. He confided to me that it was going to be hard for him to die, because his sons seemed entirely devoid of any business sense. 'Just think,' he said, 'today, I sent Gabriel for the paper. He comes back, I look—yesterday's paper. Some street urchin had sold Grasberg's son, an intelligent man, yesterday's copy. So how can I die peacefully under such conditions?' That incident has stuck in my mind, and ever since then I've been afraid that I might be sold yesterday's news. Old Grasberg, at Father's request, offered me a position at the Provisioning Authority. It involved wearing the same blue armband which the community officials wore. The most important thing, though, was the *Ausweis*, which guaranteed freedom of movement.

Did you work for money or for allowances?

For both. The allowance was daily. In addition to a few miserable groszy, the Provisioning Authority workers received a daily half-kilo loaf of doughy bread, and either beet marmalade or artificial honey. I didn't take advantage of it.

Didn't you have to?

I gave it away to friends. At home I ate food bought on the open market and most often smuggled. But officially, everything was distributed through the Provisioning Authority. Products were paid for with coupons assigned to everyone living in the ghetto. Shopkeepers stuck the coupons onto sheets of paper given to us by the controllers. They would try to cheat us; they would stick anything on and try to persuade us it was a coupon.

Controlling coupons could drive you crazy. The sheets stank of some fish glue, which disgusted me. There were always a few coupon cards left over, so my colleagues in the Provisioning Authority and I printed a satire on the back of them called 'Zarty na karty' [Quips for Chits]. I would never have thought that they would have such an influence on my literary work.

Were your activities restricted to 'sniffing' coupons?

Not at all. As the most skilled among my colleagues, I often sat at the window and dealt with clients. Lots of colourful types came by, like the two grannies who were saleswomen.

Why do you remember these grannies in particular out of the thousands of clients?

Because they were apparently in the same situation. Each of them carried in front of her on a strap a small tray of disgusting sweets, made locally, which she sold by the piece, because who could have afforded to buy themselves a couple of ounces of sweets? To sell one or two pieces was the best these two old ladies could hope for. There was no difference between the sweets, but there was a distinct difference between Granny Fajga and Granny Cyrla. Fajga was boring and unlucky. She kept complaining that she'd had a misfortune, that she'd fallen over, that her goods had been stolen, or her sweet money taken by force. I dreaded her visits because she'd describe, in a tearful voice, all the awful things that had afflicted her family. They were true, but that same terrifying truth applied to almost everybody.

Granny Cyrla, on the other hand – short, shrivelled, huge nose and bright, shiny eyes – entertained us with stories about her adventures. She talked with a cheerful self-irony, and her Polish created additional humourous effects. She had a saying which played a big part in my life – I'd repeat it at the most difficult times. It went, 'There's no evil, that won't come out for good.' ['*Nie ma tego złego, co by nie wyszło na dobrego*.'] Had she spoken correctly, it would have been banal. But as it was, it could have been a motto for all human existence. We'd wait impatiently for Granny Cyrla's arrival and support her financially, to the disadvantage of her unfortunate competitor. Their fate was identical, and their attitudes — pessimism and optimism — didn't have the slightest effect on what awaited them. Granny Cyrla, as she perished in Auschwitz or Treblinka, couldn't have had the slightest idea that something might be done 'for good' to her. At least, not in the sense that she would become the positive heroine of my story. Had she known, she would have doubtless given a sceptical smile and wrinkled her brow understandingly, 'What does it cost me? Write to your heart's content, but please take another delicious sweet.'

From what you say, it seems that you were very overworked. Did you have any time to yourself, or did you just go between work and home? Before the war, you went to a boys' school, and you've just talked about your male friends, not about girlfriends. But the ghetto must have been the period of your sexual awakening.

I wasn't quite 18 then, but the hot-house atmosphere at home condemned me to a monastic life. I adored my father, but I often hated him for eternally looking at his watch, for his eternal dread that something bad might happen to me. This sometimes gave rise to open hostility, because every time I went out was greeted with open disapproval. In the meantime, weird things were going on with me. For no apparent reason, I'd get a rush of blood to the head and think I was about to faint. My dreams were unashamedly erotic. I grew pale and lost weight, which was good for me, actually. Only family anecdotes remained of the fatty I had been.

In the building opposite, there lived a pair of doctors and their young, maybe 20-something, daughter – a dentist. It's hard for me to say now whether she was really beautiful or whether she simply seemed that way to me. Any time I met that red-haired girl with her beautiful body and slender legs, I behaved like an idiot. Despite my stupidity, I noticed her quick, arch glances and smiles.

I don't know which one of us took the initiative, probably me. I started to complain to my parents that I had toothache, even though my teeth were fine. At my next meeting with my neighbour, I appeared in the role of patient. How I managed to stutter out a request for an appointment, I don't know. It was a feat which, beside all my other wartime deeds, seems insignificant. The dentist (whose name, unfortunately, I can't even remember today) casually said, 'Come at nine. Today, if you like.'

After dinner, I again mentioned my toothache, and the appointment with the dentist.

'What time are you going?' Father asked.

'At nine,' I said nonchalantly, going beet-red. Father gave a slight smile, and when I was leaving, he came to the door with me and patted me on the shoulder.

She opened the door wearing a white apron, cool, matter-of-fact. I felt let down, that nothing would come of this. She invited me into the office. I noticed that the adjacent room was dark and completely quiet. I sat down in the chair as though waiting for the anaesthetic. She lit a lamp, I remember her leaning above me and appraising my teeth. 'So where does it hurt?'

'This one,' I mumbled, pointing to any old tooth.

'Are you sure?' She shook her head. 'Nothing hurts, does it? You're embarrassed,' she said, leaning – accidently, perhaps – on my arm.

I'm not exactly sure what happened next, because I lost all sense of time and place. I remember only her hair aflame in the lamp's bright light, her white face, and her lips on my lips. And later, the touch of her hand, my own awkwardness, and pride that it had finally happened.

When I returned home, not too late and not too early, my parents were playing rummy with friends — a game known as idiot's bridge. 'So what happened?' my father asked, looking at me searchingly and unsmilingly. I nodded that everything was fine.

'Was there something the matter?' my mother asked solicitously.

'There was, there was,' answered Father. He looked at me knowingly and calmly picked the trick up. I ran into my room and, shaken but happy, threw myself onto the bed.

A beautiful story, and possible only among the ghetto's plutocracy, because how could it have happened in terrible overcrowding? But to go back to the Provisioning Authority, what happened to the people who worked there?

You know, after the war, I often recalled, even in dreams, that little room where we worked under the supervision of Dr Anna Wohl, older sister of Stanisław Wohl, director and professor at the Łódź film school. If you were to line up my peers from the ghetto in a row, with an SS man standing opposite us pointing out with his finger who was to survive, his finger would have stopped at me, and only me.

Truth to tell, I had enormous advantages over my colleagues. They were circumcized Jews, of a Semitic appearance, and on top of that, they were not very well off. And money played a fundamental role in deciding survival – greater even than that of appearance. I was a non-Jew, uncircumcized, well-off, with an Aryan appearance, and I spoke the purest Polish. There were six of us boys in the Provisioning Authority: not one survived, except me.

And Mrs Wohl and her family?

That's another matter. She survived, even though she looked Jewish, and ended up in France teaching chemistry at some university. Her parents also survived. Her father, Natan Wohl's, uncle, Henryk, was Director of the Treasury Department at the time of the January uprising of 1983. Natan, himself, was a known financier, a wise and attractive man. He and his wife had an interesting adventure with a Polish policeman, who came to their hideout near Warsaw to blackmail them. Mr Wohl talked to him in his own way, and the result was that the policeman didn't take any money, but returned a second time. After that, he became a regular guest, practically a member of the family, and he saw the Wohl's through the whole Occupation.

It's interesting. Right after the war, when I was looking for Anna, I found myself at the Wohl's Łódź apartment, on Cegielna Street, I believe.

I had a memorable conversation with Natan. He asked me what I thought of the new government in Poland, whether it would last. I said that it would, unfortunately, and that I reckoned it would go on for dozens of years. Natan was upset. 'So that's what the new generation thinks', he said. 'Doubtless you're right, but its terrible to live and die in such a reality'. At the time, I couldn't judge to what degree he was right. I was proud as a peacock that the great Natan Wohl wanted to hear my opinion.

I've noticed that you are very impressed by wealthy financiers: Grasberg, Wohl, your father.

Oh, yes, I don't hide the fact. I think the art of making money is an art not so much beautiful as admirable. It probably comes out of my lack of any talent whatsoever in that direction. Never, other than in the exotic conditions of a position at the Wołomin glass-works, have I ever been able to earn a single złoty except from writing or editing. And I'm not taking a lofty artistic view of this, quite the contrary, I could weep for being such a zero.

It's explained partly by the fact that you never had the opportunity to shine as a businessman: before the war, you were too young; after the collapse of communism, forgive me for saying this, you were a bit too old. But rather than theorizing, tell me how your father coped with being shut up inside the ghetto.

Very badly. I describe the last months of his life in the second part of this book, but I want to tell you about one incident which was a harbinger of the later dramatic events. In the Warsaw ghetto, there was a strict rule ordering us to bow to every uniformed German. It was unpleasant, but by comparison with the other horrors of ghetto existence, it was rather childish. I always bowed first to everyone, even though in many cases it was to people who did not deserve respect. What's more, I bowed to strangers because, on account of my shortsightedness, I was afraid of making a gaffe. Why, after all, living in a lawless, ignominious world, should I consider doffing my hat in front of strangers as the worst humiliation? My father saw this differently. For him, it was a matter of principle. His temperament and inborn tendency to fisticuffs had been reinforced by the time he spent studying in Germany. As you know, the German fraternal code of honour demanded active intervention in the case of the slightest insult, which included not only gestures and words, but also glances (the so-called 'fixing with a glance'). With such an attitude, to bow to a German soldier-boy assumed almost mystical proportions. So we tried to persuade Father to spend most of his time at home, especially in winter, when it was impossible to walk around without a hat on your head. Father felt ill, in any case, and at least wasn't raring to take walks down the ghetto's infernal streets. He usually sat in his armchair, deep in thought, smoking one cigarette after another. One winter's day, we left the house together to see to something not far away from home. Even though he had aged a lot, he was still an imposing figure in his fur hunting coat, soft grey hat, and the ever-present cane in his hand. All of a sudden, a German soldier appeared in front of us – a boy of about twenty – standing in the middle of the pavement, closely watching the passers-by. He obviously demanded obeisance. Without even thinking, I doffed my hat, and looked at my father as I did so. I froze, because the expression on his face bespoke disaster. The German took a step in our direction, and there they stood, facing each other, taking each other's measure: my 56-year-old father and that shit in a Hitler uniform. I don't know how long it went on: it seemed ages to me. Then the German shouted, '*Du, nimm ab dein kapelusz* [hat]!' I don't know why he used the Polish word *kapelusz*, stressing the '*ka*'.) Father didn't even budge: he just kept fixing him with his gaze, fraternity-style. I looked with terror at the German's pistol and at Father's cane. Finally, the German turned and walked off. To this day, I don't understand his retreat. Could he have been scared off by being stared at by an elderly man? Maybe some human instincts awoke in him?

Have you ever thought how you would behave in a similar situation today?

I know for sure that were my daughter watching, I would not remove my hat.

FIVE

Fifth Conversation

Where was the Provisioning Authority located?

At 12 Leszno Street, opposite number 13, where the so-called 'Thirteen' — Control Office for Combatting the Black Market and Profiteering (the Gestapo agency in the ghetto) — was located. Nearby, at number 2, was the Sztuka Café.

Would you like to make some comment on cultural life in the ghetto? Hundreds of outstanding people, after all, were in there.

I'm often asked whether I knew Janusz Korczak. I did. The portrait of him as a martyr on behalf of Jewish children has been preserved. I, however, remember him mainly as a tireless organizer, a man who could make the rich subscribe to the cause of orphans. He went around in a military uniform of no particular distinction, looking old, stern-faced and unsmiling. He had a small beard. He wasn't particularly friendly. His goal was to save children and he was ready to do anything to achieve it. He organized concerts at his children's home. I once went to one of those concerts. I got the tickets from Father, who had undertaken to help distribute them. This 'help' consisted of taking from Korczak several books of tickets to sell, and, because he didn't want to put himself out, he'd simply pay for the lot himself. So I always had a vast number of tickets for myself and my friends, but, truth to tell, I wasn't all that keen on these events.

The concert began with Korczak sitting at a table on the platform and having a moving conversation with God in public. The Jewish God is cruel, so Korczak argued with him fiercely, demanding that He finally do something about the fate of His chosen people. This improvisation lasted a long time and created an incredible impression. Directly after, the famous actor Michal Znicz came onto the platform and sang some song by Jurandot to the effect that if you are a Jew, you're already a goner. The contrast between Korczak's monologue and this piece of doggerel seemed to me grotesque. Then, Znicz and Minowicz performed other cabaret turns. Finally, Marysia Ajzensztadt came on.

Many people still remember her. The writer Helena Szereszewska in 'Krzyż i mezuza' [Cross and Mezuza] recalls that Marysia's performances were the single pleasant memory she and her daughters had of the ghetto; for one brief moment, they'd forget the daily nightmares.

Marysia Ajzensztadt didn't survive; I feel very sorry for her. That girl, daughter of the cantor and director of the ghetto's musical ensembles, had the most beautiful voice imaginable. She was also pretty and very graceful. She didn't want to be separated from her father at the *Umschlagplatz*. And she could have been saved, because everyone in the ghetto knew her and was ready to help her. She performed everywhere she could, mainly at the Sztuka Café. At the time, I was critical of her for dissipating her talent. Today, however, I'm sorry for all the times I missed hearing her sing.

In one of your memoirs, where you write about the Sztuka Café, the name Wiera Gran appears. I came across a book she wrote once which was published in Paris, Sztafeta Oszczerców [A Pack of Slanderers]. A shattering work because it's entirely devoted to an obsessive polemic against accusations of ostensibly immoral behaviour. Did you ever come across Wiera Gran?

Only as an enthusiastic spectator. She was my favourite singer, and a beautiful woman. 'Letter, first love-letter', – her sensual voice still resounds in my ears.

Could you comment on the accusations levelled against her?

I regard them as arrant nonsense. Wiera Gran was the most popular singer in the ghetto, and I never heard a single bad word said against her. On the contrary, she was known for her helpfulness and philanthropy. I find the allegations that she 'gave' herself to the Jewish gestapo completely groundless.

Can you prove it?

The burden of proof is on the accusers. The fact is that conditions existing in artistic circles in the ghetto made it impossible to be choosy about the company you kept. As a famous diva, you could not isolate yourself from the authorities. The authorities, on the other hand, were shady characters. The main patron of the Muse was Abraham Gancwajch, president of the Control Office for Combatting the Black Market and Profiteering, probably the most powerful man in the ghetto, regarded as the chief resident Gestapo. Ringelblum wrote of him that 'he constantly organizes parties for Jewish writers and artists and provides good food, which, in these times, is the most important thing... Even Dr Schipper allowed himself to be invited for Sabbath fish... many artists receive monthly salaries from him! *Gazeta Zydowska* [The Jewish Newspaper] was full of references to the wonderful Gancwajch and his worthy wife.

But surely Wiera Gran didn't need Gancwajch's financial assistance.

Certainly not, but refusing to take part in events organized by him or his adjutants could have had terrible repercussions for her. Knowledge of the ghetto's 'Who's Who' wasn't easy. There was no shortage of Gestapo men like Izrael First in the community, either. How could a girl in her 20s find her way around that jungle?

One can assume that these occasions went on until morning because there was a curfew operating. In such a situation, can't one suspect that...?

Neither I nor any of my acquaintances took part in such gatherings. Wiera Gran mentions one of her performances during dinner. She collected 500 złoty which she gave to a good cause. I never heard anyone accuse her of bad conduct or of using her connections to dishonourable ends.

Where is Wiera Gran today?

The accusations destroyed her life and ruined her career. She got persecution mania, the proof of which is the book you mentioned. And to think that she had a signed contract with the Paris ABC theatre before the war! The date of her departure was set for 1 September 1939. After endless lawsuits and other horrendous struggles, which lasted for practically the entire postwar period, Wiera Gran still lives, to this day, in Paris. The writer Stefan Kisielewski told me that he'd met her some years ago. She looked beautiful, and was, as that old goat put it, still eminently '*couchable*'. I never knew her myself, but I often think about her with a certain embarrassment. I'm ashamed of those who took the moral high ground and threw stones at her without mercy.

We were speaking about the prominent people, the ghetto kings of life. Did the rich maintain their 'splendid isolation' until the very end?

Probably not completely. I witnessed incredible scenes. For example, when the liquidation action began, the president of the Provisioning Authority, the millionaire Abraham Gepner, walked through the streets giving 20-złoty pieces to the crowds of beggars. It had no practical meaning, because by then, those people could count their lives in hours. But Gepner was paying off some lifetime debts. Towards the end of the ghetto's existence, such situations weren't unusual. Even though I was still not an adult, I felt increasingly bad myself. I knew that we had some enormous moral duty to the dead people lying in the streets covered with newspapers, whose corpses were cleared by Pinkiert's funeral department, and even more to those still alive, whose pleas for mercy could be heard from inside the barracks for the homeless, the windows of which bristled with scores of outstretched hands. Perhaps this book will be a kind of payment for that obligation.

Gepner, who refused to leave the ghetto and perished with the insurgents in the bunker, is one of the true heroes of that time. The fate of that other old man, Alfred Nossig, was the total opposite.

It's worth talking at length about Nossig because his actions are chilling. He lived in the same building as me at 39 Chłodna Street. Every day, despite myself, I would look into his flat, which was on the same floor as ours in the opposite wing. When I discovered that the short, scrawny, lame old man was Dr Alfred Nossig, I almost died! He was a famous person, a Polish–German–Hebrew poet and dramatist with a mystical bent, as well as a sociologist, economist, philosopher, sculptor, medallist and a known activist, first as a Zionist and then in the pan-European movement. What I knew about him then came from my reading of Feldman's *History of Polish Literature*, and I also knew that he'd been connected with Paderewski for a long time and had written the libretto for his opera *Manru*.

How old was this renaissance man when the ghetto was opened?

Nearly 78. He lived with an old serving woman who worried about his meals (which were, as far as I could see, opulent) and about his clothes (he was always well dressed). He exercised for half an hour every morning (his old-man's scrawniness made this a grotesque sight). We called his displays — always performed in front of an open window — the '*Danse Macabre*'. After gymnastics and a hefty breakfast, he went to work, because despite his advanced age, he was the director of the community's emigration department. He came back rather late and his servant gave him dinner which he usually ate alone, although sometimes in the company of his mistress.

His mistress?

That's how it was. The author of works redolent with the spirit of the 'Song of Songs' had a mistress – not an old one, at that, and in the evening hours, every now and then, he gave himself up to the life of the senses. My observations of the events played out behind a not very well drawn curtain testified to it. Or, maybe, it seemed that way to my overdeveloped imagination.

On normal days, he sat at his desk until late – writing, writing, writing, with his nose to the paper. He never paused for a second; apparently, he didn't need time to think. It was said that he was preparing a memorial about the future of the ghetto for the Germans.

I never saw anyone other than the above-mentioned woman paying him a visit. Nossig took no part in the life of the building, never exchanged a single word with anyone. He never noticed any of us as he slipped by. It was as though any human contact repelled him. He behaved like a healthy man in a leper colony. Everybody paid him back with sincere antipathy: there was gossip about Nossig's connections with Hitler's special forces, which seemed absurd at his age. There was no end of gossip then. I bowed every time I met him, to which he reacted with some indeterminate movement of his skinny neck — it might have been in response to my bow or else a nervous tic.

Did you run into him after the boundaries of the ghetto were changed?

No, I lost sight of him. But later, from a ŻOB [Jewish Fighting Organization] announcement, I learned that Gestapoman Nosik [*sic*] had been shot on 22 February 1943. Apparently, he had provided the Germans with information about Jewish 'bunkers' in attics and cellars. At first, I thought it had to do with two completely different people. It turned out, however, that the sentence was carried out in Nossig's flat at 42 Muranowa Street. There was no doubt about it.

I recently came across a trace of Nossig in many publications, not just from the war period. I learned that he'd been a German agent since 1913, and that his area of operation was penetrating Polish Jewry. After the First World War, he was often in Warsaw, even though the Polish Government knew that he was a paid agent of Wilhelmstrasse. Afterwards, he passed himself off as an intermediary between Poland and the Third Reich, stressing that he had excellent contact with Hitler. He'd tell the writer Roman Brandstaetter* about his mission of saving Jews. In the end, he found himself in the ghetto.

Are there any sources for the last period of his life?

Adam Czerniaków's invaluable *Diary of the Warsaw Ghetto* includes many references to Nossig. One learns from it that Nossig appeared in Warsaw right after the Germans came in. 'I was visited by the *Tausendkünstler* [juggler] Alfred Nossig', the chairman of the Jewish Council notes on 17 October 1939. He had his guest's current address as 21 Krasiński Street, Flat 35. On 9 December of the same year, he writes: 'Morning in the SS...Later on, ordered to give a job in the community to Dr Nossig.' This notation reveals no liking for the newly acquired worker. Two weeks later, Jewish activists held deliberations on the question of Nossig. As Ringelblum relates, 'because of the sensitivity of emigration problems, it was decided to surround Nossig with honest people.' In Czerniaków's diary, there are many fundamentally unfriendly remarks about Nossig. But the most appalling is something that Czerniaków couldn't have known— a six-page denunciation of insurgents to the German

---

* Roman Brandstaetter (1906–87): Polish-Jewish poet and playwright.

authorities. The 80-year-old traitor threatened the insurgents, at the very end, that the Gestapo would avenge his death.

I think that somebody competent should examine this amazing – and unique among Jewish intellectuals – fraud and renegade.

Nossig is a monstrous example of the unreciprocated love of Germans by Jews.

I can give you another example, this one grotesque. The example is the case of my aunt, Lili Piszczkowska. Her adoration of the Germans knew no bounds. When they appeared at her luxurious apartment after September 1939 and requisitioned her valuable dinner-service, she announced that she was very proud that her porcelain would be of use to the lofty aims of German officers. The fact that she was subject to the same restrictions as all Jews didn't alter her opinion one iota. She didn't go into the ghetto, however, and one day, as a result of being denounced, found herself, together with her half-witted husband, on Szuch Avenue. And there, at Gestapo headquarters, she gave the performance of her life. She started telling the interrogators that the decision to annihilate the Jews was just, that she adored Hitler and honoured the whole killing machine. The officer, hearing these words spoken in impeccable German by my aunt, an educated person, was dumbstruck, and ordered the old lady to be thrown off the premises. Love of Hitler saved Auntie's life, or rather, delayed her unfortunate end. An irony of fate ordained that after the war, angry with the world because the Germans had lost the war, Lili went to England to her son. The son either didn't want to, or couldn't, support her, and Lili died a servant to the wicked enemies of Germany.

It's dreadful and funny. A borderline personality. But you speak of it in a distanced way. I've noticed in general that you're careful in your judgement of people placed in extreme positions. Actually, each day in the ghetto was a test of human decency. There was the Council, the community, the police, all these institutions and others, too, like your Provisioning Authority, were open to corruption, forced to collaborate in some way. That makes it difficult to judge.

I have always felt better playing the part of advocate rather than that of prosecutor. Did you know that the elite of the young legal profession went into the police? Students of people of high moral calibre, like Berenson, Brokman, Neufeld, Schönbach. At the beginning, it was justifiable, because it was a question of security forces, of maintaining order in the ghetto. A crowd of many thousands cannot get by without security forces and internal organizations. They couldn't know that their function would shortly change. That they would be used for deportations. That they would be the main helpers of the Germans during the liquidation of the ghetto. That role of the police was shameful, requiring them, after the war, to give proof of their personal innocence. Many educated people, I'm not speaking about the rabble who also went into the police force, found themselves trapped. At a time like this, any person of decent character should resign, throw his cap and his identification papers away. Because how can you justify colluding with enemy action against people?

Yes, but the boundaries are slippery — one policeman sees to administrative goals, another shoves people onto the platforms, and sometimes saves someone among those he's routing out of their houses.

I wouldn't condemn anyone for simply belonging to the police force, but for actually participating in crimes. There are a number of people still living in Warsaw who have a few things on their conscience. They're pensioners today, one doesn't need to dwell on them, but the problem is a major one.

Did you know Marcel Reich-Ranicki, who was active in Poland and who has been a leading literary critic in Germany for many years? One hears a lot about him lately, because it turns out that he has a complicated and ambiguous past.

Reich-Ranicki, whom I see from time to time when I'm in Frankfurt, is a few years older than I am. He comes from an intellectual family, and he was a scholar and music-lover since his youth, which I very much envied. He lived near me on Chłodna Street and had a sizeable record collection. He would invite guests to his flat for concerts of recorded music. Scores of people who couldn't fit into the small apartment stood on the staircase listening to the music. I met Reich very often, and all I know about him is that he worked in the community. I can't say I was crazy about him, that's all. The rest is just slander.

SIX

Sixth Conversation

As far as I know, your official literary debut was in Łódź in March of 1945. But you regard as your real debut the works you wrote in the Warsaw ghetto in 1942, in particular the much-celebrated poem 'Ptak' [Bird].

That's right. After the war, I had more or less forgotten about those early works, and then, 33 years later, I picked up a copy of *Les Temps modernes*, Jean-Paul Sartre's monthly, and, to my amazement, found there, at the front of the issue, a poem with the following comment: 'In the Summer of 1942, a famous magician performed in the Warsaw ghetto. The following poem, from the pen of an unknown author, was found in the archives of the Jewish Historical Commission.' The work was called 'L'Oiseau' and the first verse went:

> Quelque part, à la belle étoile
> Dresser sa tente un mage célèbre:
> Devant l'entrée un signe étrange,
> Symbole de mystérieuses ténèbres.

And I started reciting it by heart:

Out in the open, nght on the street
The celebrated magician pitched a tent
Above its entrance hung a curious portent,
Symbol of a terrible secret

Inside, the jeering crowd grew still
While he, in a turban of stars,
Gazed upon the dying embers
And, like a shaman, lifted up his hands.

Thus began the seance: a juggler
Of plates and fiery rings,
A heavy table pirouetted
Like a dancer on the arm of the Master.

Later, the swallowing of fire
And glimmering, thin swords.
In the dark the master seems to have paled
Then once more burns like a torch.

To top off somebody thrust
A glittering sabre into the supple flesh
Of the magician who, gored through,
Smiled and bowed with grace.

For the finale the great magician carefully
Concealed something with his top hat,
Tipped it –a bird took wing
And immediately soared into the horizon.

The bird limned the air like the tailing of a missile,
And like a bullet streaked above the wall.
Veiled by clouds he remained
A faint but translucent emblem.

The magician gazed a farewell to the bird.
In his eyes were tears; in his head, a roar.
But when he turned to look upon the crowd gathered there,
'The crowd was staring at the sky and weeping.*

Yes, it was I who had written that poem which had made its
way, in translation, into a French periodical. I wrote it one
summer evening and on the following day, read it to one of my
friends at the time – a very excitable young man who fell to his
knees, much to my embarrassment. This gesture, a thank-you
for the dedication to 'Ptak', was my first literary success.

---

* Trans. Nancy Esposito.

But let's return to the present, to the moment when I recognized myself as the unknown author. I made myself known to Irena Kanfer, the translator, and since then, 'Ptak' appears under my own name. It shocks and surprises me each time I see this poem in print. Did *I* write that? So that boy in the photograph who gazes down at me, his eyes filled with fear, was me?

Was this your only encounter after many years with your ghetto writings?

No, it was the second. An acquaintance of mine, the noted graphic artist George Him (co-creator of famous works from the prewar Levitt–Him studios), was putting on an exhibition in London about the Warsaw ghetto. Knowing that I had spent nearly two years of my life there, he asked me to help him collect materials. In connection with this, I visited a lot of people and institutions (without much success, truth to tell). I visited Professor Bernard Mark, at that time director of the Jewish Historical Institute. We had a long conversation, and since Mark (a historian of the uprising) had never been in the ghetto, he tried to get what he could out of me. I told him how I had conceived the poem 'Ptak' in those days inside the ghetto. He was familiar with it from Michał Borwicz's anthology and was surprised that it was the work of a satirical poet.

'Didn't some of your satires come out in the Warsaw ghetto?' he asked.

'Yes.' I explained:

> I worked extensively, almost daily, in that genre then. Even though I did not have an outlet in which to publish my poems, they nonetheless attained popularity by being duplicated on machines by many people whom I did not know. On more than one occasion, I was proud to hear them being quoted in conversations, or I would see them on scraps of paper handed from reader to reader.
>
> They were mainly personal satires aimed at particularly tiresome ghetto officials. Here's one which I've somehow managed to remember. This one, too,

---

* For example, in the anthology *Le Luth Brisé* (Paris, 1963).

has an avian subject. In order to understand it, you need to know that a particularly hated director of the community housing authority was called Fogel. When the scandal about the allocation of housing grew too hot, the community decided to appoint a well-known lawyer called Adler to the position. *Fogel* (bird), *Adler* (eagle) – the names cried out for a winged parable. The poem's epithet came from Wyspiański, 'Ptak ptakowi nie jednaki' [One bird isn't like another...] and it went something like this:

A Bird sat high on a rock
Doling out spaces to the other animals.
Wanting to be held in high regard,
He took the eminent title of Commissar.
But when he began his allocation,
Loud cries of complaint went up:
The lion was granted a hovel too strait for a pig
But the rat inhabited an oversized cave.
A certain dog had to share with a cat
The tiniest grotto around.
Everywhere friction and discord.
In the midst of it all the Bird grew stout.
Giving little quarter to sneers,
The animals pushed the sinister Bird off the rock,
And now perhaps it will all work out –
The business of rooms will be assumed by the Eagle.

I depicted the ghetto dignitaries in short epigrams. For example,

His office with people is always aswarm
Unless you 'know' someone, you won't find your way.
Nobody knows what he lived off before the war,
But everyone knows what he lives off today.

Or,

He isn't a robber,
Trickster, or liar,
But he always had a slight weakness
or our occupier.

As I was reciting these trifles to Mark, I suddenly remembered something. 'Wait a minute', I said, 'I wrote and produced a review in the ghetto along with two friends! What a pity that not one of the 50 copies of it has survived. '

Tell me how the review came about.

It was like this: I was working for the Provisioning Authority at the time, and, needless to say, the work was extremely boring. So, along with two lawyers who held managerial positions there– Kazimierz Herszaft and Tadeusz Teszner – I decided, for the sake of variety, to write a review about the Provisioning Authority. I felt very honoured that two colleagues senior to me in age and rank were willing to have me as coauthor, but by then, I had kind of a reputation, and therefore some respect.

What kind of review was it? Live actors or puppets?

Live actors, of course – the authors and several other of the office-workers at the Provisioning Authority. To be precise, the terms 'miscellany' 'or satirical programme' might be more appropriate for it.

I gather from what you say that the piece was performed.

With great splendour. The première took place on 17 January 1942 at 12 Leszno Street, with the audience consisting exclusively of Provisioning Authority administrators and staff. The review satirized the internal conditions at the authority and, to some degree, the local ones. I can no longer reconstruct the text, which we copied later onto expired ration-cards. Our printing press was an old hectograph on which internal Provisioning Authority memoranda were copied.

The jokes and sayings became part of our everyday language at the office – our personal property. Some of the more notable ones were leaked to the outside.

The second performance was at the same place, and the profits went to a good cause. Despite the relatively high price of tickets, the public came and the show was a success. The third and last performance was held in the apartment of Dr Henryk Glücksberg, the community's councillor. The Jewish District's directors were all present, including President Czerniaków who recorded the event in his diary entry for 24 January 1942. It was a rather festive event. The ghetto dignitaries swallowed our satire, or at any rate, did not register their disapproval. Even President Czerniaków, a dour man, smiled several times.

Did professional cabarets exist in the ghetto?

Of course. I'll tell you about just one of them. At about the same time as our review, a group of professional writers organized a 'proper' literary cabaret. The cabaret was located right by us at 2 Leszno Street, in the ghetto's most elegant café, the Sztuka [Art]. The café was very popular because Wiera Gran sang there. An excellent piano duet, consisting of Władzsław Szpilman and Adolf Goldfeder, accompanied Gran, and her greatest hit was a rendering, made by Szpilman, of Różycki's *Casanova*, entitled 'Jej pierwszy bal' [Her First Ball], with words by Szlengel. The satirical programme took the form of a *journal parlé* and was performed by Władzsław Szlengel, Wacław Teitelbaum, Leonid Fokszański, Józef Lipski, Pola Braunówna and, apparently (I don't remember him in the part) Andrzej Włast, once the great director of 'Morskie Oko'* and author of hundreds of songs. Szlengel, Teitelbaum and Lipski delivered the satirical news, and Braunówna performed her bitter song, 'What does "Jew" mean, mummy dearest? Something shameful, something cursed?' The only poetry in the programme was presented by Leonid Fokszański. I had got to know him quite well by then, and it was he who gave me my first professional advice. He was an attractive man and a talented writer, and the poems which he wrote in the ghetto were, without doubt, his crowning glory.

I remember, as through a mist, Fokszański's poem 'Wszyscy się zmieszczą' [There is room for everyone] and another, 'Chicago', alluding to the situation in the ghetto. I can still see him reciting these works simply and naturally and without a shade of pretension.

---

* Popular cabaret in 1920s Warsaw.

It is interesting that, despite its dangerous proximity to the ghetto wall, the Sztuka Café was popular right until the end. When, in April 1942, the sinister news broke about the 'displacement', we at the Provisioning Authority were preparing a second instalment of our review, and a fourth instalment of the cabaret was running at the Sztuka. During the liquidation *Aktion*, almost all the participants of both shows perished. The 28-year–old Fokszański died in a particularly dramatic way; Szlengel, too, met a similar fate later on. He left behind some searing poetry which was published after the war under the title *Co czytałem umarłym* [What I Read to the Dead]. Braunówna, Lipski, Włast, Teitelbaum and Goldfeder perished, as did the wonderful Marysia Ajzensztadt, who had performed at the Sztuka for a certain time and whose death I still cannot get over. Wiera Gran and Władysław Szpilman survived. Of our humble entertainment, which does not compare with the cabaret at Sztuka, I am the sole survivor.

Let us return to your visit to Professor Mark. Did it yield any results?

Yes and no. Mark heard me out, after which he telephoned one of the clerks at the Jewish Historical Institute, asked him to come to his office and explained something to him in Yiddish which I did not understand. A minute or so later, an older man came in with a copy of our skit *Żarty na karty* [Quips for Chits]: one of the 50 copies which we had run off ourselves on the duplicating machine and which had been found when Ringelblum's archives were being dug out. I had tears in my eyes as I held that little book in my hand. Here I was, receiving a token of survival from a world which had been exterminated. Unfortunately, this was my first and last glimpse of the text of our review. I was categorically denied permission to borrow it, and it later transpired that the copy had vanished without a trace. Perhaps one of the workers at the Institute had taken it abroad? Or perhaps, because of its connections with provisions, the rats had taken an interest in it?

SEVEN

Seventh Conversation

You knew Adam Czerniaków, head of the Judenrat, an organization which was almost as controversial as the police, personally, didn't you?

Czerniaków is going through a period of great rehabilitation at the moment, but in the ghetto, some regarded him as a positive presence, others as a harmful one. Was he offering ruthless resistance, or cooperating with the Germans? It's an eternal debate – and an unresolvable one.

I saw Adam Czerniaków frequently. I didn't feel particularly well disposed towards him. He was a large, gloomy man, always dressed in dark colours – very solemn. I never remember him smiling: he looked like a funeral director. I knew him from scribbled sonnets which were distributed in the ghetto, and published by him before the war in *Głos Gminy Żydowskiej* [The Voice of the Jewish Community], as well as from his speeches, and I have to say that neither his poetry nor his oratorial skills were his strong suit. He had a penchant for complex, flowery metaphors. In the speech he gave at Councillor Z.'s funeral, he spoke of people of diamonds and people of wax. He included the dead man among the former, finding evidence of his great soul in the fact that he wore high boots.

And he didn't?

No, Councillor Z. did, but the reason why he left this earth was overindulgence in alcohol. That posthumous glorification irritated me to high heaven. The single thing that was praiseworthy about him was his beautiful daughter, Bronka. Apart from that, he wasn't hero material.

Do you have anything positive to say about Czerniaków?

A great deal today, but in those days, only a few isolated things. For example, I remember his mania for establishing gardens. It was a noble mania because the ghetto was a stony pandemonium devoid of any trace of greenery. So Czerniaków created a café-type garden, at the opening of which a certain Władysław Lin [Hermelin] performed his couplets. He was known among shopkeepers as the best humorist, and among humorists as the best shopkeeper. My father and I listened to his creation dedicated to Czerniaków and found it somewhat questionable as literature.

What do you think of Czerniaków's diaries?

When I learned that he was working on them, I thought they would be sheer tedium spun out by a writer full of his own importance. After I had read them, I realized that I had been too hasty in my judgement. The *Diary* is a turgid document of its times, and its author a figure of tragic proportions. I even noted down a thought from the *Diary* which is worthy of immortality. 'Watching some people, I come to the conclusion that life is too short to enable them to reveal the whole gamut of their stupidity and malice.' Working at the community, Czerniaków had ample opportunity for such reflections. He was surrounded on all sides by evil. With the exception of a few decent people, who very quickly crumbled, the community was top-heavy, especially among its leadership, with an element devoted to amassing a fortune. A former senator of the Republic of Poland, Czerniaków had clean hands. He witnessed appalling things – beatings and other cruelty. And today, that aphorism of his is more important to me than his unsuccessful poetry. I have to admit that Engineer Adam Czerniaków was an honest and wise man who was worthy of respect, and it was not his fault that he all too often found himself in embarrassing situations. Even if he had some faults, he erased them with his suicide.

What do you mean when you say 'embarrassing situations'?

In May 1942, the Germans decided to make a film in the ghetto which was supposed to have been called *Asien in der Mitte Europas* [Asia in Central Europe] and depict how well Jews were living. The title was rather absurd, if you consider who regarded themselves as Europeans here. Czerniaków, of course, had to be the main actor in this unusual visual document. Footage was taken of his office, of the elegant meals they forced him to eat, with the commentary that the head of the Jewish Council was eating delicacies while the population was living frugally. And he, poor man with his Jewish face, seemed to confirm this.

That must have been terribly humiliating for him.

Not only for him. People were afraid to walk the streets when the film was being shot, because personal documents were confiscated and you were ordered to retrieve them from a certain address. Without documents, you ceased to exist, so everyone obediently went. Once there, it turned out that you had to take part in some staged party, laugh and dance. 'The Jewish population is having enormous fun' — the commentary ran. There were even more disgusting incidents, for example, orgies between old men and young girls who were forced to appear naked in baths. And staged funerals.

Did you take part in anything like that?

Only by accident. My landlord at 16 Chłodna Street was one Herman Czerwiński, a newspaperman, and also a prewar intelligence agent, apparently. He had a heart ailment and died — I was present at his death. A few days later, his funeral took place in the Jewish cemetery, which was outside the walls of the ghetto – a separate enclave. We all went to his funeral out of solidarity with his widow, a very pleasant woman. The ceremony took place in a civilized and dignified fashion because the Czerwiński's were people of some stature. Suddenly, cries broke out as a lot of cars drove up to the cemetery carrying high-ranking officers together with the plenipotentiaries of the head of the Warsaw District, Leist, the Commissar of the Warsaw ghetto, Auerswald, and others, among them, film-makers with cameras whose orders were to film a typical Jewish funeral. They began to direct the behaviour of the widow and mourners. The widow had to howl, the guests had to fall to the ground, the women to weep, claw at their faces and tear their hair. I fell and ran with the rest. I'd give a lot now to see myself in the one and only film in which I've ever appeared.

Does the film exist?

Apparently, it's been found, but I haven't had the good fortune to see myself from ghetto days. I've never come across it.

Tell me something about everyday and social life. I read in a book that the closest contact was between neighbours from the same building, at close quarters in an overcrowded apartment.

Contacts were difficult; social life most often centred on staircases. The older people especially didn't wander around the streets unless there was a reason. Even though the curfew began at eight in the evening, most Jews didn't leave their houses after six. So I rarely saw Władysław Sterling, about whom I have written separately and with whom we were friendly. We met Professor Ludwik Hirszfeld on several occasions, but it was not a particularly close acquaintance. I became quite friendly on my own account with a much older gentleman, a clerk at the Provisioning Authority. He was called Mieczysław Hertz. I later realized that he was the father of Zygmunt, the editor of the Paris-based journal *Kultura*. I was recently reminded of him through my correspondence with Czesław Miłosz. Before the war, Mieczysław was the president of the Łódź industrial and trade chamber and, in his youth, the author of a successful play: *Ananke*. He was very pleased that I remembered that fact. Zygmunt, in turn, was very moved when, after the war, he heard about my close contact with his father, who did not survive the ghetto.

Among the lawyers, we met the famous Leon Berenson and the defender of Gorgonowa, Mieczysław Ettinger, who taught law courses. He was the son of an even better-known lawyer, Henryk Ettinger. There's an anecdote about that. A long time before the war, when the son appeared in court for the first time, a judge, famous for his jokes, quipped, 'So young and already an Ettinger.' I was very pleased when, after my father had died, Ettinger said to me, 'Warsaw without the distinctive figure of Gustaw in a *droshky* will no longer be our Warsaw.' Other famous people I saw included the director Andrzej Mark, the painter Roman Kramsztyk, and the conductor Marian Neuteich.

What about distinctive characters? There must have been no end of them in the ghetto.

I'd like to mention someone we already knew from before the war: a little man called Lewinski, thin as a rake, who ran a door-to-door lending library. Even though it was potentially risky, because lice could get into the books, my father, who was often laid up for weeks at a time, used his services. My mother remembered from before the war that this Lewinski, under the pretext of lending books, also sent out girls of a very different profession to deliver them. The fees were, as you might expect, considerably higher on those occasions. Lewinski himself ran the service in the ghetto. Just a week before his death, my father was showing off his muscles to Lewinski. I remember that well because father died shortly after that, while the puny Lewinski lived and lived...

Our neighbour was a certain Mr Gruszka (pear), or was it Śliwka (plum)? A shoemaker by trade, he was a political commentator by calling. He spoke bizarre Polish. Each morning he'd stand at the door, exchanging views about recent events with neighbours. To this day, I can hear his dramatic, squeaky voice saying, 'I'm telling you, Russia is mobilizing itself against England.'

I also met my overgrown, somewhat retarded schoolmate Stückgold. This fat, insolent boy, taller by a head than the rest of us, always carried condoms in his pocket and had a rich erotic life. After he had seduced some young girl, his father, a shopkeeper, had to give a gold watch and chain in compensation. I met this boy, reduced to a skeleton, begging on the street. The Grasbergs found him some kind of manual work. He was all by himself – no parents, no money – but we managed to keep him alive for a few months because at least he earned enough to buy his rations.

As for well-known local characters, I saw the ghetto's idiot-philosopher Rubinsztajn, nicknamed '*Ale glajch*', which means 'it's all the same'. Rubinsztajn preached the downfall of all riches, the equality of everyone in death. He was known for a joke he made when he'd throw some coin onto the ground and scream: '*A cwajer in di erd! A drajer in di erd! A firer in di erd!*'* Everyone liked it. His distinctive feature was the speed with which he moved from place to place. He'd make some remark and run off, followed by a small crowd. He was undoubtedly psychotic, but he had something of the street philosopher about him and his buffoonery had tragic underpinnings.

---

* A two down on the ground! A three down on the ground! In the end, a Führer down on the ground!'

Tell me, did you have any kind of contact with the resistance movement?

None whatsoever. Now and then I'd hear something about the activities of illegal organizations — for example, about the arrest, in April 1942, of Jerzy Neuding, a socialist activist and a friend of my uncle's — but a resistance movement as such came later. Our resistance was limited to sabotaging German orders. As I recall, the first such timid action came in February 1940 when, in filling out German questionnaires, we'd write 'White' instead of 'Semitic' under the heading 'Race'. I know that Poles boycotting the expression 'Aryan' did the same.

Any thought of a Jewish Thermopylae was far from my mind in the ghetto, as you may have realized. My sole thought was escape, which doesn't mean that I didn't want to save face. I thought my face worth saving if only as a souvenir.

Were you forced to make hard choices, dramatic ones in a moral sense?

The liquidation of the ghetto began on 22 July 1942. At my house, we had already made plans for our escape. Two or three days beforehand, we received orders from the heads of the Provisioning Authority that workers, as well as community workers, should help the police with deportations. That was a decisive situation for me. I knew I could not do that. Director Drybiński, whom I had always regarded as a nice person, declared that people who refused to help would lose their jobs, as well as the privileges I've already spoken about. He met me on the street and started screaming that everybody else was at the *Aktion*, why wasn't I there? How dare I! (Perhaps I'm doing my colleagues a disservice, but that's what Drybiński said.) 'I am most certainly not taking part in this *Aktion*,' I said.

'So you won't be working?'

And instead of going as a punishment to the gathering place, I ran to a nearby photography shop and begged the owner to take my picture. He did so with shaking hands and promised me the prints by evening in exchange for bread.

Did you think of yourself as a hero?

No. I was going to be leaving the ghetto the following day. There was no guarantee, however, that our escape would be successful. If it didn't succeed, I'd be left in the ghetto without an *Ausweis* [identity card] and without an armband, condemned to certain deportation. But the very thought of taking part in that *Aktion* was so offensive to me that the risk was worthwhile. In addition, I had the feeling that this was the end of the ghetto world, the twilight of the ghetto gods. When I was sleeping on the floor at the Provisioning Authority, I was woken by a familiar voice. It belonged to a friend of my father's, Councillor K. An important figure in the ghetto, he was president of the Cooperative Bank and member of the Provisioning Authority board. And this great man, K., says to me, 'Kazio, I heard that you and your mother are leaving the ghetto. In the name of your dead father, I beg you to help me get out of here as well, find some hideout on the Aryan side.' I, all of 18 years old, was supposed to help this great man! This encounter strengthened my conviction that I had to get out of the ghetto, if not this way, then that; if not today, then tomorrow. Ghetto privileges meant nothing any more. I left Leszno Street firmly behind.

From a slightly earlier period, I remember one scene which is symbolic for me – a mass of spectral figures, starving people crazed with fright, condemned to annihilation, flowing down Leszno Street. And above them, on the balcony of the Evangelical Reformed church, cut like a niche into the wall of the ghetto even though it lay beyond its boundaries, was the figure of Pastor Skierski. He was staring at the crowd with an expression of indescribable horror and compassion on his face. I wanted to give some sign that I could see him, that I was there. It was hopeless, since from his position above he could only see a black ant-heap of people. But for me, his presence was a sign that there, on the 'other', side someone was thinking about us, keeping vigil: that I would find friends there who would help me survive.

I'm surprised that you left it so long to plan getting out of the ghetto. The borders were closing in; you were forced to move from 39 Chłodna Street to number 16. The atmosphere was worsening. In November 1941, the Nowy Kurier Warszawski *[New Warsaw Courier] carried the first accounts of the execution of Jews captured crossing ghetto borders.*

On the contrary, you should be surprised that we planned our escape so early on. You need to bear in mind that for a long time, people in the ghetto knew nothing about the concentration camps; they didn't believe in the planned annihilation. We learned about German preparations from the socialist activist Edward Strzelecki, when he visited my Aunt Pańska, and also from Mrs Boryńska's son, a railway worker, who came to fetch his mother one day because he thought it unsafe for her to remain in the ghetto. In the summer of 1942, it became known that the evil hour, in other words, the *Aktion* of the liquidation of the Warsaw ghetto, was approaching. Rumours became a reality when the German authorities started taking the best-known people hostage. Thanks to Olek, who had a permanent pass to the Aryan side, my mother and I had two sets of 'Aryan' papers. We also had somewhere to go directly after leaving when, one day, we and the Oszerowski family got out through the law courts.

EIGHT

Eighth Conversation

Do you remember the exact date you left the ghetto?

It was Wednesday 29 April 1942 – the eighth day of the first *Aktion* of liquidating the Warsaw ghetto. Olek arrived in the morning, smiling as usual, and relayed the news that my mother and I were to be at Judge Kupść's in the law courts on Leszno Street at 11 a.m. You don't easily forget a name like that even after many years.

We had spent the four previous nights amid a crowd of workers and their families at the Provisioning Authority. It was dirty and disgusting there, but undoubtedly safer than at home. At daybreak, we were lying side by side on the floor, hearts pounding as we listened to shots coming from Leszno Street and to the roar of passing trucks. If they stopped at Number 12 it could mean death.

The threat was growing. From reading ghetto memoirs, I remember the atmosphere of mad, animal panic.

Something had clearly altered the system of deportation. Apparently, its tempo so far was considered too slow, even though the dwarf Lejkin was going crazy trying to supply the giant Szmerling as great a quantity of humans as possible to fill the freight wagons at the *Umschlagplatz*. German divisions, as well as Ukrainian and Lithuanian ones, were brought in for the *Aktion*. All hell broke loose. Entire streets were blocked off. People were dragged from houses and thousands of the unfortunate ones were shoved onto platforms; the remainder were herded, amidst gunfire, to the *Umschlagplatz*. The Jewish police had gained powerful help, but even that was too little for the Germans and the avid executor of their orders, Mark Lichtenbaum, who became head of the Judenrat after

Czerniaków's death by suicide. Czerniaków's death shattered me. I took it as a sign that any hope of surviving in the ghetto was lost and the only way to salvation was flight. It was Lichtenbaum who had ordered the workers of the community and the Provisioning Authority to take part in the liquidation *Aktion* with the overworked Jewish police.

The previous evening I had picked up the photograph. It wasn't bad, and, most surprisingly of all, I have it to this day. Sixty years later, it stands on my bookshelf, a reminder of the improbable truth that this Mieczysław Chiemelewski is me. The photograph was the final thing I needed, as I already had in my pocket a certificate arranged by Olek saying that my documents for an 'Aryan' *Kennkarte* [identity card] had been received. All that remained was to provide a signature and the prints of both forefingers, and I would have at my disposal an identity document good for five years.

First, though, you had to get out of the ghetto.

After Olek's visit — he had managed to make it through the round-ups on Karmelicka Street — my mother and I had to get to our last apartment at 16 Chłodna Street as quickly as possible. Luckily, we didn't run into the *Aktion*. The depopulated streets bore traces of recent round-ups, here and there the trampled remains of clothing, old hats, broken dolls... The crowds of street vendors and beggars, so characteristic of the Jewish section of town, had vanished – they were the first to be deported. Stray individuals were sneaking through in various directions. Someone was pulling a cart full of bedding, perhaps to some workshop,

Why?

The frantic effort to find menial jobs in the German manufacturing establishments, which were springing up like mushrooms after rain and exploiting free Jewish labour, was still going on. The authorities were honouring their *Ausweis* for the time being. People would pay a fortune for a place at Schultz's or Többens.'

Chłodna Street had so far escaped the liquidation *Aktion*, if you ignore the bloody massacre in the apartment of the famous antiquarian Dr Albert Schulberg, in which many people perished, including Professor Franciszek Raszeja, a surgeon who had come from outside the ghetto on a consultation. That massacre had occurred on 21 April in a neighbouring house and gave barely a taste of what was to happen on the morrow. The street which constituted the fashionable part of the ghetto was completely deserted; the houses, with their tightly drawn curtains, looked dead. The Lithuanians, the so-called 'Szanlis', paraded on the Aryan side, shooting at every Jew who appeared at a window. One of our neighbours broke down and committed suicide just by stepping out onto the balcony.

Does that mean the apartments were completely empty?

Only the chief tenant was left, Mrs. Czerwińska, widow of a community official whose spectacular funeral, stage-managed by the Nazis, I described earlier.

Why did you go back? Weren't you completely ready?

We wanted to wash for the first time in many days. As well as that, Mother wanted to take some souvenirs of Father, documents and photographs. She packed them all into two briefcases – indispensable props for our disguise.

And what did you take to the Aryan side?

I was interested only in my books; I was losing the second quite considerable collection I had acquired in the ghetto. I took with me the first 1870 Polish edition of *The Pickwick Papers*. I had had it for two years and read it at the times I felt saddest. I lost it during the course of my travels just after the war.

Explain to me why it was possible for so long to leave through the law courts.

The courts served Poles as well as Jews. The entrance on the Polish side was from Ogrodowa Street and on the Jewish side from Leszno Street. It wasn't safe to be there, and entry was unsafe. Armed gendarmes patrolled those leaving via Ogrodowa Street, and, in addition, there were plainclothes policemen milling around.

What was it like on 29 April?

There wasn't much activity that day, but more than I'd imagined there would be. It's possible that people were arranging documents for jobs in the workshops. We'd scarcely entered the lobby when some shady character attached himself to us, muttering about our illegal presence in the courts. It was puzzling because we were wearing armbands and nothing betrayed the purpose of our visit. On impulse, I gave him 20 złoty in the same way that you might give alms to a beggar. The blackmailer went off without a word. Had we got into negotiations with him, our whole plan of escape would have gone nowhere, as I realized later on.

It was still half an hour before eleven o'clock. It made no sense to stay in the lobby any longer – we had to get to Judge Kupść. It turned out to be very easy, and Olek, his mother and brother were already waiting in his chambers.

Is that where you turned into Aryans?

The dispassionately objective Judge Kupść put into a drawer our photographs and documents, which he was going to return after the war. As I learned later, he had to destroy them shortly afterwards for some important reasons. This is how we were left with no mementos of our past: the few which survived came back to us from distant friends (this is why there is such devotion to iconographic materials in this book).

In the Judge's chambers, we got rid of our armbands and everything connected with our stay in the ghetto. I was now Mieczysław Chiemelewski (only for a short time, as I've told you) and Mother was Natalia Irena Godlewska. We had our life-histories down cold long before we left the ghetto.

I didn't know Olek's mother or brother. Fortunately, they were quite Aryan-looking. They also seemed satisfied with our appearance.

Did you leave only with the Oszerowskis?

Of course not, it was a whole production. The actors in this performance were several lawyers (I remember lawyers Płoska and Pilecki, in particular) and other people known at the courts. The last to arrive was Łuczyński, a friend and partner of Oszer Oszerowski, who, in accordance with the will, looked after the family until Olek reached maturity. I immediately realized that he was the leader here and held all the strings. At a signal from him, we walked out into the corridor in a specific order, the five of us in the middle surrounded on all sides by the others. We looked like lawyers leaving the building after a trial, briefcases in our hands.

How did you behave?

Old Łuczyński played the director. 'Relax!' he ordered. 'Laugh. I'm going to tell jokes!' And started to tell one about a young lady who thought she'd left her nether garments at her doctor's when actually she'd left them at the dentist's.

We exploded with laughter a second before we walked through the doors leading to Ogrodowa Street. I was still giggling when I suddenly noticed the faces of German gendarmes watching without interest the lawyers they knew well. The five of us aroused not the slightest curiosity. But this wasn't the end of the adventure, because the first person we came across was the blackmailer we'd met in the lobby of the courts. What bad luck, I thought. But instead of handing us over to the gendarmes, he smiled knowingly and winked. When he'd gone, I asked Judge Kupść to explain. 'It's obvious,' he said. 'That guy assumed you were blackmarketeering Poles who'd gone into the ghetto to transact some business. It takes one to know one.'

How did you feel in the 'normal' city after the hell of the ghetto?

It was strikingly quiet. In a year and a half in the ghetto, I'd only seen the streets on the Aryan side once, from the windows of the car taking me and my mother to the cemetery, from Wronia Street to Żytnia. We had received a special dispensation, with the help of the community, to bury Father in the Reformed Evangelical cemetery.

And now we were walking towards Marszałkowska Street – in smaller groups, so as not to attract anyone's attention. But no one bothered about us here: people were moving around in the most normal way and there was no fear in their eyes. I, too, began to feel relaxed.

NINE
Ninth Conversation

Did you celebrate your successful escape from the ghetto? Where did you live?

We went into an inn, together with the group of lawyers who had accompanied us. I was euphoric to such a degree that one of the lawyers told me off for being reckless. We'd only just begun, and I was acting as if it were all over. After settling the account, the Oszerowskis went their own way, and we went to Maryla Roszkowska's fashion studio on Marszałkowska Street.

Who'd arranged those quarters?

Mother. When I think about it, I remember the shattering image in Aleksander Ford's film, *Ulica Graniczna* [Border Street]. An empty flat – everyone has either been killed or deported – and suddenly the telephone rings. A dreadful, terrifying sound. Despite the cataclysm, the telephones worked, and right before the liquidation *Aktion*, Mother contacted Mrs Roszkowska, whom we had known for a long time. In a na vely conspiratorial way, she asked her whether we could drop in for an hour. Mrs Roszkowska understood and extended an invitation.

Was a fashion studio in the centre of the city the best place to hide?

Unfortunately not. Hell was only just beginning. The women who were employed there observed us with curiosity, and from their expressions, one could tell they weren't as stupid as they looked. In a word, we were nervous, and Mrs Roszkowska also showed her own fear when she told us someone was coming to live with her, so that after about a week, we were forced to leave this hideout.

Our papers were good: we were officially in order, except that I still hadn't received an *Ausweis*. We started to look for somewhere to stay, and chose the EKD [Electric Access] rail-line, along which trains went to Milanówek and Grodzisk. The choice was logical in the sense that we'd never been in those parts before the war, had no acquaintances there, so there wasn't much risk of our being recognized. We decided on one of the three Podkowa Leśna, and rented a room in a very primitive house belonging to very simple people, Mr and Mrs M. Their great source of pride was that they owned a toothbrush — one for the whole family. (That roving toothbrush was not used every day, just on special occasions.) The house had one great virtue: it was situated at the very edge of the forest. I felt safer because of that, since having a window on the groundfloor meant I had a possible escape route. (Fear has stayed with me to this day. For example, I can't sit with my back to the door in a café. Almost certainly, it dates from those times.)

Things would have been all right had I not been a young man without a job. Nor was my mother, who was pretending to be my aunt, any age. So, in order to make the situation more acceptable, I made up some pretend work for myself to which I went three days a week. I made a show of going to the station, messed around there for a while, then went into the forest, where I spent many hours. I even had my own tree-stump there.

I'd sit on that stump in the quiet of the forest — those forests were dense then — and write or read. Many of my poems came from there: poems which I remember with amusement today, as they were very serious, very bombastic. Nothing came of that bombast, but I thought that I was creating immortal works. Afterwards, I would go back in time for a late dinner.

How long did your creative activity go on in the forest?

I don't know exactly. I remember only that it was late summer. We left the ghetto on 29 July, then we spent a week at Mrs Roszkowska's, so we would have been in Podkowa Leśna in August.

Did you make contact with any of your Warsaw acquaintances?

From time to time we'd go to Warsaw, but it was really my mother who maintained external contacts. It was easier for her and the risk of mishap was less, at least during the round-ups of unemployed young people. We lived like this for about a month. I remember two things about that time. First of all, the landlord's daughter had amorous leanings and I awoke such feelings in her that from morning onwards she'd sing at my door: 'It's a sin not to love on such a night / Let's make love while there's time.' She was an eyesore, and hard to shake off.

The second memory is more dramatic. Mother was out and I was sleeping, when suddenly a commotion awoke me. It turned out that an infant had been left in the forest near our house. I heard voices saying, 'It's a little Jew; it's circumcized.' Our landlady insisted that the child be taken to the police. I doubt that the so-called Blues – the Polish police— showed it any mercy: quite the contrary. I fear that child's fate was sealed. It made a great impression on me. Even though I had money, I couldn't say in that situation: 'Stop! I'll take care of it.' I couldn't, because of my own and my mother's safety. But it caused me enormous pain.

Then you moved.

Yes, because our relations with the landlord were starting to become complicated. While it was summer, we could pretend that we were on holiday, like other people. But when autumn came, it was more difficult to think up convincing stories.

At a particularly difficult time, we decided to answer an advertisement we saw attached to a tree-trunk in Podkowa Leśna, or, more likely, Milanówek. We went to see about renting that room. The house was modest but comfortable, and was also near the forest. I remember that the room had a heavy curtain instead of a door. But we could see that cultured people were living there: there were good pictures on the walls and everybody had a toothbrush, despite the normal poverty of Occupation.

How many people were living there, apart from you?

Not many, but the prevailing atmosphere was quite strange and not very pleasant. I felt a tension straightaway. A woman of around 60, the widow of the owner, a professor, was in charge. A young couple lived there as well – the landlady's stepson, a man of about 30, lame and unprepossessing, and his fiancée, a pretty girl. Both were intellectuals from an academic background. There was also a dog, a big, friendly brute, with whom I immediately established a rapport. In Konstancin, I had three or four dogs and have never been afraid of them. I have always adored dogs and been liked by them in return.

We rented this room without a door for about two weeks. Our relations with the landlady were strictly formal, with clearly defined hours for using the bathroom and kitchen. I had minimal, but friendly, contact with the young couple. At around 7.30 one evening (curfew was at 8 p.m.), the curtain suddenly opened and the landlady appeared, saying, 'Please leave the house immediately. You are Jews.' This was a little strange, but she might have come to this conclusion because we whispered to each other behind that curtain and may have revealed something. Of course, we denied it, but said we'd be happy to move out if she would be so kind as to let us stay the night, because curfew was approaching. (It was very risky to be out on the street at night carrying things.) The woman said absolutely not, we had to pack immediately and clear out without leaving a trace.

This upsets the idyllic picture of Polish society being made up of pure altruists.

Picture the scene. In the porch, the young man and his fiancée watch without a word as my mother and I, suitcases in hand, prepare to go off into the forest. They remain silent. As we leave, I say, 'Even supposing we were Jews, our documents are in order and one more night should make no difference. Why can't you let us stay until morning?'

'I said no', the landlady replied. 'Please leave.'

Then the dog ran up to me and bit my thigh. It had either been told to attack, or had instinctively picked up the hostile atmosphere and joined in.

Dusk was falling (it was probably September) and the rain was pattering down. My wound bleeding, we went out into that dark night.

I have found myself in worse situations during the war, but I remember this one with awful clarity. It was a terrible memory, especially the sight of that young man, who neither uttered a word nor did anything. He was totally neutral, which, at the time, depressed me even more.

So we went out into the night, carrying our suitcases, blood pouring down my leg, my mother weeping. It was very late – around 7.50 p.m. – a few people were still out, but the trains were no longer running. I suggested that we should leave our bags somewhere in the forest and sit it out until morning – perhaps they wouldn't find us.

Then, all at once, there appeared a little old lady – straight out of a fairy-tale. She looked at us and, on impulse, my mother, still weeping, said, 'Could you let us spend the night with you?'

The little old lady said, 'Of course, you are welcome.'

And now comes the fairy-tale part – forgive me for mixing genres, but that's how it was. We followed the little old lady across the threshold of her fairy-tale house – pure gingerbread! There were two small rooms, very clean and with lots of pictures on the walls, very na ve ones painted by the lady. She brewed caramel tea, offered us fried potatoes and made up a bed for me. My mother bandaged my wound. I lay down in bed and in the light of the carbide lamp saw something very strange on the table next to the bed – the most beautiful catalogue I have ever seen in my life. It was from the Louvre, luxuriously bound in Moroccan leather, a hellishly expensive edition, with superb illustrations of works of art. I looked at it until morning.

The following day, Mother slipped the old lady, against her wishes, a good sum of money, and we went out into the world once more to fight for our survival.

Where did the catalogue come from? The kind heart? What is the point of this fairy-tale?

I don't have an answer to the first two questions. But the point is that a few months ago, I saw an obituary in the newspaper. A certain elderly professor had died, and his name suggests that it was that young man standing on the porch. He was a well-known scholar.

Of the Humanities?

Yes. Think of it: I have lived in Warsaw for so many years, so did he, and I never met him, even though we moved in similar circles.

Perhaps he didn't remember your name.

Probably not, but I remembered his surname – which was unmistakable – very well, and I also remembered his unusual first name. I read his work, but I never saw him. After he died, I realized that, for many years, I had had the urge to go up to him and say,

Professor, I'm the young man who was thrown out of the house by your stepmother, and you just stood and watched. I've no doubt you remember this as a very unpleasant episode. I don't know what your relationship with your stepmother was like, but judging by the tension in that house, probably very bad. And that is probably why you found it impossible to react to our exodus in any way whatsoever.

You realize that you are telling me this story right after the one about the infant found in the forest, when you found it impossible to react. Any basically sensitive person who feels he should do something has a guilty conscience when he doesn't.

Exactly.

'I am convinced,' I continue, in my fictitious speech to the dead professor,

that you couldn't react as you undoubtedly would have liked to have done at the time. There was something going on between you which prevented you from reacting. So I just wanted to say, I've thought about this for many years, don't worry, because as I was walking in the forest I met a little old lady out of a fairy-tale...

A good fairy-tale, because the previous one was bad.

'...and so you see Professor, not only did I survive, but I am in good health, quite well-off, so don't feel bad on my account – if you do feel bad at all. That incident had a very happy ending, because we managed to survive the war.'

That's what I wanted to say to him, but I didn't know how he would take it, because there was a small fly in the ointment here. There is a fundamental difference between an 18-year-old boy who doesn't undertake raising a Jewish child because he doesn't have the means to do it, and a grown man who tolerates base behaviour in his own house. All that was required of him was an attempt to intervene. But maybe he knew that would turn out badly? Perhaps his reluctance was appropriate?

No it wasn't. I can imagine it theoretically, but it wasn't appropriate. He could, at the very least, have shaken your hand, or called the dog off. He could have made a strictly formal human gesture.

That gesture you're talking about reminds me of an episode which has symbolic significance. I was lying on the ground, on the way to a camp, in front of a house which was occupied by the German Army. Having been thrown out of Filtrowa Street, we were lying side-by-side on the ground with bullets flying over our heads.

During the uprising?

Yes, probably on 9 August 1944. It was an unusually dramatic situation. I remember taking my father's beautiful gold watch off my wrist and handing it to my mother, saying that I felt I was not going to get out of this alive. I told her to give the watch to Helenka, my future wife, with whom I was very much in love. Amazingly enough, my mother, who was not normally a willing participant in such conversations, took the watch. Then I noticed that the Germans were looking at us through the fence. A young man in a uniform, of about my age, climbed onto the paling. I looked at him; he looked intently at me. Then he climbed down and threw something in my direction – a bottle of water. I didn't particularly need that water just then, but it was one of those gestures which prevented one from falling into nationalistic, chauvinistic madness. That gesture, at such a terrible moment, said that the Germans were not animals, simply depraved people.

TEN

Tenth Conversation

How did you spend the winter after your pretend holiday in Podkowa Leśna?

We had to go back to Warsaw. A family we knew called Czuruk had promised us accommodation. Unfortunately, when we came to their building, the doorman told us that they had all been rounded up a few days earlier. You never went anywhere spontaneously because the Germans liked to set traps, so you had to get the lie of the land first. That news was a dreadful let-down. I don't know why they had been rounded-up – perhaps for sheltering Jews. In any event, their fate was tragic – not one of the family survived. The next address that we had turned out to be useless. The woman who'd promised us a room had changed her mind, even though it was a normal business transaction and not an act of altruism. We paid a lot of money.

Did you have enough money for basic necessities?

I smuggled some gold out of the ghetto in the heels of my shoes, but of course that was a drop in the ocean in terms of our needs. We sold all kinds of memorabilia in order to provide some additional security for ourselves, which, because dishonest people often took advantage of our helplessness, was disproportionately expensive. I remember the loss of Father's most beautiful cigarette case, embossed with a ruby. I valued it because Father loved golden cigarette cases. The one with a ruby I sold to a man recommended to me for his honesty. I also asked him to make up a set of documents. The transaction was such that what he paid me for the gold, he took back for the papers. It was daylight robbery, but fortunately the man had enough decency not to denounce us.

What happened to the apartments of people who'd been arrested? Were those premises sealed?

Not usually. I've already mentioned that after a raid, the Germans continued to keep watch and wait for other people who might show up. In any event, the Czuruks' apartment was out of the picture, and we had nowhere to go. We left our miserable belongings somewhere for safekeeping, and wondered desperately what to do with ourselves. Our situation was so hopeless that, contrary to good common sense and basic safety, we went to a boarding-house – which was tantamount to giving ourselves up to the Germans.

So boarding-houses still functioned?

Naturally. There were more than 20 such places in Warsaw. If you glance through a document which is in my possession, a telephone directory for 1942 issued by the Germans, you'll quickly be able to check that. That book is quite a curiosity, because prewar addresses and contemporary ones are mixed together in it. Every Jew listed in it, then being held in the ghetto (the book was issued before the liquidation), has, in addition to his own name, the name 'Israel'. And every Jewess has the name 'Sara'. They are included so that Jews could be immediately distinguished from non-Jews. But there is some confusion because, for example, Professor Hirszfeld figures in it as Hirszfeld, Ludwik, *Universitätsprofessor*, with an address on the Aryan side. And then: Hirszfeld, Israel Ludwik, and some address in the ghetto. (A microfilm of my book found its way to the Holocaust Museum in Washington.)

But to get back to our story. We went to that boarding-house on Marszałkowska Street, number 137, I believe, where a very pleasant young Polish woman registered us. Our documents were in order except for the *Arbeitskarte* [work card], which no one asked to see anyway. We stayed there for a few days, so terrified that neither one of us closed an eye; we sat, fully clothed, on the beds, listening for the slightest sound in the corridor.

But you must have tried to find some housing?

As soon as the time approached when you could go out into the street, we scuttled around Warsaw looking for a place. We could have tried advertisements, but under those conditions, when so many Jews were in hiding and there was so much hysteria, unless you had some kind of recommendation it was no more than an idle dream.

And then one day, walking the streets in desperation after another sleepless night at the boarding-house, we met a man with whom we were very friendly: Zygmunt Kolski, a friend of my father's. They'd known each other for many years: both of them started their careers at the Bank of Poland before the country had achieved independence in 1918. The Kolskis were Jewish through and through. They were living in their prewar apartment on Krakowskie Przedmiescie, almost opposite the Church of the Holy Cross. I remembered them because in May 1935 they telephoned Father to suggest we watch Piłsudski's funeral from their balcony. We took them up on the offer, and thanks to that, as a child, I saw the Marshall's funeral and his chestnut mare. Goering, Laval and many other people were there, too.

The Kolskis knew nothing of what had happened to us since the outbreak of war. Mr Kolski pulled us into an alley so that we could have a quiet conversation and then offered to take us in.

What did he do after war broke out? Didn't he go into the ghetto?

No. Despite the fact that his mother's and wife's maiden names were not solidly Polish, Mr Kolski was safe. In the eyes of the whole building and his neighbours, the family passed for pure Aryans. They looked it, especially Mr Kolski, who was typical gentry. Hearing about our troubles – the previous night there'd been an air raid and we had all gone into the shelter, where the boarding-house residents had had a good look at us, which wasn't safe – he brought us to Krakowskie Przedmiescie. There he did another beautiful thing: he opened his wardrobe wide and said, 'Take what you need. From now on, all this is not just mine, it's ours.' Actually, I didn't need suits: I needed a sense of security. As it happened, our lives, though safe for the time being, didn't change much. The tension in the Kolski's apartment was as great as it had been in the boarding-house. My mother slept on the couch, I in an armchair. We lived like this for three or four nights.

Couldn't the Kolskis, who were living relatively normally, have helped you through acquaintances? Couldn't they have found a safer hideout for you?

In fact, I was better able to help them. They were totally isolated from the outside world and had no contact with other people. They acknowledged their neighbours, shopped close to home and didn't go into town. Mr Kolski asked me to have new documents made changing his mother's and wife's maiden names. All the other details remained genuine. I managed to do so without much difficulty because I had made contacts in the meantime with honest falsifiers of documents. So, when my mother and I moved out, I felt that I had done them a real service.

Was it of any use to them?

Yes, because they survived the Occupation, though unfortunately they both died in the early 1950s.

How did you find a place to live?

We looked separately. By chance, my mother bumped into Fräulein Marta.

Who was Fräulein Marta?

As I mentioned, I had several governesses before the war. I was attached to them, and, above all, to Marta Holzmann. She started teaching me German when I was perhaps 5 years old, and she stayed for the next four years until I went to school. Marta was a relatively young woman, a German born in Poland. Not particularly pretty herself, she had two very attractive sisters. Emma worked as a secretary and was a good woman; Hilda, on the other hand, was rather flighty, as they used to say. I went for walks with her on Ujazdowska Avenue and they were happy times, because the girl was beautiful and very good to me. She lived in Marta's apartment on Sosnowa Street, where there was, shall we say, a not very convent-like atmosphere. I often went there with Marta.

When I asked Marta if she had any boyfriends, she said yes, a certain Prince Crispin. He was undoubtedly a product of her imagination: the result of reading penny romances. She once even pointed out a man in a limousine, saying it was the Prince. In practice, she would canoodle with casual acquaintances on park benches, always asking me not to tell my parents. She was very nice.

She remained on good terms with my parents when she left, although we only met sporadically. Just before the war, I remember, my father was approached by some legal authorities asking whether he'd be prepared to pay the thousand złoty Marta Holzmann had been fined for attempting large-scale smuggling. My father put up the money even though it was a large sum in those days.

I had no contact with Marta when the war started. I heard from someone that she'd married, was a *Volksdeutsch*, and her husband, whose name was Stolarek or Stolarczyk, had remained a Pole.

How was it possible to make such an 'asymmetrical' decision?

It was one of the common ways of assuring your future whoever won the war.

The couple had three sons; they ran an inn. My mother got a scare when she met Marta on the street, because meeting people one hadn't seen for a long time, and *Volksdeutsche* at that, wasn't one of life's pleasures. Marta, however, flung herself at Mother with feeling, wept at the news of Father's death, enquired about me, too, and offered help. Mother assured her that we didn't need money, and then Marta dragged her to her restaurant on Obozna Street. Mother came back laden with all sorts of delicious goodies. We never saw Marta again. I tried to find her after the war because I was fond of her, but I didn't succeed and won't now.

Why were you so scared of her when she owed you a debt of gratitude and showed, as far as one can tell, genuine friendliness and interest?

It was her husband in particular we were afraid of, because bad things were said about him, perhaps without basis. Also, for people in our situation, contact with somebody who knew everything about us was not a good thing. Feelings had to be put aside for the duration of the war. But I wanted to talk about this in order to be fair to Marta. She behaved impeccably towards us.

It was about this time that I began to wory about my health.

I suddenly became aware of my heart. Every once in a while, I'd feel as though some ferocious bird was flapping about inside my ribcage. I went to a doctor – Rudzki, I think – and told him my symptoms. He examined me very carefully, and then declared that I had a serious weakening of the heart muscle and that I had to be careful not to overexert myself and, above all, not to get too excited.

The perfect prescription for someone in your situation.

Exactly. I wandered around town in a desperate fashion. It was unbearable at the Kolskis'. I knew our chance of survival was slim, so I decided to treat myself well before I died. I went out for nice little lunches, and even ordered vodka to bolster my courage. Something prompted me on one accasion to go into a bar on Filtrowa Street near Narutowicz Square. (You'll say I'm being metaphysical, but my entire life at that time had something supernatural about it.) I went in and asked if I could use the phone. But, of course, the telephone was on the counter and everyone in the place could hear. I picked up the receiver and pretended to dial a number and start a fictitious conversation about an apartment. It went something like this: 'So what about our room? No good? No conveniences? There's nothing more to say under the circumstances.' I was speaking all this nonsense loudly when the waitress joined in. She told me that on the third floor of this very building, 83 Filtrowa Street, there was an elegant room for rent at Colonel and Mrs Koprowicz's. I finished my pretend conversation and climbed the stairs to the third floor. A small, elderly, suspicious woman opened the door. I told her that I had heard about the room and that I needed accommodation. She asked me where I was from and if I had references. Then she interrogated me about whether I was Jewish, because so many people were hiding the fact. I burst out laughing and said that was absurd. At that precise moment, Professor Bartel came to mind. Oskar Bartel had taught me history at Rej's and lived in an apartment in the courtyard of this building. Would this reference be enough, I asked. (I should add that the professor was the president of their housing cooperative.)

Under different circumstances, I wouldn't have dared asked

for his help. In the first place, I didn't know how he would react, but there was a more important reason. Professor Bartel had his own major problem in the shape of his wife, a Jewish woman whose surname was Neuteich, and now fate had decreed that my entire existence was to depend on him.

I ran straight to his apartment. He opened the door in slippers and dressing-gown and, as soon as he saw me, he stretched out his arms and cried out in a Lwów accent, 'Ka-a-a -ziu! You're still alive!' I'd always liked him; we hugged each other and I nervously stammered out what I wanted, saying I was sorry to bother him. He looked at me with his characteristic expression and said, 'Kaziu, you've offended me.'

'Why?'

'Because how could you, a student of mine, possibly ask whether it was all right for you to call on me?'

Did he write a reference?

He didn't write anything. He said that Mrs Koprowicz could talk to him any time. I went back to that woman, who at first glance I had taken for a shrew (in this case the first impression was wrong), and repeated my conversation with Professor Bartel. 'In that case,' the Colonel's wife said, 'You're very welcome here.' The room was terrific, not very expensive, and my mother and I moved in there.

Were there any other sub-tenants there other than you?

A married couple arrived at about the same time as we did (I don't recall whether they came before or after us): Stanisław and Zofia Nawrocki. They were still young, around 30. He was well-built and masculine; his features were not quite Aryan, but neither his manner of speaking nor his behaviour suggested that he was Jewish. She was pretty and racially neutral. We were on good terms with them.

Stanisław spent every day outside the house, and Zofia waited and worried. One time, when he'd not shown up after the curfew, she broke down and, through her tears, told us everything about herself and her husband. She was a Jew from Katowice, a teacher. Stanisław, an engineer by training, was up to his ears in underground activities. He had graduated from military college before the war, and was acting as the head of training for a serious Home Army group. He had taken part in many operations. We tried to comfort her by saying that a man like that could find a way out of any situation. And then, when it was already very late, there came a knocking at the door. The Koprowiczs opened the door to a dishevelled Stanisław. As he was taking off his coat, a Jewish armband fell to the floor.

That must have been quite a shocking sight.

I nearly died of fright, but Stanisław made nothing of it. He explained that some kind of conspiratorial matters had taken him to the ghetto, which he'd left by jumping over the wall. This was probably true. His explanation was accepted without reservation and the armband was burned.

I lost contact with Zofia and Stanisław when I went to live in Wołomin. I remember visiting them after the uprising in some dwelling at the edge of Milanówek. Several Jews were hiding there, no other tenants were in, but they returned at nightfall with Stanisław and it appeared that they were coming back from blowing up German trains. From their whispers I learned that the guerrilla action had been successful. Then I noticed my bed was uncomfortable – I could feel something hard in it. Ammunition. I was happy to leave that sanctuary. I later learned that the Gestapo had arrived a few days later. They found only the Jews and shot them on the spot.

It's ironic that the Koprowiczs, who chose their tenants so carefully, should have ended up with just Jews.

That wasn't the end of it. Not long before the uprising, a Mrs Borowska moved in there with her children. She was also Jewish, although you wouldn't have suspected it from her appearance. My instinct for these things was unfailing.

And the Koprowiczs had no idea? What was it like living there?

We had ideal relations with our landlords: they were delightful and very friendly. They did, however, have their little shortcomings – Mrs Koprowicz, as was clear from my first conversation with her, was rabidly anti-Semitic.

Did she try to engage you in conversation about it?

As you probably suspect, we didn't engage in such discussions. I have to say, however, that people's verbal pronouncements, regardless of how disgusting they might be, didn't bother me as much as their actual behaviour. Mrs Koprowicz was a good woman who mouthed the current obscenities like a robot.

Was she uttering German propaganda, or stereotypic Polish prewar anti-Semitism?

Both of them had strongly anti-German leanings. The Colonel, every inch a country squire, was dovish at heart and, despite his advanced years, would gladly have led an uprising against the Germans. His wife badgered the poor old man, complaining that if it weren't for that old geezer she'd still be enjoying life. Her aggression probably came partly from that.

Was it hard to take?

It wasn't easy to put up with, particularly when the ghetto was burning. I experienced terrible moments watching the sinister glow. You can probably understand how I felt hearing anti-Semitic mutterings on the trams: 'They were amassing those arms against us. If it weren't for Hitler, they'd take control by force after the war.' Or, 'Truth to tell, sir, the Germans are doing the job for us.' And each evening, I'd remove Jewish ashes from my clothing.

You found yourself, inevitably, a witness to that apocalyptic sight.

I didn't watch it, but for nearly three months, the echoes of cannon-fire, the smoke which stung my eyes, the evening glow and the endless waves of unconfirmed, fragmentary information kept bringing home to me what was happening behind the ghetto walls. I had never felt as desperate and alone as I did in those days.

Did you feel safe from an official point of view? What was the situation with your Ausweis?

It seemed to be going forward. One day I met Jurek L. – a friend from the ghetto law course – in the street. He was active in the Home Army and a very distinctive type: big, red-haired, with a talent for sports and soldiering. His father was an officer in the Anders Army. I told him my problems and he promised to arrange an *Ausweis* through the deutsche Ostbahn. I gave him 5,000 złoty – a sizeable sum – and waited for news. A few weeks later, just as I was beginning to get worried, a middle-aged man came to Filtrowa Street; he mentioned Jurek's name and handed me a certificate. I looked at it and saw a blatant forgery, so badly done that a patrol-man checking documents would have had to be blind not to spot it. I made my views known and the man acted dumb; nevertheless, he took the *Ausweis* and went away. A few days later he reappeared, declaring that an *Ausweis* in my name was lying in the office of Dr Engelhardt, the German head of the Ostbahn rail office at the Warsaw-West station. It was a difficult situation because apparently, Engelhardt had not long been arrested by the Germans for falsifying documents. Then the man offered to remove my document from the sealed office for another 5,000 złoty.

This was bordering on blackmail. Did you give him the money?

I did, but I decided to take matters into my own hands. I set off for the rail office at Warsaw-West to look for traces of Dr Engelhardt. No one knew anyone of that name. I walked along the tracks to another office building and the same thing happened, nobody knew anyone by the name of Engelhardt. They sent me to another place, and on the principle of 'third time lucky' I went, even though I felt uncomfortable about it. I got the same response. At that point, I became really scared – what was I doing here, by myself, on the rail-tracks? Terrified, I ran up to a cluster of carriages and jumped in one of them. As the empty carriage started to move, another man also jumped into it. I heard shots. I asked him what had happened and he said that an alarm had sounded because someone had been seen wandering along the tracks. I'm sure that was me. That's how that story ended. Ten thousand złoty wasted, the certificate gone to hell, and I nearly lost my life.

What part do you think your friend played in this dubious affair?

I never saw Jurek again. I looked for him because I felt there was something strange about all this. I later heard that he'd died heroically in an attack on a bank. When he learned that his mother and younger brother were dead, he fell into a depression and wanted to die himself. He died like a hero, but I would rather he hadn't involved me in this eposide.

I came across a reference to him in a memoir by an American woman, Mary Berg, which came out just after the war. (The famous poet Julian Tuwim thought highly of this work.) I didn't know her personally, but Mary had spent a few months in the ghetto. She lived on Sienna Street, which, under existing conditions, was the centre for the fashionable young set. Jurek belonged to the circle which she describes, as did the beautiful and seductive Jaqueline, my juvenile sweetheart from the pre-war summer colony in Rytro. I wanted to get in touch with Miss Berg, but her publisher dissuaded me. Apparently she didn't want to correspond about wartime subjects with anyone.

What made you leave Filtrowa Street for such a long time before the uprising?

Olek Oszerowski, who lived on the corner of Asnyk and Niemcewicz Streets, was my neighbour. It was at Olek's that I met a schoolmate of mine: a Jew, Włodek S., who was a year or two older than me. I was tremendously pleased to see him and forgot to be careful. I allowed him to accompany me right up to the door of the house. It never occurred to me for a moment that something might happen as a result of this meeting. But it did, and soon.

Włodek's Gestapo connections were revealed later on. He was being blackmailed by a policeman and his wife, with whom Włodek was having an affair. The policeman was making a profit out of his Jewish acquaintances. By that time, I was already working in Wołomin, and I came to Warsaw only on Saturdays and Sundays. One day, my terrified mother was waiting for me at the entrance, so I didn't even look into the apartment. She told me what had happened. There had been a loud banging at the door in the night. With the help of the doorman, a group of blackmailers had identified me and gone straight to the Koprowiczs, asking where Marianowicz was.

Would you have given that informer your surname? Did they come to blackmail you for money or to denounce you to the Gestapo?

They might have got my name from the doorman, or I myself could have given it to Włodek. I was naïve and criminally negligent. Fortunately, I hadn't mentioned my mother. The raid was almost certainly about money, although everyone who was blackmailed invariably ended up at the police. In any case, those thugs were asking about me. They knew everything. My mother's presence surprised them, however. They dragged her out of bed and told her to get dressed, probably in order to scare her. At first they didn't say anything about a ransom, but they took her downstairs to the telephone. Before that happened, however, Koprowicz stepped in. He declared that Mrs Godlewska was his cousin, that he would vouch for her, that this was an idiotic mistake, and so on. This took them somewhat off guard: the Colonel was emphatic and, on top of that, my mother was convincingly Aryan in appearance and her documents were entirely in order. Everything seemed to indicate that there had been a mistake. The German in the group telephoned someone, telling them what had happened and asking what they should do. He was ordered to release my mother.

Without a ransom?

Yes. Ironically, the whole incident bolstered the Koprowiczs' faith in us – they didn't believe we were Jews and regarded it all as provocation on the part of the Germans. As a result of this situation, my mother had to stay at the flat, but I could no longer live there. Mother sought Professor Bartel's advice. He conducted a propaganda campaign in the building, starting with the doorman, explaining to everybody that it had all been some kind of ghastly mistake and that it was absurd to suspect Mrs Godlewska was a non-Aryan.

It was lucky that a few weeks earlier, thanks to Ryś Oszerowski, who had good connections at the *Arbeitsamt* [job centre], I managed to get a lead on a job. Funnily enough, sometimes you would get assistance from Jews who were in hiding. The youth I'm talking about was a beautiful boy, very popular with girls. The director of the *Arbeitsamt*, a veritable monster, needed him as bait for the girls, which didn't bother the young Don Juan because he liked to enjoy himself.

Did you have to bribe the German?

Of course. You had to give a bribe for everything in those days, not a large one – about a thousand złoty, perhaps. Having someone to back you was more important. I received three offers of work through good backing. The first, thanks to my fluent German, was an offer to work as an interpreter at a camp for Jews in Rembertow.

I can imagine how thrilled you were at that!

Exactly. I don't think it would have been possible to dream up anything worse. There was also another job which was no better. The third one, which interested me, was the position of porter's helper in a glass-works in Wołomin.

And so, one day, when my back was to the wall, I went to Wołomin and presented myself at the office. This is where a completely different chapter of my life under Occupation begins: an epic bordering on the tragic and the grotesque.

ELEVEN
Eleventh Conversation

The two old, formerly Jewish, glass-works in Wołomin had been taken over by the German economy in the General Government and called Ostindustrie or 'Osti'. General Odilo Globocnik, chief of the SS and of the police for the district of Lublin supervising the annihilation of the Jews in the General Government – a person with a ghastly reputation – was its head. The works were one of the important branches of Osti, which had basically been called on to exploit the Jewish workforce, but when that was liquidated, lost its *raison d'être* and became a prime candidate for liquidation itself. It was left with only the works in Wołomin which employed Aryans.

A book about these works came out in the 1980s. I know that, for all kinds of reasons, you don't have a high regard for it, but actual historical facts are given there.

Yes, I read it with interest. The glass-works in which I held the responsible position of porter's helper was called Vitrum and did well before the war. It had been established in 1903. The last owner, who was there for a long time – from 1915 right up until the outbreak of war – was a certain Rynglewski: Ringelbaum was his real name. He had a partner called Flanzreich. Together they owned three glass-works.

And the second works?

This was smaller and called Praca before the war. A different, cooperative system existed there. The workers formed the management and wages were apparently higher there than at Vitrum.

Was a cooperative like that unusual before the war?

I've no idea. During the Occupation, of course, such a thing would have been impossible. But the people remained the same even though both works came under the administration of Osti in the shape of SS Oberscharführer Mues.

What do you have to say about Wołomin, which is regarded as a mafia stronghold today?

In the second half of the fifteenth century, it was a yeomanry settlement called Wołunino. Then nothing for a long time. In tsarist times, it was apparently a penal colony, where dangerous criminals and their families were sent. During the Occupation, it was a terrifying hole. Not a day went by that someone didn't perish, and nobody even bothered to find out why. The Polish police didn't bother with such details as a corpse by the fence. The term 'mafia' wasn't known in Poland at that time, but two or three competing gangs operated there under the guise of being independence fighters.

Can you distinguish those gangs from the genuine underground movement organizations?

I don't think anyone can. I'll speak further about my contacts with various groups if you want me to. But, other than personal information, I don't know anything. I have tried, without success, to obtain facts from various institutions, including the Polish United Workers' Party. It is known, though, that the strongest groups were the Home Army and the communists, that various gangs were in operation, and that there was no shortage of individual acts of sabotage.

When I think about the people I knew in this context at the glass-works, I recall someone called Kostrzewa. He was an elderly, unqualified worker: a semi-idiot who was either cross-eyed or had leucoma. He wore a pair of ragged dungarees and always had a hat on his head. He doffed his hat fervently at the sight of authority, and when he saw a German, he doffed it so low that he almost hit the ground. His obsequiousness was so irritating that Mues, the works boss, couldn't stand it any more and punched him in the head. I think it was the only time I remember that Mues allowed himself to use his fists. Kostrzewa was no weakling: on the contrary, he was tremendously strong, physically, and that's probably why he was kept on at the works. No one could compete with him at unloading coal-wagons.

Once, when I was laughing at this pathetic figure along with a group of workers, I discovered, by chance, that unloading coal-wagons was also Kostrzewa's favourite night-time activity on the rail-tracks after work. In other words, he belonged to the most active thief-saboteurs in the Wołomin area. 'And when he runs into a German', a worker that I knew told me, 'he chokes them to death with those great paws of his as though they were chickens, or breaks their heads with his spade. He's famous for bursting out laughing on those occasions. He's got a weird sense of humour, that sonofabitch!'

I know I'm supposed to admire Mr Kostrzewa's unloading activity, however…

I know what you mean, but remember that everything which went contrary to the Occupation's aims, that is, everything which was illegal, was regarded as an act of patriotism. I see in this the roots of social corruption, because what is illegal today was, for years, patriotic. Not paying for a ticket was heroism on a grand scale. Forty-five years of communist rule, regarded as an idyllic time by some, was, in reality, a period of intense hatred of official structures. Patriotism again meant not paying, or else cheating. And all at once we have a free Poland and we have to go back to normality, to paying for things.

Did writing your memoirs make you want to go back to Wołomin after the war?

I went back twice. The first time was quite a long while ago, in connection with a lawsuit over a stolen car. The weather was dreadful and I scarcely saw the town. The second time was in the 1980s, when I was thinking about this memoir. What I saw was mud, ugliness, neglect – it was ghastly even compared to Occupation times. I ate in those wartime restaurants twice a day and remember that they were first-rate. At The Niespodzianka [Surprise], they served pig's knuckles, roast pork, ribs – delicious! A Mrs K., the very wealthy owner of neighbouring forests, came to buy glasses at our works. She was either from Tłuszcz or Ostrołęka. She was middle-aged, tall and fat, and always came wearing a huge hat. She evidently found me attractive, because whenever she showed up, she would invite me to The Niespodzianka's competitor, The Oaza [Oasis], whose speciality was hare with beetroot. The dish was very expensive – beyond a worker's means. To go with it, she would order not rot-gut but fine vodka. She would gaze at me with hungry eyes (despite the large serving on her plate) and say, 'O, Lord, if I were only 27 years younger.' (I was lucky she wasn't!) In any event, the food was up to standard. In the Polish People's Republic days, however, when I went to the Wołomin restaurant, I left in a hurry without ordering anything. And the slums were 50 years older and unrepaired.

I know I made you move on ahead to the present day, but tell me about your first visit to Wołomin and being hired.

Wait a moment, I can't just stop right now. Let me tell you the well-known writer Tadeusz Konwicki's recent joke. We were talking about Wołomin and my wartime romantic adventures there. Tadeusz thought for a moment and then said, 'Be careful when you go there, because someone could throw their arms around your neck shouting, 'Daddy'. 'Who?' I asked. 'Geezer' [Dziad], the leader of the Wołomin gang, for example!"

That's surely not a reason for you not to go to Wołomin?

That's it. Finish. I'm going back 50 years. I arrived in the evening, dressed like most of the young people pretending to be in the Home Army. It was perhaps a bit risky, but good for somebody in my situation.

I can't imagine a time, however bad, when fashion wasn't important.

I adhered to fashion which dictated, in order to look like everyone else, high boots, breeches and jacket. I had also grown a small idiotic moustache. Unfortunately it was blond, so you could barely see it. I was well dressed and spoke fluent German. I was told to return the following day. I spent the night in the local hotel, or, more accurately, in one of the guest-rooms above the station restaurant. This was basically a hovel with an outside toilet.

But so what? I had come, after all, to work. My papers were in order and I had never been in Wołomin before, so who was there to recognize me? I didn't realize that by parading around town in my high boots I attracted everyone's attention, and was constantly being watched no less by people from the Home Army than by those from the Polish Workers' Party. Every new arrival to a small place like this one aroused that kind of interest.

In any event, the following day I was hired. I had a responsible position as deputy to the porter – a vulgar, drunken Ukrainian illiterate.

Day or night shift?

Day. One of my duties was to run and open the gates at each sound of a car's or wagon's horn. Nothing was mechanized; it was all indescribably primitive. People pushed wagons along the tracks with their bare hands.

What did the works actually produce? Special glassware for the Waffen SS?

God forbid. The army comandeered huge amounts of wine, liqueur, champagne and vodka glasses, and other glassware, for its own use. The manufacture of bottles was straight out of the nineteenth century.

Blown?

Of course. I can still see those people blowing bottles with their mouths, the heat and glow of the glass-works' oven... A fascinating scene, a veritable image of hell. We did produce a small amount of bluish pressed glass, as well, but the quality was a lot worse. It was intended for mustard jars and other such inferior use. We made jars, bottles, tumblers – a whole assortment of domestic glass. The Germans used vast quantities of our products. They smashed wine glasses, so they ordered huge consignments of a thousand pieces at a time, packed in large cases with wood-shavings, to be exported to the Reich and the Occupied countries. Apart from these mass-produced objects, the works also made limited editions of fine art glassware for such SS dignitaries as Kurt Daluege, Oswald Pohl, or Heinrich Himmler himself.

After some time I was promoted. I got to know the boss of the works, Oberscharführer Florenz Mues. His rank was equivalent to that of staff sergeant and he was a powerful businessman. The first time we met he asked how I came to know German so well. I said that since childhood, I had had a gift and a liking for foreign languages and that I spoke English and French equally well. He was impressed. I said that because

I've always held that modesty is not always a good idea and that it's good to boast about something from time to time. This probably brought about my speedy promotion to staff member. From being a lackey who had to open heavy gates every five minutes, I became a gentleman before whom the miserable porter was a nothing. I was responsible for supervising and organizing everything that went on in the works' yard.

Did your duties also include dispatching the wares?

Not at first, but after a while they did. As yard manager, I had to see to the loading of wagons, which involved a constant running around and making sure that there were enough hands to do the work. There were only a few Germans and they didn't handle that very well. Apart from that, there were many matters not tied directly to production, but also to warehousing or getting rid of by-products. The coal used in the ovens left behind it heaps of coke and dust which had to be cleared from the yard. I quickly found local enterpreneurs who needed fuel and went into business with them.

Who got the cash?

The money went to the works – that was the official channel. But I got a percentage of each transaction. After a time, prices were fixed for these various exchanges. Payment was not just in cash but also in vodka.

But you were producing empty bottles. Where did the vodka come from?

The company had a German contingent. The alcohol monopoly gave us a certain number of full bottles in exchange for our glass, and the works payed with them. We created a fixed system of values and tariffs for every service provided. For example, the railway station was supposed to get two litres of vodka for pulling wagons up to the terminal. In fact they got one litre, and we kept the other for ourselves. That was the agreement we reached with station-master Kapusta and train-dispatcher Wojcik.

We?

I say 'we' because I never operated on my own. The other clerks and I very quickly created a network of people who shared a common understanding. Today, we might have been called a gang. A gang, not a mafia, because we never used force.

But you were corrupt?

Well, of course! I felt safer being one of a group of felons. Paradoxically, I would have felt vulnerable had I not taken part in this scam. I wasn't thrilled by it, nor did I need the money. But I was a felon from the Third Reich's point of view, of course.

It's obvious that you didn't have moral scruples about it.

What scruples? When I was working at the window in the Provisioning Authority, sometimes a baker would come who had to account for his coupons and who would offer 50 złoty, for example, for me to overlook his discrepancies. The suggestion would infuriate me.

What if he'd offered a thousand złoty?

I wouldn't have accepted that, either. It would have been completely unthinkable. It was only in Wołomin that I changed my tactics, not out of a desire for gain but out of fear of breaking binding regulations.

Can you describe the structure of your gang?

The head book-keeper, Mazurkiewicz, was the leader. A huge presence, 4ft 11ins tall in his hat, he was highly intellectual, hugely charismatic and fluent in German – a thoroughly nasty character. A man's head and torso on the legs of a dwarf. I, too, was one of the ringleaders because I had access to the outside world on account of my position. So was Mazurkiewicz's assistant, also an intellectual, by the name of Głowacki. And then there was a cashier, Mr Esch, a *Volksdeutsch*. We had complete faith in him. He would give us a press conference every day on what he'd heard on the radio. He hated the Germans. He would say that if the war would only end, he would murder them all. He had become a *Volksdeutsch* for a very specific reason. His daughter belonged to some kind of organization, listened to the radio and got caught redhanded. Mr Esch went along to the appropriate authority and said he'd sign any anything provided they let the girl go. And that's what happened. The Germans went for it. We adored him, but at the same time we didn't let him in on all our scams. He was too honest.

There were women in the gang as well. Mrs Urbańska, the

personnel manager, and Mrs Płoszczańska, secretary to the director of the works, neither of them young, but still on the make. There was also a typist and stenographer, Helenka Bilecka, who was young, pretty and shrewd. I was instantly attracted to her, but she took no notice of me at first. What could a person in her position have in common with a miserable gate-keeper? I just looked longingly at her from a distance.

Why do you think your organization worked so well?

I think our natural instincts for self-preservation played a part. We all felt threatened and without really knowing why, we wanted to stick together. Mazurkiewicz was, as I mentioned, the force behind it all. He was made to undertake great tasks. It was he who once said to me, 'Listen, Tolek [that's what they called me then], we have to start making money because our wages are laughable.' I couldn't tell him that I wasn't interested. And that's how it started: with the coke, vodka, wagons and illegal allowances.

We were quite blatant in our dealings, as a result of which we nearly got caught when the works' director was away. We were loading a wagon once 'on the workers' behalf' (this was a kind of bonus included into a percentage of broken glass) when SS man Jacobi questioned us, insisting that a wagon like that had just been sent out.

What saved you?

Mazurkiewicz's presence of mind. He started shouting that money had been stolen from the safe. Jacobi rushed into the office, where Mazurkiewicz had hidden several thousand złoty. In the meantime, we sent the wagon out, and when Jacobi came back into the yard, the money was miraculously discovered and the *corpus delicti* had vanished. Jacobi was a born loser. He didn't stand a chance with us.

You were playing with fire.

That's an understatement. I don't know to this day whether it would have been safer to stay in that gang or to have left it. Mazurkiewicz and his associates were by no means benevolent altruists. I don't want to make them out as villains, but it certainly wouldn't have been healthy to have got on the wrong side of them.

TWELVE

Twelfth Conversation

I regarded the glass-works as a good place to work because a new management, under the auspices of Ostindustrie, had only just been put in place, although production had continued the whole while. It was a comfortable position and safer than going into a long-established place where I would have drawn attention to myself. Probably because of the organizational chaos, after I'd only worked there a few days, I was given the task of bringing money from the bank all by myself. The amount was to be 300,000 złoty. I left early in the morning. The director of the Bank Emisyjny in the Praga district of Warsaw told me that there was no money in the works' account, just a niggardly 30,000 złoty. (They didn't want to pay out more than that.) I took the money and went to Wileński station. On the platform, I ran into Miss Bilecka, the typist at the works, who was also going back to Wołomin.

I'm amazed that you were entrusted with fetching such a large sum of money. You could have stolen it and gone into hiding . How did you transport it?

Apparently I seemed trustworthy. I carried the money in an unprotected briefcase. Somewhere between Kobyłka and Wołomin, the compartment doors opened simultaneously on both sides to reveal masked assailants with pistols. There was a shout: 'Hands up!' One of the assailants stuck a gun in my ribs and said, 'Just the briefcase!' They took the case, which, contrary to expectations, contained not 300,000 but just 30,000 złoty, and ran off. When the train stopped at the station, I called the *Bahnschutz* [station security officer] and reported the attack, asking him to take personal details from all the passangers. I thanked God that I had witnesses, in the shape of my colleague from the works and several other people, to testify to the situation. If no one had witnessed the attack, I would have had to have taken 30,000 złoty of my own funds, and that would have been it. But in this case, I had no other choice than to curse my luck and tell Mues what had happened. I reported the incident to him when he returned from Warsaw. I won't pretend I wasn't very frightened. 'So, we live in lawless times,' he said. 'Anything can happen, it's as well it was only 30,000. You were upset, weren't you?' And as consolation, he gave me a carton of cigarettes called 'Juno', the advertisement for which ran: *Aus gutem Grund, sind Juno rund.*

So, even this incident didn't have an adverse effect on your career?
Apparently not. It had its bad, but also its good, side.

Were there no further repercussions of this attack? Surely the works director's reaction of giving you a carton of cigarettes wasn't typical.
That same evening – and you'll recall that I was living in a hovel of a room above the inn – there came a loud banging at the door. I was told to come down immediately to the restaurant where Captain Moszyński, Polish police commandant, was waiting.

You'd reported the incident to the German railway security. Was that the last contact you had with the German authorities?
For the time being. My 'partners' were the Polish police. I got dressed and went downstairs with my heart in my mouth, because our native authorities did not have a good reputation. I walked into the smoky, noisy bar. An elegant man was sitting at a table in a corner– an older man with a grey moustache, the typical ideal Pole with excellent manners. I remember he made a very good impression on me. He asked me to describe the whole experience. He didn't take notes, but just sat silently, only asking whether I'd like something to eat. I ordered and a glass of vodka appeared on the table. Moszyński asked whether I had noticed anybody following me from the bank to the station. I said no, because it hadn't even occurred to me to look back.

'Oh, I think you might have looked back.'
'But I didn't.'
'Listen to me very carefully: Warsaw is an enormous city, crimes like this vanish there like stones in water. Wołomin is a

little town where everybody knows everybody else. It isn't advisable for plans of assaults to have originated here. You might have sensed that people from Warsaw were tailing you. Had you turned around, you would have seen them.'

'In that case, Captain, I'm willing to look back. Now I recall that I did look back and was worried because someone probably was tailing me.'

'Yes, yes, that's relevant to the inquiry, the Captain said. 'What's most important is that the whole affair originated in Warsaw and not in Wołomin.'

And that's where the case rested. The following day, I had to sign a statement to that effect. When I got to know Moszyński better, he told me that that first conversation had been very important. He hadn't known with whom he was dealing, so he was sounding me out carefully to see who I was and whether I could be counted on. After our meeting in the bar, I was no longer under surveillance, and my guardian angels hadn't been the police but the Home Army men. As I came to find out, Captain Moszyński had some kind of responsible position in the Home Army and the Germans later shot him.

He was endangering himself.

Yes, like a whole mass of other nameless people whose number can't be established now. I talked about this with present-day residents of Wołomin, but those days are as distant and as incomprehensible to them as the Punic Wars.

So your contact with the Polish police ended well. You were lucky that the Germans didn't conduct their own investigation.

Unfortunately, they did. Three months later, when I was starting to feel really safe in Wołomin, and living with the woman who was to become my first wife, I received a summons to the Kripo (the Kriminalpolizei) on Ujazdowski Avenue, not far from Szuch Avenue – Gestapo headquarters. At first, I didn't know whether to run away or brazen it out. Fortunately, my nerve didn't fail me, and I decided to trust in my appearance and papers. No one could prove I had connections with the assailants. I said goodbye to my girl, and without telling Mother, went to Warsaw. Before I left, I armed myself with a packet of illegal English cigarettes.

Why?

You write about the theatre, so you should be able to see what an important part props play. I felt that those cigarettes would improve my image. I wanted to give the impression of being a man who could afford to smoke contraband cigarettes and who was therefore afraid of nothing. The cigarettes served as a kind of fetish, in the same way as, for example, a cane or a handkerchief do to an actor playing out some role. That touch 'fixed' me in the part I was playing.

It must have been a difficult experience.

The summons and my papers were methodically scrutinized at the door. Then I waited quite a while to be shown into the office. When I went in, I brashly offered a cigarette to a low-ranking officer. He took it with some hesitation; I lit it for him and he told me to give a detailed account of the incident. This conversation put me at ease. Then I was taken to the cellar where, surrounded by armed Germans, I was confronted with an identity parade.

A dozen or so ghastly-looking prisoners filed before me, and I was supposed to identify the assailants. (This would have been almost impossible, because they had had masks on their faces). The two officers never took their eyes off me. Fortunately, I did not have to pretend anything, because I recognized no one. The Germans must have realized this from my expression because they finally gave up. On my way out, I signed a statement, lit a cigarette and walked out, scarcely believing my luck.

THIRTEEN

Thirteenth Conversation

Tell me about your private life in Wołomin? It's hard to believe you didn't play around, fall in love.

Several hundred Poles were employed at the glass-works – actually, there were two glass-works, our large one and a second, smaller, one. The main boss was a Mr Brachvogel – an educated man and a great expert. Once, as we were strolling through the square, I asked him to explain the local conditions to me, because, as a newcomer, I didn't have much idea of them. He reassured me that I'd manage, that one didn't need to pay much attention to the Germans because they were in our hands, and he added: 'Look how many young and beautiful women there are here. You could have any one of them. You're an elegant young man from Warsaw, exactly what they're waiting for. You can pick and choose.'

You were 19 years old; you probably didn't need to be told twice.

It was nice to hear. I also remember a conversation with a simple, not particularly pleasant, servile Polish clerk – let's call him Nowak. I walked around the square with him as well; he was telling me who was who, and then we started to talk about women. There was one very beautiful woman there whom I nicknamed (to myself) Goblet. Goblet's husband had been deported to a camp. Nowak maintained that his wife was chaste. Filled with pride by what the boss had told me, I bet him that she'd be mine within the week. Nowak took the wager. I was a bit scared because I was basically an unassuming young man from a good family who was not accustomed to dragging women into bed.

Nowak himself ended up badly on account of love. He was pale, whey-faced, characterless and with a wife and small child to boot, yet he went totally nuts over one of the workers, a woman already in her thirties who had incredible sex-appeal. In his passion for her, he forgot everything. He would sit at her place, singing songs, in a squeaky tenor voice, to the accompaniment of a guitar. One day he was found by the raiway track, with that guitar, dead. He had been returning from his lover and a guardsman had shot him because it was forbidden to cross the tracks at dusk.

And you, yourself – did you have any erotic encounters in Warsaw after your initiation by the dentist?

None after leaving the ghetto. I can't imagine any such adventures in a situation like mine. Although one of my friends told me after the war that when he was in hiding, he couldn't stand it, and made use of the renowned services of Mrs J., widow of a well-known actor. She ran an elegant house of ill-repute in her own private apartment. After the initial interview, Mrs J. organized a rendezvous for my friend with a young person who turned out to be a novice. The poor girl, weeping profusely, told him her story. He wept too – he had reason! – but he didn't give up the purpose of his visit.

I didn't distinguish myself with such determination and didn't have such melodramatic adventures. I was hungry to the point of obsession, but as I have already pointed out, I was raised in the conviction that you had to adore the woman first. Meanwhile, in the matter of the wager over Goblet, I had to work fast.

This coincided with a decision to change apartments, because it didn't make sense to stay in Wołomin 's pseudo-hotel. I found out that there was a room with a certain Mrs Korol, a widow of a railway bookings-clerk of Russian or Ukrainian descent. Her senile mother and 20-something son, Sergiusz Korol, lived there, too.

How did the Germans react to people of this sort of ethnicity?

They tolerated them, just about. However, Korol, like the whole group of his friends, boys as well as girls, was a so-called White Russian. They all had identity cards issued by pro-German Russian committees.

Mrs Korol, Sergiusz's mother, was grotesque – skinny, sharp-nosed, with her hair in a bun. The Korols lived on the second floor of an old house with two entrances in the long premises of the enfilade. I had a walk-through room. There was something like a bathroom, but without plumbing. A basin of water stood in there, brought in by Sergiusz. That was his only job. Not one of the Russians – literally, not a single one of them – worked. I think they lived exclusively by renting rooms. The Korols asked quite a lot for the room. I could well afford it, but they didn't need to know that. In addition, Mrs Korol suggested that I eat soup with them (she pronounced it 'shoup'). I agreed for the sake of peace. Mazurkiewicz, the head of book-keeping, asked whether he could get a place there, too, and I arranged it with Mrs Korol. He took 'shoup' also. When Mrs Korol brought us plates of that substance, we poured it into a special pot and disposed of it discreetly in the outhouse.

These circumstances facilitated the seduction of Goblet. She wouldn't have come to the hotel out of concern for her reputation, but a private room – no problem. When I commenced the assault, the citadel proved extremely weak.

Did this take place in the enfilade?

It was a problem because the room was open. Even worse, Mrs Korol lived in a constant state of fear and spied on us. I remember her coming into my room once at a particularly inopportune moment, but, being a broadminded landlady, she just said, 'Love each other, children, love each other,' and walked out. She was forever walking by, walking in, walking out – it was apparently her favourite form of recreation.

This continued for some time. The beautiful Goblet was very stupid. I remember that she responded to my every provocative gesture – undoing her buttons or whatever – with 'what a fate.' I've remembered that all my life.

It wasn't such a terrible fate.

She chose it herself. You couldn't exchange two words with her, so it all became a bit boring and tiring. I remember we broke up after she asked me to translate a letter from her husband in Auschwitz. It was written in German because of camp censorship. There were no specifics, just generalizations, but it made a deep and not very pleasant impression on me. Her husband wrote that he was always thinking about her and

living in the hope that she was faithful to him. I translated it and
thought it made no sense for me to continue this romance. I was
very young and quite sensitive. When I terminated our
meetings, however, Goblet fell into a rage and began to tell all
and sundry that I had a wife and three children in Warsaw. This
was one of the only times in my life that I broke up with a
woman with bad feeling on both sides.

Mazurkiewicz wasn't sexually abstemious, either. He found
himself an office girl, quite a pretty one, and that's how we
carried on in that enfilade. He liked to drink. On one occasion,
we went over to friends for a vodka and were coming back after
curfew when he suddenly started singing legionnaire songs at
the top of his voice. The streets were empty, patrols were out,
and the drunken Mazurkiewicz was bellowing out, 'We, the
First Brigade'. I could have hit him in the face, but came up with
a better idea. I persuaded him to hurry up.

'Why?' asked Mazurkiewicz.

'Because someone is waiting for you at home.'

'Who?'

'A siphon. A siphon is waiting there crying, and tears are
falling from its beak: drip, drip.'

At this, Mazurkiewicz fell to pieces and, starting to cry, let
me take him by the hand and lead him home like a child.

At that time, totally against my nature, I was writing
drunken orgiastic poems.

Did you ever publish any of them?

No. But I remember a fragment of one of them: 'Why are
your eyes so dark, Krystyna?'

I recall that Krystyna was one of the girls who came to see
Sergiusz. She was also my lover, hence the reference to the song
'Oczy czarne' [Dark Eyes].

What did she look like?

She was small, dark, and strikingly pretty, although she had
some teeth missing, which marred her looks. No one knew
where she had come from, so it was assumed, probably
wrongly, that she was Jewish. She travelled a lot, trading,
apparently. I suspect she didn't avoid contact with German first-
class passengers. Even though I was very inexperienced at the

time, I felt a certain professionalism in her way of making love, although she didn't make any financial profit out of me. She was always pleasant, smiling and not stupid. She was infinitely more attractive than the lazy Russian girls. Without question, it was I who benefited from our relationship, because I tried not to disappoint my experienced teacher's expectations.

How did this erotic life affect your feelings for Helenka?

You're running ahead. I'm only talking about the first weeks in Wołomin. My relationship with Helenka was still asexual, although we had become friends and were on first-name terms. Helenka started coming to me for English lessons. She was talented – a quick learner. Seeing that I was educated, she wanted two things from me: to learn English and to learn to play bridge.

I didn't know at the time that whenever I taught some girl, I would inevitably find myself in bed with her. Helenka was the first example of that. She came over often – I even had to throw her out when Krystyna or some other girl came on a more specific mission. We had a brother–sister relationship.

You kept company mainly with young Russians.

It wasn't especially fascinating company. As I mentioned, none of them worked: it's a mystery to me what they lived off. They met for two reasons only: to sing wartime Russian songs and to copulate. Surprisingly enough, they weren't drinkers.

When I went to bed to sleep, they'd come into the room and bellow those songs of theirs. Whether I wanted to or not, I was forced to join in. Because of that, even though I don't know Russian, I learned by heart all the words to songs such as 'Katiusza', 'Taczanka', 'Tuczi nad gorodom stali'. The copulation, however, was nothing like an orgy, even though it took place in public and without shame. It wasn't an orgy, because orgies involve some kind of passion or lust, and in their activities could be sensed an enormous, all-encompassing boredom. They knew each other by heart, so their songs and couplings were conducted in slow motion and something approaching despair.

Very Russian, apart, perhaps, from that puzzling lack of passion. Where did they get those wartime songs from?

Probably from prisoners of war. I got to know some of those

girls in a biblical sense. I couldn't have done otherwise. But why am I telling you these disgusting things?

For fun.

It seems I am sexually inclined.

And conversationally, too. That's good.

I'm glad it's good. I remember being very ill once. I had a horrible attack of flu and fever. Suddenly, their 'Egeria' showed up in my room. She had a very good position, earned money, and rarely came by, so they had great respect for her. She suggest an alcohol rub – at her house. She was very big and attractive. Half-dead from that sickness and all the horrible noise, I agreed. She rubbed until crack of dawn. I don't know how I survived it.

But you got better.

Yes. You had to be as strong as an ox to survive something like that, especially with a weakened heart muscle. It's a feature of youth that you get over things fast. So that was the local talent at that time.

Meanwhile, what was your mother doing?

Mother had rented a room, not far from Wołomin, to which she'd come from Warsaw, allegedly on holiday. She went back and forth, spending a few days of the week on Filtrowa Street at Professor Bartel's suggestion. She visited me sometimes, reacting with great indignation to the least evidence of debauchery. You can imagine what happened when I took up for good with a shoemaker's daughter. God! It was a bolt from the blue to her. She never got over it.

But she herself had been ostracized by your distinguished family.

This explains her reaction. Had she been a countess by birth, she might have reacted differently. Lower-class people tend to be very snobbish. Helenka's background was not of the slightest interest to me.

She came to me for lessons and we grew ever closer, but not intimate. Then one day, during an English lesson, I was waiting for my mother to arrive from Warsaw. From my window at the Korol's house, which was opposite the station, I kept glancing at the platform. When she didn't get off the last train, something inside me snapped. I was sure that the Germans had caught her. I was concerned about her anyway, especially after the night-time incident on Filtrowa Street: now I thought it was all up. It would have been a tragedy, even though my mother often got on my nerves.

But she was also your last relation on earth.

It would have been very hard to accept her loss.

Your mother travelled back and forth between Warsaw and Wołomin. Weren't you afraid that she'd lose her nerve and reveal herself in some critical situation?

I counted on her not doing anything rash or stupid, but indeed, anything could have happened.

At that moment in Wołomin, for the one and only time during the Occupation, I went completely to pieces. I felt a sudden, all-encompassing need to tell someone my story and, disregarding the need to be careful, told Helenka everything. I was very young, although my papers made me out to be three years older than I was, and on top of that, since the 4 October 1941, I hadn't been able to grieve over my own situation or over the death of my father, whom I adored. We lived under such tension that there was neither time nor opportunity to release that deeply suppressed, buried feeling. All of this erupted in me when my mother didn't come that night.

I had a need to tell this to a woman. (I always needed to be close to women: I couldn't live without them.) Each night spent alone, each moment without a woman, was a moment wasted, and I'm not talking about sex here. I needed that closeness like air. All my life I've been dependent on women.

So when that lovely, graceful, intelligent and understanding girl found herself at my side at that moment, I confided everything to her, in general terms – that is, without disclosing my surname. She listened intently and then burst out laughing. She told me that when she was setting out for Wołomin, her anti-Semitic father warned, 'Take care you don't give yourself to some Jew in hiding.'

And I never even noticed that we'd become as close as it's possible to be. It was very moving: in some sense, unusually pure and human. The next day, I woke up a different man – still depressed, desperate, but with the feeling that something very important had happened to me. I had fallen in love.

And what happened about your mother?

It turned out that she'd simply got talking with some friend and missed her train.

So a trifling event had a serious consequence: you took up permanently with Helenka.

At first I visited her at a house on the outskirts of Wołomin belonging to an acquaintance of her father, a master-shoemaker. I went there to dinner; we talked; I observed the proprieties. After a short while, however, we decided to shed all pretence and lived together under Mrs Korol's hospitable roof.

How did Sergiusz's friends react to this change?

With tolerance. They immediately excluded me from their company and ceased imposing on me. They somehow vanished from my sight and dispersed completely.

Were you happy?

Certainly. Thanks to a woman's closeness and thanks to the presence of a spirit.

Your father's spirit?

FOURTEEN
Fourteenth Conversation

I have a very early memory which is most important to me. I am very small, lying in a cot somewhere by a window. It is summer in the countryside. There is a buzzing of bees. All of a sudden, a huge, terrifying spider appears on the wall next to me. I scream for help. My father rushes into the room and kills the spider. My father-protector who will not allow any harm to come to me... You know, during the Occupation, I felt him watching over me. My mother kept repeating that as well – we summoned his presence in that way. He functioned in my mind like a guardian angel who would lead me out of hell. Two manifestations of his presence were striking.

The first was in shoemaker Ruciński's house on the edge of Wołomin, where Helenka rented a room. It was a rural paradise of a little house, except that the shoemaker raised pigs and the aroma which wafted in from the sty was not very romantic. That didn't bother us. Most often, I'd stay the night on the sly, and with the lifting of the curfew in the morning, I'd go back to my house.

How were your relations with the landlord?

Usually, I'd sit down to tea with the shoemaker's family and chat about things. We were joined by their other tenant, a somewhat colourless, uninteresting, middle-aged woman. I'd tell all kinds of stories about my life – these were, of course, pure fabrications of the Marianowicz legend – and she once decided to tell us about a marvellous adventure that had befallen her in Vienna.

She had worked there for a few years before the war as a secretary in the Polish consulate. She knew none of the places I mentioned and had seen practically nothing, since she was interested only in saving money. Her duties included dealing with matters involving Polish nationals. Once, a rich man from Warsaw took up residence in the Metropol Hotel, where the Gestapo was located after the Anschluss. When he came down for breakfast, his wallet, containing a thousand dollars, was stolen from his room. (You could buy a small house for that amount in those days.) The injured party immediately reported it to the consulate, who in turn contacted the police, as they were acquainted with all the hotel rats. Several joints were searched and the wallet was found.

She phoned the hotel with the happy news, and the gentleman sent her a bouquet of roses and asked her out to dinner, that very evening at Vienna's most elegant restaurant. She dressed herself up as well as she could and went. After dinner, they took a ride through night-time Vienna and went on to see some cabaret. She saw more in that one night than she had in all of her two years working in Vienna. For her, it was an unbelievable adventure and she would never forget that gentleman. By chance, I asked his name. Gustaw Berman! This had a profound effect on me. Imagine how I felt, to suddenly hear a story about my father in a shoemaker's house on the edge of Wołomin. I didn't know whether it was a coincidence or a provocation. But no, the woman couldn't have known anything about me.

And the other time?

It happened not long after the first, a few weeks later, when Helenka already knew my situation but not details such as my surname. Every Saturday afternoon she travelled to Warsaw to spend Sunday with her family. When she returned, she talked about what was happening on Stępińska Street. One particular Sunday, her uncle and aunt came to lunch. Her uncle had some status in the family because he was a retired doorman of the Bank of Poland and had made enough to buy his own house in Żabki or Marki. As usual, Helenka's father was badmouthing the Jews, and on this occasion, the uncle contradicted him. 'You know, Stefan, I don't agree with you, because everything I've attained in life I owe to Jews.' Her uncle's father, Helenka said, had been a caretaker at 8 Szkolna School Street (I pricked my ears at this because I knew that address well). A certain young man lived there who was a bank manager (in 1918, on the eve of independence, my father's career had begun in this way). Her uncle was at a loose end until one day, this gentleman called to him and said, 'Listen, Frank, you don't have to hang around like this, come to the bank and I'll find you a job.' He got him a job as errand-boy, and he worked his way up to a position as door-man. He owed all this to that man, whose name was Gustaw Berman.

Again, I was deeply affected. I lived under such stress that I immediately interpreted this as a sign that my father was watching over me, that I didn't need to be afraid. I subconsciously explained it in this way, even though all my life, I've kept my feet firmly on the ground.

It's interesting that a sceptic like you should have had such odd experiences.

It's as though God were trying to prove to me 'there are things in heaven and earth...' Take the Korols' house, for example. Sergiusz wrote poems. He had no literary or academic background, but he had a certain ability. He saw me as an oracle, so I told him about the Skamander Group poets and the avant-garde, but mainly I corrected his work, thereby becoming indispensable to him. He even printed a small volume of poems on the duplicating machine and distributed it among his friends. I remember one phrase which had a certain poetic power: 'A barber with a devilish whisker through a dirty window-pane glimpsed the day...' The line stayed in my subconscious to the point that I called one of my books 'Barber with a Devilish Whisker.' (The association of ideas came from the fact that the hero of the book was a barber specializing in shaving corpses, and a barber like that ran such a business a few doors from the Korols' house).

Sergiusz talked to me a lot, especially about Jews, which made me think. He talked in a friendly manner, anecdotes mainly, but I wondered why he was telling these stories to me in particular. He questioned me, in particular, about Jewish poets: Słonimski, Tuwim, Wittlin. He also confided that, after the liquidation of the Wołomin ghetto, he had a Jewish lover whom he was hiding on the Aryan side for sexual purposes. He was surprised, however, that at the moment of his most ardent advance, the girl would go on reading the paper.

I have always been very clean since childhood, so despite the inconveniences, I was often at the basin giving myself a wash. Once, when I was standing there naked, Sergiusz came in. He wasn't a homosexual, but he looked at me with more than usual interest. I didn't care, because I wasn't circumcized.

I read in a book about operations to reverse circumcisions. I don't know what it entailed. Have you heard about such things?

There was a well-known surgeon in Warsaw, called Dr Michałek-Grodzki, who specialized in two kinds of operations – sewing on foreskins and nose-jobs. The foreskin operations were seldom successful: the wounds festered and the chance of success wasn't great. The nose-jobs weren't always successful, either. My friend, Olek Oszerowski, went in for such an operation. He used to ride a bike, and in order to explain the plaster on his face to his landlords, he said that he had had an accident. Then he told them that the operation on his skull had been essential because his nose had broken, and so forth. Before all this, he'd been a handsome blond man with somewhat Semitic features and a nose that suited his face. When the wounds healed and the bandages came off, he had an upturned nose like Kosciuszko. He looked a complete idiot. He could forget all about making it with women. Fortunately, his surgically remodelled nose drooped with time and made him look more like a normal person.

Thanks for this tragicomic digression, but I can't wait to hear the rest of the story about Sergiusz.

On one occasion, Helenka and I were in bed, and with her good eyesight she suddenly noticed something strange on the stove. She climbed onto a chair and removed an item which looked like a bugging device. No one was in, so we followed the wire and found the end of it attached to a receiver on Sergiusz's desk. If I'd had the wherewithal at that point to behave calmly and logically, I would have checked whether the device worked, but in my frenzy I broke it. I was terrified. Sergiusz was a fairly talented amateur electrician and knew how to play a variety of tricks. For example, when the downstairs door opened, a bulb on his desk would light up. He'd constructed other such gizmos.

We ran outside and walked through the forest towards the Nałkowski house by the meadows to calm ourselves down and work out our next strategy. After a while, I decided that I couldn't run away; I had to stay. I couldn't give up the factory because I really had nowhere else to go and it was hard to imagine a better place, and I dreaded to think how many problems I would have trying to get new papers. On top of that, the police would be notified of my disappearance and the consequences could be disastrous.

So, I went back home and waited for Sergiusz. He didn't return for a long time, which allowed me to think the matter through carefully. I told him it was time to show our hands, that I was aware he knew a lot about me – way too much – and I showed him the device. He hotly denied everything, claiming that the receiver came from a telephone which had been taken apart years ago. I stuck to my guns, telling him that after discovering the device, I had informed my friends in Warsaw and, if so much as one hair on my head was hurt, they would know who was responsible. Sergiusz changed his tactics then, and gave me his solemn word that he wouldn't hurt me, wouldn't betray me, and that I could regard him as a friend. He gave me his hand. I sensed he meant what he said, and stayed. He never broke his word, in fact, but knowing his suspicions was an added threat.

I wonder whether Sergiusz had connections with the Gestapo?

Possibly, but as a certain episode proves, he didn't have their trust. Usually, when I came back from the factory, the windows of my room and Mazurkiewicz's were dark. And then, one evening, I saw lights, and German cars in front of the house. What was I to do? If I ran, it would be the end of me. I didn't know why they had come, but I walked in and, acting the simpleton, na vely asked, 'To what do I owe the pleasure of your visit?' The room looked as if an earthquake had hit it: everything was in disarray; stuff had been thrown out of cupboards, and so on. The officer conducting the search said it was just on the offchance, because they were actually searching the Korols'. He did question me, however, about the large amount of vodka that I had. Indeed, we had a bit too much of it. I said that I was a non-drinker, but that I and my fiancée, Fräulein Bilecka, both received allowances of it from the factory. They couldn't prove anything against me. I brazenly suggested they check with the factory head. They left me alone, and after turning everything upside down in Sergiusz's room (it took them about two hours), the officer said as he was leaving, '*Ausser Wanzen haben wir nichts gefunden*'.*

You didn't get much peace there.

No. There was another terrible episode, too. Helenka and I were again alone in the house when we heard the doors to the apartment opening, then the one to our room, and a completely drunken German soldier staggered in. He saw Helenka – who was probably wearing a robe – and his eyes lit up. Without a moment's hesitation, he moved towards her with obvious intent. It was a nightmare. I pulled him away, explaining that we worked in the SS factory. His hand went to his revolver. I had a momentary inspiration and yelled in a German *Feldwebl's* [sergeant's] voice, '*Raus! Sofort!*' [Outside! At once!] He stood to attention and walked out of the room with measured strides as if he had suddenly sobered up. I've hardly ever been so frightened. Mainly because I was helpless in the face of an armed brute.

To finish the Korol story, tell me what happened to Sergiusz.

He was shot as a spy by Warsaw freedom-fighters. I think it was actually a misunderstanding. His documents showed that he belonged to General Własow's** organization, and that probably sealed his fate. We will never know what the real story was. Mrs Korol outlived her son. Somebody told me that they had seen her in Wołomin after the war; she was apparently obsessed with telling everybody that her son was innocent. Who knows...

---

* We've found nothing other than lice.
** General Andriej A. Własow (1901–48) was a German prisoner of war who, in 1942, organized an anti-Soviet army.

FIFTEEN

Fifteenth Conversation

Could you describe the political divisions among the factory workers?
What powers did the individual political factions have at their disposal?

I really don't know because I didn't belong to any group, and my contacts, especially at first, limited themselves to hints and allusions. I did, however, figure out that the Home Army chief at the factory was Klos, chief foreman at the works: an introverted man, not much given to revealing himself. I had much better relations with Lipert, the head of the Polish Workers' Party [PWP]. He was a solid old man who commanded great authority; he made a good impression on me from the very beginning. Over time, we cooperated with each other.

Isn't it odd that a bourgeois like you should have fallen into such company?

My outlook at the time was very radical and my attitude towards the middle classes more than critical. Don't forget, too, that I was involved with a girl who not only sympathized with the PWP but was an activist.

Was that the result of her upbringing?

Without a doubt. As you know, she was a shoemaker's daughter, her mother a factory worker. Like the rest of her young companions (Helenka was pretty and a lot of boys milled around her), she found herself in PWP circles. This was already 1943, and the popularity of communism had spread as a result of such events as the Battle of Stalingrad. Helenka didn't belong to the Party, but she took part, for instance, in the action of getting Jews out of the Warsaw ghetto. A married couple, the Legiecs, headed this.

Were they Poles or Jews?

They were Poles to the core, of working-class origin. They

belonged to a national faction, a group which had nothing to do with Moscow, just decent people with leftist leanings, like foreman Lipert. And while we are on the subject of foremen at the works, there was another one who worked nights – I won't give his name – whose distinguishing characteristic was his incredible sexual activity, carried out in the orderlies' room. He was remarkably well-endowed; he could do it to infinity and became famous as a result. Legends were created about his wonderful 'dong'. The women in the factory lined up at night and he serviced their needs, sometimes a dozen or more of them per night. That was all he was interested in; when he was needed elsewhere, the workers would come to the orderlies' room, saying they were sorry, but they had to interrupt him a moment. The women waited. Some paid for his services.

It was interesting from a behavioural point of view because he was physically grotesque and not young – he had to be at least 50. I doubt if any one of these girls so much as exchanged a word, a kiss, or any kind of embrace with him. He'd be useless at those things; he operated exclusively with his 'dong'. Other than that, he was a good Pole, and nothing could be held against him on grounds of patriotism.

Let's leave the factory foreman's night-shift, and go back to you. I know what political outlook you held then. How did your career in the factory progress?

At an amazing rate. From lowly drudge to site-worker, and then I was entrusted with the duties of shipping clerk and warehouseman all in one. That was a solid position, but I was not entirely happy with it because I had not the slightest ambition to make a career for myself with the Germans. But I couldn't turn it down because that would have aroused suspicion.

Who controlled or oversaw you? (I'm not sure how to put it.)

There were comparatively few Germans at the works, but I do remember a few of them. There was, for example, the one I've already mentioned, that disgusting character, the watchdog SS man Jacobi, a fanatical Nazi who, for some reason, had always been passed over for promotion. He looked like death: he was old and thin, and his false teeth were forever dropping out of his mouth. He walked around the yard, snooping and denouncing. His qualifications and position greatly outranked those of the ordinary soldier and he fulfilled the role of deputy to the chief, his factotum. As I have already said, Mues, although only a non-commissioned officer, in practice, held the position of a higher ranking officer. There were rumours that he had been a bigwig in the SA* and had been demoted for some impropriety. He was a money-grubbing tradesman, interested only in women. The higher-ranking German officers treated him as an equal. Mues had a wife who would come from Paderborn once in a while, a beautiful, attractive woman. (I still remember her gorgeous legs.) However, her relations with her husband weren't very good.

You've remembered her very well.

That's because of a certain incident. Mues once came to me with a proposal that I give his wife French conversation lessons. (I had told him that I knew several foreign languages.) I was terrified, because his wife was decidedly friendly towards me. You have to understand that if the chief's wife had ideas beyond conversation itself, her husband's coming into the room at an inopportune moment could have meant the end of my life. I got out of it somehow, and Mues probably came to the conclusion that my vaunted knowledge of French was just a bit of bragging.

Can you describe Mues?

He was 37 or 38, tall and blond. His one flaw was that his left shoulder was slightly lower than his right. His wife was often accompanied by an elegant older man – her official lover. (Apparently, there was an arrangement.) Mues also had a German lover by whom he had a child. She would take it in turns with his wife to come to Wołomin. She was less attractive than his wife, but pleasant, in her own way.

What about the other women?

There were about 300 women at the works, but why commit *Rassenschande*** when there were plenty of obliging German women in the General Government?

---

* Sturmabteilungen der Nationalsozialistischen Deutsche Arbeiterpartei: paramilatary organization founded in 1920; declined after 1934.
** Betrayal of the race (i.e. of its purity). This was a crime under Nazi rule.

That's interesting, because in the case of Polish women, material benefits – money, nice food, clothes – might have come into play.

They might, but they would definitely have been only random cases. This reminds me, however, of a certain rather macabre episode. I remember that in the autumn of 1943, a freight-car appeared at the glass-works with an unusual load: used clothing to be distributed to the workers. They were not just any old rags, but suits and outfits in good condition. They had been disinfected, but quite a few of them had reddish stains which couldn't be removed. They were bloodstains, and the clothes had belonged to western Jews murdered in the camps.

The clothing was thrown onto the floor of the warehouse and the workers chose suitable items for themselves during their breaks. I avoided the place, even though everything was above board. What, after all, is the harm of using the clothes of dead people, one might ask. But this argument didn't sit well with me, because my imagination associated the clothing with people I'd known or been close to.

Did the workers who had been given these things by their German employers realize to whom the clothes had belonged? Did the red stains draw comment?

Of course. It was talked about, but with no emotion or interest. The fact that the clothes had belonged to Jews evoked neither commiseration for the former owners nor joy that they had fallen victim to the Reich. The attitude to the clothes was purely utilitarian; the comments were exclusively about their usefulness.

Didn't that enrage you?

I bore no ill-will towards those who made use of the Jewish clothes. One might say, like the poet, that the people of Warsaw, like those of Rome and also of Wołomin, 'trade, play, make love, as they pass by the heaps of martyrs' [Miłosz] – often in the clothes of those who fell victim to genocide.

SIXTEEN

Sixteenth Conversation

Can you describe the topography of the glass-works in which you spent so much time.

It covered an enormous area, with a railway siding, several workshops and warehouses, all of it surrounded by narrow tracks along which workers pushed carts of bottles. The carts were filled by loaders (women), who threw bottles in with enormous skill and much noise. It was so primitive that when an innovation was introduced involving the lowering of cases of glasses and goblets from the warehouse down a ramp (to save carrying them downstairs), everyone thought it was the eighth wonder of the world.

At one time, there was also a building for office workers – about a dozen were employed. It's not worth talking at length about Mr Knack, who was head book-keeper for a short time. He moved around a bit, womanized, and ran off who knows where because it turned out he hadn't a clue about book-keeping.

Was he German or Polish?

He was an adventurer of unknown origins, probably Romanian. He was very handsome.

His replacement, no doubt, was your not very handsome flatmate, Mazurkiewicz.

I've already spoken about Bolesław Mazurkiewicz, he of the short legs and inspired book-keeping. Mazurkiewicz established a whole network, because after a few weeks, he demanded a deputy, and for this position he recommended an acquaintance of his – in fact, his best friend, although they always addressed each other formally to maintain the illusion that they knew each other only slightly. The deputy was a Mr

Głowacki, an intelligent man who spoke good German.

Mues's secretary, Mrs Zula Płoszczańska, was already working there when I was hired. She spoke excellent German and had very good qualifications, which you could detect straightaway. She was about 50. After Mr Głowacki came Miss Urbańska, well over 40 but still attractive. She was a mysterious figure: at first I thought that she was either Głowacki's wife or mistress, but apparently not. I should stress that none of these people had Semitic features. All of them spoke impeccable Polish.

Jan Wolak was hired as head of supplies. He was an elegant middle-aged man, but my hair stood on end when I heard his Jewish accent.

Could Germans tell a Jew by the way he spoke?

They hadn't a clue about these distinctions. The detection could only have come about as a result of Polish ill-will. But the clerks, Esch or Wojakowski, weren't capable of denouncing anyone.

They were decent people?

Through and through. But there were also little anti-Semitic groups in Wołomin. I remember once, when Helenka and I had already been living together for quite a while, a distraught Mrs Płoszczańska came over and said that she trusted us 100 per cent and needed our advice about an important personal matter. She admitted she was Jewish, the widow of the administrator of the Rothschild estates in Austria, a Frenchman called Bonhomme. Some young people in a local underground fascist organization had started to blackmail her. Their leader was the son of a well-known builder. This young H. demanded that Mrs Płoszczańska carry out his orders, the first of which was to translate *Mein Kampf* into Polish so that, after the war, he could absorb into his life the principles contained there. If she didn't do this, he said, he would denounce her. She had two choices open to her: to feverishly translate the writings of Hitler, or to run to goodness knows where. We advised her to take the second option. She did so, and as far as I know, she survived the war.

Do you know, by any chance, what happened to that young fascist?

Ironically, he suffered a martyr's death at the hands of the Germans. I told you that in Wołomin, killings were routine. An important German functionary, nicknamed 'Cucumber', was murdered one day. As a result, the Germans carried out the biggest organized round-up in that town's history. The whole of Wołomin was surrounded from dawn onwards, and the guards were in walkie-talkie communication with each other. Each house was searched from attic to cellar. The residents stood in their yards for many hours, grouped according to degree of suspicion. A few dozen people, among them young H., were taken away in handcuffs. These were people in whose houses arms had been found. I hit on an idea which led to about a hundred men being rescued from the round-up.

How did that happen?

I went to Mues and told him that the round-up would be an excellent opportunity for the glass-works, which was always short of workers. Since we couldn't manage to recruit people in the normal way, we could at least pull a few men out of the round-up and have them work for us. The head of the glass-works thought this an excellent idea and ordered a carriage for me, with Jacobi as escort. He told us to tour the round-up points, and gave us a free hand in the task of finding a hundred workmen.

It sounds like a fairy-tale. Wołomin must have remembered you for this.

We drove from point to point, pulling people out. The gendarmes on patrol expressed no reservations about the less suspicious people. Some of the people we picked actually did start to work; others ran away without even registering. Later on, to my embarrassment, the mothers and wives of these people blessed me in the street. I also recall several other interventions: some successful, others not. Once, for example, an old labourer from the glass-works came begging me to save his two sons whom the patrol had caught with apparatus for distilling illegal liquour. I learned that one son had been shot on the spot and the other was being kept in prison. The third son had long ago been taken to Dachau. When I asked Mues for assistance, he first raised his hands helplessly, but then said that the following day, Haupsturmführer Police Captain Lange was coming for glass, and I could try to talk to him.

Weren't you scared?

I was, because Lange aroused fear. He was 6ft 8 ins tall, with a face like a bulldog – the mere sight of him made you feel weak at the knees. Overcoming my fear, I went up to that bruiser, who was standing, legs akimbo, watching goods being loaded onto a truck. I appealed to him in the name of all the workers and told him the entire story. He grunted something and pointed to a German who noted down the name of the detainee and the details of the case, together with those of the Dachau prisoner. This in itself was great progress.

And what happened? Did Lange turn out to be human after all?

Wait. It was miraculous, because two weeks later, the son came back from the concentration camp. That had to be the result of Lange's intervention. It was said, after the war, that Lange was Austrian and a social democrat sympathizer in the service of the Polish resistance. It is hard to believe that someone of his bearing should prove to be a decent man.

Did you intercede in the case of young H. as well?

Yes, although with mixed feelings because I knew the situation with Zula Płoszczańska. But I couldn't refuse his father, who wanted me to go with him to the head of the works and translate the conversation for him. Old H. had brought with him an étui weighing several pounds and made out of splendid, museum-quality silver. He offered this and other marvels to Mues as a bribe for intervening on behalf of his son. Mues listened, looked greedily at the silver, but told the old man to take the box away and said he promised nothing. He also revealed that the situation was the responsibility of the local authorities and the solution was to be found in Warsaw. H. achieved nothing. His son's name was later found on a list of those shot.

Who replaced Mrs Płoszczańska?

Fräulein Zarembska came in her place. She was rude, unattractive, and her qualifications were vastly inferior to those of her predecessor. She was on friendly terms with the SS because, in addition to Jacobi, there were few more shirkers from the Volkssturm. One was a homosexual who gazed shamelessly at me, complimenting me on my very graceful legs and treating me like a girl. I entered into conversation with him about the current situation, as he was fairly intelligent. We spoke on one occasion about Marshal Rommel, who, in the eyes of the Germans, was a military genius (before the catastrophe in Africa and Montgomery's victory at Alamein). I said, somewhat provocatively, 'You see, Rommel had scarcely left Africa, and you got kicked in the bum.' He smiled at this and said, 'You are quite wrong. We didn't get kicked in the bum because the Field-marshal left Africa. Rommel left Africa because we'd been kicked in the bum there.' The remark took my breath away, because it was an unusually bold comment for a German to make. Apart from him, there were a couple of other fellows who no one took any notice of. For a while, we had the young Oberscharführer Grützner who looked like a filmstar. He was reputed to be a mass-murderer and sadist, notorious for his work in death camps. This reputation, coupled with his dazzling looks, made a ghastly impression. Mues quickly got rid of him because he didn't like the fact that he was of the same rank, and, on top of that, he probably didn't enjoy having a degenerate like him at the works.

That boss of yours was strange.

I had mixed feelings about him. He acted like a high-ranking officer. I only ever once saw him in a cold sweat from fear, and that was when the gate-keeper announced the arrival of Globocnik. Who wouldn't be afraid of that monster? I caught a glimpse of him once and I don't blame Mues.

In retrospect, though, I think he was simply an operator. He'd say, '*Zwei Jahre GG und doch eine reine Weste*', which can be roughly translated as 'Two years in the General Government and my hands are still clean.'* Actually, his hands were dirty, because he was no mean swindler. He'd often spout all kinds of terrible things about Poles and Jews, but I had the impression that he was actually play-acting and that he had really had it up to here with the war. I could sense that his attitude to me was positive. He'd brag to other Germans that a high-class chap like me was his warehouseman. He used to say I was a '*Pfarrer im*

---

* Literally, 'And I still have a clean waistcoat.'

Urlaub', a vicar on holiday, because he thought I had a priestly manner. The best example of his friendliness was the stand he took in Helenka's and my conflict with Miss Zarembska, which I'll come to later.

Fräulein Zarembska brought her older sister to the works. Fräulein Zakrzewska was a pudgy blond who straightaway attracted Wolak. The last on the list was the supplier, Mr Witkowski. As soon as I saw and heard him, I thought it was all over for him. He had the wrong appearance and spoke with a thick Jewish accent.

It still puzzles me that none of the Poles working there noticed these unmistakable signs of ethnicity.

I didn't hear any comments made about Witkowski. I barely knew him, but if I remember correctly, he worked up to the end.

This speaks well of the residents of Wołomin, at least, of those without fascist connections.

Certainly. In connection with this, I remember one particular situation. One of the cleverest workers, a young woman called Zosia with whom I was friendly, looked at me intently one day and said, 'You know, sometimes you look like a Jew.'

'What does a Jew look like?' I laughed.

The answer should have been obvious: 'Exactly like you!' But Zosia said nothing, and we never returned to the subject.

That's a bit odd, because in contrast to Witkowski you must have looked like a full-blooded Pole.

Yes. But to get back to Witkowski. I was shaken at the sight of him and thought he'd be the nail in our coffin-lid. How could I warn him and save others' lives at the same time? It occurred to me to send him an anonymous letter, telling him of existing dangers at the works. The idea had its merits, but I somehow couldn't bring myself to do it. I decided to get advice from someone older and more experienced. So I went to see Councillor Loeffel, who was in hiding in Warsaw. He was the husband of my friend from the Provisioning Authority and, despite the difference in our ages, he'd always liked and trusted me. I told him briefly what I had in mind and he dismissed it without a moment's thought. 'Perhaps it makes sense,' he said, 'but a decent person never resorts to anonymous letters.'

That was unusually moral for those times.

You would come across principles like that in the older generation. I listened to him and virtue triumphed.

Do you think Witkowski had ended up at the works by accident?

Probably. There were lots of Jews in hiding milling around, and the works may have had the reputation of being a good 'safe place'. Apart from the *Volksdeutsch*, Esch, and the Pole Wojakowski, there were only two other authentic Poles: stenographer Bilecka (my future wife, Helenka) and Krystyna (whose surname I don't remember), who later became Mazurkiewicz's wife.

In any event, we knew nothing about each other at first, and no one, apart from Mrs Płoszczańska, revealed anything.

Was the relationship between the office workers such that no one talked about the background of Wolak and Witkowski, for example?

It would have been risky, particularly in front of Mazurkiewicz. I had all kinds of suspicions, but right up until the end didn't know who was who. The raid on the works, however, was the acid test which all my colleagues failed by betraying fear out of all proportion to the situation. They were paralysed – especially Mrs Urbańska – and their panic unmasked them.

It happened after Stalingrad, when the Germans completely changed their attitude towards us. They had grown afraid and decided to see to everything themselves. The changes were political in nature. For example, I was stripped of the position of warehouse and shipments' manager and transferred to accounts as book-keeper for the payroll. The duties of the remaining workers were also strictly curtailed, and the entire office moved to a counting-house outside the works.

And that's where the raid took place?

It was summer. I was sitting in a room with cashier Esch, Mazurkiewicz, and a couple of other people. Esch was distributing wages through a special window which opened on to the corridor; the room's other two windows looked out on to the pavement along which all the workers walked to pick up their pay. I knew all their faces, so I was surprised suddenly to see strangers and signs of unusual activity. 'What would happen if someone were to attack us?' I asked Esch. He replied that under no circumstances would he surrender the cash-box – he'd rather die on the spot! At that precise moment, a boot appeared at the threshold and a voice barked out 'Hands up!' Masked men started to come in through the window. The brave Esch, instead of heroically defending the cash-box, meekly did as he was told. The aggressors took the box and the typewriter. All the office workers were stood up against the wall with their hands above their heads. Mazurkiewicz – a dwarf, I'll remind you – jumped a tall barrier in a single stride – something even an athlete couldn't have done without training. Fear makes you do such things. The rest of us stood trembling by the wall. The bandits ran off. We heard gunshots. (The German guards, we later discovered, shot one of them. The corpse lay under our window.)

Did the police show up at once?

Almost too quickly. Some young man was visiting Mrs Urbańska, her son, I suspect, who also stood by the wall with us. The investigation began, and it was then that I saw paralysing fear, out of all proportion to the event, on everyone's face. That confirmed my suspicions that not one of my colleagues was 'in order'.

How did the investigation take place?

An SS man rushed in with the dead bandit's documents. The police questioned us one by one, and, in the meantime, the documents vanished into thin air. The same idiot SS man came back and admitted that he had given them to one of us. But to whom? He thought about it for a long time and pointed to me. Nobody had seen anything; everybody's face had been to the wall; there had been complete confusion; Germans were running around everywhere. It could have cost me my life. On top of that, Mues, who could have spoken on my behalf, wasn't there. They questioned me for half an hour or so, and then that same SS man reappeared. It turned out that he had put the documents deep in his own pocket to keep them safe. In any event, we somehow survived this attack, but it revealed that every one of my colleagues had something on his conscience, even Mazurkiewicz and Głowacki, who had so far camouflaged themselves extremely cleverly. Helenka, who had observed this from the sidelines, later told me that I was the only one who had behaved with relative calm, though it was I who was under the greatest threat. My strong nerves saved me during the entire Occupation; the others had madness in their eyes. I no longer had any doubt that they were Jews.

Have you any idea who conducted that raid: were they members of some underground organization or just bandits?

I have no idea. It was impossible to make sense of the jungle that was Wołomin. They were certainly not Home Army or PWP, because I would have known them.

Were your suspicions about the non-Aryan background of your colleagues confirmed after the war?

Completely. We all met up with each other more than once afterwards, with the exception of Mazurkiewicz, who made an unforgivable blunder at the end. When the Germans were disbanding Wołomin on the 3 August 1944, he appeared in company with Mues and the whole German commission at the works, and together with them, advised on the evacuation of various items to Germany. This was probably correctly seen as a hostile *Aktion* against Polish interests.

But the simple act of working for the Germans wasn't considered collaboration.

No, because everyone worked. But helping Germans to steal Polish property was an unforgivable crime. Immediately after the war, I visited Lipert, who was First Secretary of the PWP district committee in Warsaw. He worked in Praga. He was holding some kind of conference when we arrived, but his secretary announced us and he popped out of his office and hugged us, happy to see that we were alive. He asked whether I wanted to study, or perhaps leave the country. He opened up a whole range of possibilities to me. I understood that he fully accepted my employment at the glass-works, and that I didn't need to have moral scruples about it. My intervention at the time of the round-ups, and, in particular, with the documents, was well regarded. About Mazurkiewicz, I heard him say, 'If I ever found that bastard, I think I'd kill him.' I repeated it to that delinquent, who then fled to Israel. He wrote to me later asking whether the situation had changed. I made a few enquiries, but the verdict was still merciless, so Mazurkiewicz stayed in Israel.

Did you correspond further with him?

We exchanged a few niceties. In the early 1950s, my wife got a letter from his wife, Krystyna. She said they were living in Tel Aviv, that Józef had a good job and that they had a very nice tenant.

And the others?

Głowacki lived in Łódź for a while after the war, then emigrated. Mrs Urbańska married a colonel from the Polish Army and moved in party circles. Wolak left the country immediately. It turned out that he was extremely wealthy, had property in Israel and had found himself in Poland before the war only by accident. He and his wife, Mrs Zakrzewska, returned to their homeland. I don't know whether any of them are still alive.

It's nice, though, that you met up after the war on good terms.

Not with everyone: we had a serious conflict with Miss Zarembska. First, she quarrelled with Helenka, and then she told Mues that I had threatened revenge on her when the Germans lost the war. (I'd have had to have been suicidal to have said anything of the sort.) Mues called me in to his office and reported what she'd said. I gave him my word of honour that this was a lie, and he believed me. He said that he demanded loyalty on the works site; what happened elsewhere was not his concern: 'You can shoot Germans if you feel like it, but not at the works.' He added that he knew something about me. I had a moment of panic, then he said that I was the son of a minister of the Polish Government in London! I was rather pleased, because it testified to my Aryanness! I assured him that I wasn't, but he was firm. He didn't press the matter further, just demanded formal apologies from the two clerks. That's how an episode which could have cost me my life ended. Had fate taken me to Paderborn, I would have looked in on Sudetenstrasse to see whether Mues had survived the war and how he had taken to denazification.

Do you think Miss Zarembska denounced you out of stupidity or malice?

I think it's certain that she wanted to unload her fear through aggression. I doubt if she had given any consideration beforehand to what she was doing. But never mind that. In any event, soon after the war had ended, we met that nice Miss Zarembska on the pontoon bridge linking Warsaw to Praga. She was walking along with a big bag on her arm. We stood facing each other, and she threw herself on my wife, hugged her, and then began kissing me, as well, feverishly explaining her previous actions. She justified herself by saying that she was Jewish and had felt like a cornered animal at the glass-works. She opened her bag, which was full of gold dollars, declaring that she wanted to share this wealth with us to make up for her moral transgression. We weren't interested. Later, she went to Israel with her sister, Zakrzewska, and her brother-in-law, Wolak.

Esch, the cashier, survived the war by only a day. Following the liberation of Wołomin, children ran after him shouting, 'Hun! Hun!' He was so upset by this that he went home and died.

The fact that the eight of you functioned there, right under the eyes of the Waffen-SS, was a kind of miracle, and, in terms of the Germans, a strange irony of fate.

I regard the fact that we worked with impunity, and for such a long time, in an industrial establishment of Ostindustrie which was devoted to the commercialization of the extermination of Jews in Poland, as a rather subtle paradox of history.

SEVENTEEN

Seventeenth Conversation

It's paradoxical enough that you all survived the war, working next to each other and mutually ignorant of each other's backgrounds.

Yes, imagine various legends, made-up life-stories, and at the same time, we functioned symbiotically, made friends even.

Is friendship in the normal sense of the word possible when everyone is lying to everyone else? Like the friendship between double-agents in the spy novels of John Le Carré?

I don't regard myself in the least bit like a hero in a novel, but what I lived through then was entirely unique, historically speaking. It would have been impossible both previously and later. The tragic elements of the Holocaust are fading with time, particularly in light of the fact that so many terrible crimes have been committed since then. Humanity in our era has equalled Hitler's cruelties, though it hasn't created such an excellent industry for killing. Interpersonal relations under the Occupation, on the other hand – between Poles and Germans, Poles and Jews, Germans and Jews – were *einmalig* [unique], and not to be understood by those who hadn't gone through it themselves – like the encounter of eight adults, each one of whom was pretending to be someone other than he or she really was. It was a macabre version of Chesterson's *The Man Who Was Thursday*. So, was it possible to make friends under these conditions? Not really.

Strange things must have been going on with people's emotions in those days, either the feelings were repressed or they exploded, like your love for Helenka.

I needed that love as much as I needed air to breathe. I sensed immediately that Helenka was my great opportunity and best *Ausweis*. It was not an accident that I entrusted her with my secret.

I knew of her actions in the ghetto and her pro-Semitic sympathies. In addition, something else had happened earlier which gave me food for thought. Some Germans came to the works for glasses. They had brought with them a poorly dressed man and left him in the car. He interested me, so I went up and began to talk to him. He asked if I had a cigarette. The tone of his voice interested me and I asked him who he was. He replied that he was a Jew, a specialist in airport construction on the international level. 'I design those airports, and as recompense, they don't kill me', he said. 'But they give me very little to eat and I have nothing to smoke.' I went to Helenka and told her about the encounter, as she had better access to supplies than I did. A moment later, I watched her come out of the office barracks and, in full view of the Germans, hand the prisoner a whole carton of cigarettes and tins of food. You could see how important it was to her. Nobody else would have done that. A small thing, but telling. I knew Helenka was a human being, that she could be trusted. I also got to know and like her family. Her mother was a pleasant woman, and her father, despite his avowed anti-Semitism, was all right, really. I became friends with her brother the moment I met him.

Apart from Helenka and her family, you weren't close to anyone, then?

It's hard to compare the various kinds of friendship, but I was very close to Olek Oszerowski. We saw each other less frequently after I found myself in Wołomin. It was then that the Hotel Polski affair erupted.

It was one of the most dramatic and never-explained stories of that time.

Unfortunately so. This is what happened. South American Jews sent their relations several thousand visa promises. They were intended for particular individuals, the vast majority of whom were no longer living. So the Gestapo hit on an idea: with the help of provocateurs, the news was leaked that these documents could be had for a price of 100,000 złoty per person at the Hotel Polski, 29 Długa Street, in Warsaw. After a short stay in the hotel, this ensured a legal trip to the Vittel camp in France, and from there, further transport to America. The transaction was underwritten, of course, by the fat cats at the

Gestapo. Even Guzik, the long-time representative of the Jewish Joint Distribution Committee in Poland, who was trusted in Jewish circles, was duped. This assured the success of the action, because he sent his wife and children to Vittel.

It was a horrifying piece of deception which I know fooled many people.

For a long time, the Oszerowskis were undecided about whether or not to go. The boys were decidedly in favour, but their mother had serious reservations. In the early summer of 1943, she asked me, through my mother, to meet her in a café. I went there specially from Wołomin. She was dreadfully agitated. She wanted, without her sons knowing about it, my opinion about leaving. I was placed in a difficult situation, because what could I advise when all the solutions were fraught with terrible risks? I was honest, but I spoke only about my own situation: that I completely discounted such a solution. I preferred to hide in the guise of Marianowicz than be some unfortunate Itzek or Shrul, freely giving himself into the hands of the Germans. I didn't openly say no, but I didn't conceal my scepticism. Mrs Oszerowska went into some sort of mystical state and began – in a very low voice, because we were sitting in a cafe – to talk to her dead husband: 'Oszer, Oszer, enlighten me and don't let your sons commit folly!'

But the spirit of the husband and father didn't influence the decision.

Unfortunately, they let themselves be taken in. The stay in the Hotel Polski inspired confidence: its residents moved around town legally and cards arrived from those who had gone on the first transport. The second one got no further than Bergen-Belsen, and from there, Auschwitz.

You had money – you'd sold the villa in Konstancin during this period. Were you never tempted to start some kind of negotiations in this matter?

No. I didn't try to make contact with the people at the Hotel Polski. Quite simply, I was afraid – the affair smelled of the Gestapo a mile off. There was something absurdly grotesque about it – a group of people living in hope when, in reality, they were caught in a trap and surrounded by spies.

That whole affair would be a wonderful subject for literature: for a novel, or better still, a play.

Undoubtedly. And without having to use gigantic scenes of extermination.

What do you think finally persuaded some very intelligent people to take such a huge risk?

A number of things: the hopelessness of that half-life in hiding; a loss of faith in survival; fear each time a door squeaked or something rustled. Have you ever been really afraid?

No, not in that way. But if I use my imagination, I can understand the impossibility of the situation.

Yes. They put all their eggs in one basket and decided that if they were going to perish, then they would do so quickly and not by degrees, and maybe, after all, they would survive.

In those days, you had to rely exclusively on your own discretion, follow your own intuition. Mine, at any rate, didn't let me down. I once stood at that kind of crossroad after the uprising: I could go to Zieleniak camp with the crowd, or I could try to escape. I told my mother that my fate was probably about to be decided. She didn't say anything. I chose to stay in the crowd. In a crowd, I could hide; those who escaped were shot down like ducks by the Germans.

We're reminiscing about the uprising, but you haven't yet told me how the situation in Wołomin was resolved.

After the dramatic raid on the cashier's office, when the fears of the Jews in hiding came to light, the Germans further tightened security. This gave Helenka and me an opportunity to help people in the resistance movement.

Acts of sabotage were becoming more frequent, particularly those aimed at German transports. The wagons of bottles were subject to attack, and so the head of the works decided to organize escorts for them. For this, people who could be trusted by the Germans were needed, but this created a problem: where were they to be found? The Germans didn't have their own resources so they had to trust their office workers – in other words, us. Their interests were not our interests, so we were presented with a wonderful opportunity to acquire priceless documents bearing the seal of the Waffen-SS. We started to recommend to Mues, as trusted escorts, people who had various problems. He didn't go into any details, but took our recommendations and hired the people we presented. This involved the production of documents.

Valuable documents indeed. Not only were they authentic but they allowed freedom of movement.

For members of the armed resistance, they were simply priceless. When Helenka and I had used up the whole contingent of our acquaintances in Warsaw, we offered our services to Lipert, and the entire operation became institutionalized.

And Mues always signed the documents?

Because she was a shorthand-typist, Helenka was in daily contact with him. She brought for him to sign the mail she'd worked on. Mues was cavalier about such things: he would sign automatically without interrupting his conversation with clients.

He didn't take any special precautions?

I don't think he was much concerned about any of this. In any event, Helenka took advantage of his indifference and always slipped in among the other things three or four documents with photographs made out in the names of 'our' people. This went on, without a hitch, right up until the evacuation of the Germans from Wołomin. It was clean work, but it could have cost us our lives had any of the Germans decided to look closely at the documents.

This went on for a few months, and then you and Helenka went to Warsaw. What led to your separation?

We would still meet every day. I lived on Filtrowa Street with my mother, Helenka on Stepińska Street with her parents. We were very taken with the mass evacuation of the Germans – whole trains and columns of cars were leaving Warsaw. It seemed clear to us that the war was ending. No one had it in mind to look for hidden Jews. Rumours circulated that some kind of disturbance was going to take place on 1 August. When I was leaving Helenka that day, I simply said, 'Be careful.' I remember watching her disappear around a corner. Then I went home and fried myself a wonderful horsemeat steak. At about 5 p.m., gunfire broke out. I looked out of the window – people were running in all directions in terror. Somehow, mother managed to sneak back into the house, and I was somewhat relieved that we, at least, were together.

Did you remain on Filtrowa Street?

Yes. A certain incident occurred there which had its own particular consequence. I've already said that there was a bar on the ground floor of our building, facing the square, thanks to which I was able to find accommodation for my mother and me. When the uprising broke out, a high-ranking German police officer was sitting drinking vodka in the bar. Insurgents burst in, shouting that they were going to take him prisoner. They had trouble, however, communicating with the offender, and someone came upstairs to fetch me because they knew I spoke fluent German. The police officer told me he was a captain, Viennese by birth, a book-keeper by profession, and a choral singer by vocation – a member of the *Männergesangverein*. He had been sent from headquarters to Warsaw to conduct an audit of police books. He claimed to have had it up to here with the whole war, and wanted only to get himself taken prisoner. Throughout all this, he cursed Hitler mercilessly. After talking to him over a period of some two or three days, I began to have some faith in him, and decided to make a deal with him: if the Russians came in, I would defend him; if the Germans came, then he had to protect us from his countrymen. He stood up – I remember that he was in his socks because his feet had swollen – and formally shook hands with me. Fortunately, there were no witnesses to this conversation, because had there been others around, I would have been ashamed to enter into such an agreement.

Not everyone would have been disposed towards amicable agreements.

A few hotheads wanted to shoot him on the spot, but the more level-headed prevailed. As it happened, it worked to our advantage.

Why was that?

At first, the Germans shot the entire male population captured on the field of battle. In truth, if I remember correctly, as of 9 August, a prohibition against shooting, brokered by the Red Cross, was to supposed to come into effect, but you could never quite tell. That day, the gate to the building fell off its hinges, a great noise broke out and a German tank rolled into the courtyard. Everyone was forced out of the building. There was screaming and the sound of gunfire. I didn't see everything because I was standing with my face to the wall. All at once, our hostage came limping out of the bar, where he had been all this time. The non-commissioned officers stood to attention and told him who they were. Our German then said that not a hair on the heads of the residents of this building was to be hurt. He climbed on to the tank and drove away reluctantly. As you see, he turned out to be a gentleman. Then our odyssey began, we were driven out of Warsaw through Zieleniak.

And before that?

A state of euphoria marked the first days of the uprising. I usually fulfilled guard-duty on the roof of the building. I saw the city in flames and the student hostel on Plac Narutowicz, a German stronghold, being severely bombarded. I was more terrified than I had ever been in my life.

Does this mean you had a negative attitude to the uprising?

It's hard to answer that in a single sentence. I was conscious of the uniqueness of the moment, but wasn't able to enter into the general spirit. I remember being on guard duty one night with the sculptor Aleksander Żurakowski, and saying to him that a terrible thing was happening – an entire generation was heroically and needlessly perishing and the city dying. I have to add that we had a radio in the cellar and already, on the first day of the uprising, I had heard Johannes Steel's terrifyingly pessimistic commentary on the 'Voice of America'. His real name was Johannes von Stahl, and he was an outstanding journalist and expert on German affairs. Many years later, I got to know him, and told him how, in August 1944, he had helped me to understand the reality of the events that were being played out. My hair stood on end when I realized, thanks to him, that the uprising had been unleashed on the offchance, and without the agreement of the Russians. Żurakowski acknowledged my comment by saying, 'I'm amazed that a member of your generation should hold such a view.'

Do you think that the uprising was inevitable, as some say?

I don't know, but I think that one can attempt to justify every bad political and military decision by saying it was inevitable. For me, the only thing inevitable about the uprising, given the conditions under which it began, was its ending.

Did you lose anyone you were close to?

Seven of my classmates from Rej's perished in the fighting, and several others were severely wounded. I often think about those fallen friends, what they might have become had they not perished almost before they had started to live.

EIGHTEEN
Eighteenth Conversation

After your individual experiences inside and outside the ghetto, you were back on an equal legal footing with the rest of the population of Warsaw.

This was the only positive aspect of my situation, because I took the mass exodus very hard. I've told you about the dreadful moments when we were lying in a heap on Raszyńska Street amid fierce gunfire and wild screams of drunken Russian soldiers. I saw them running from house to house with flaming torches and bottles of petrol, lighting fire after fire. Those were truly hellish visions.

Driven by this hoard, we reached Zieleniak, a former produce market and now a transit camp for people driven out of the Ochota district of Warsaw. Thousands of people were crammed in there, and new ones kept being brought in.

Was this camp divided into sections for various categories of people?

No, people just poured in and stayed there. The command was German, with Russians as guards. Those from Kamiński* were predisposed to stealing and rape. Everything took place in the open air. The nights were chilly at that time. There were no provisions, no sanitation and a shortage of water. I remember, however, that in next to no time, people started to organize themselves. They made bonfires, cooked, and even traded. But the terrible conditions were nothing as compared to the threat of rape, especially to young women who, time and again, would be pulled out of the crowd. I remember the wild sobbing of the girls who were raped, and the dreadful

---

* Kamiński Mieczysław: SS General, commander of a brigade of deserters and bandits, known for his cruelty towards the Polish population.

behaviour of Kaminski's Russians. The drunkenness, orgies and relentless sobbing went on throughout the entire night.

I was in a difficult situation because we found ourselves there in the company of our former housemates in Warsaw, Mrs Borowska and her two teenage children. They looked remarkably Aryan and it never, not even for a moment, occurred to me that they could be Jewish. Mrs Borowska had a husband in the United States and as soon as the war ended, she went to join him there. But in Zieleniak, she lived through hours of agony, because her 16-year-old daughter was beautiful and liable to be raped. I suggested bandaging her face like a leper's. It worked.

In the camp, food was bought with gold. A pound of bacon cost five tsarist roubles. I wandered around the camp without a moment's rest, poking around to see what I could find for the people I was looking after. I bought food with gold, then fought over slats from some ruined fence so that we could have wood for a fire. I kept bringing stuff back to our 'nest'. This hyper-activity was what enabled me to survive the whole situation. At one point, I saw a fat German in an airman's uniform. He was weaving through the camp carrying a huge milk-can and it was clear that he didn't know what to do with himself. So I went up to him and asked what the problem was, what was in the can. He said it was milk for the infants, and he didn't know how to distribute it. He was a bit dim-witted. I began giving it out without delay. The German immediately trusted me and said that he ran a *Durchgangslager* [small transit camp] in Okęcie. He suggested taking a large group of people from Warsaw.

He relied on your going there, no doubt, because he wanted to establish himself as indispensable.

Most definitely, he was shirking service on the battle-front and needed a transport of people as an excuse. The suggestion gave me a second wind. First of all, I pulled out all the young and beautiful women (I've always had a weakness for them), then mothers and children and older people whom I had happened to meet. I formed a detachment which, instead of following the normal route, was to go through Okęcie. I remember an older man with a beard standing to attention before me and saying, 'Councillor Witold Szulborski, Colonel of the Polish Army, awaiting your orders. Will you accept me as co-worker?' Gladly, I told him. So Mr Szulborski, a well-known lawyer after the war, became my valued assistant. Two days passed, and the time came for the camp to be evacuated. We managed successfully to hang back until only our group was left. Our German led us to Okęcie on foot. We were one of the first groups to leave Warsaw from that direction, and we must have looked pretty rough, since the local inhabitants cried when they saw us. I was busy working on the German. I explained that one of the women was pregnant, another had just had a baby and a third one wanted to get pregnant, and they all had to be released. In that camp in Okęcie, I managed to let a whole crowd of people out through a hole in the fence and they ran off in various directions. Instead of eating and resting, I took care of my appearance. I shaved and washed. Mother pulled a clean shirt out of a bundle, gave herself a wash, and we started to look human again.

You haven't changed at all, you always were an aesthete.

I want to stress the role that personal hygiene played in my battle for life during the Occupation. It's hard to explain exactly why, but throughout the entire war, I felt that my survival depended on cleanliness: physical, that is. If I let myself go in the literal sense – stopped washing, cleaning my teeth – it would be the same as letting myself go in the existential sense: allowing my resistance to break down, giving myself up to the enemy. For me, decent, indeed elegant, clothing and the scent of cologne symbolized resistance and endurance – perhaps out of spite and anger. I was lucky that fate didn't decree the gehenna of a camp for me. I'm afraid that, with my disposition, I would have broken down very quickly and ended up a 'Muzulman'.* But to go back to my story, I think that what happened next was intimately tied to my idiosyncrasy on the point of cleanliness.

What did happen?

The German undertook to provide two trucks for the sick (an unheard-of luxury), and a couple of hours later we moved out, without a night's rest, to the EKD [electric railroad] station

---

* Concentration camp victim in an extreme zombie-like state.

to go to Pruszkow. Of the hundred or so people in the group, many ran away along the road. I couldn't run since I regarded myself as the leader. We found ourselves at the station – Salomea or Opacz, I don't recall which – and rode to Tworki, from where we were to march to the camp. Suddenly, a Pole jumped out of our very crowded train and started shooting at us. Shooting at evacuated people was an absurdity – pure lunacy. He must have been mad. His actions changed our German from lamb to crazy beast. He started stamping his feet. All the earlier agreements, that he would let me and my very sick 'aunt' go at Tworki, quite understandably went out of the window. At the station, which was surrounded by a large numbr of gendarmes, the terrified passengers climbed out of the wagons. The German, behaving very stereotypically now and yelling and screaming, organized a colonnade which walked in the direction of the camp.

Were you standing at the front or the back of the colonnade?

It's part of my personal philosophy not to rush up to unpleasant things. It doesn't do to approach things; it's better to delay confrontation, because who knows what might happen? The world could end, for example, thereby saving us a lot of trouble.

So I hung back by the wagons with my mother. The front of the colonnade had moved on; the train wasn't moving. Suddenly, the red-haired EKD conductor ran up to me and said:

'Here's a Red Cross armband. Are you alone?'

'No, I'm with my aunt.'

'Take this other armband.'

'What are we supposed to do?'

'Put them on and get onto the train.'

'But we've only just arrived. The gendarmes will shoot.'

'Don't worry. Just get into the wagon immediately.'

So, our hearts in our mouths, we climbed into the wagon with those armbands, like doctors or nurses. The Germans were standing with their guns ready, but they didn't shoot. The conductor sounded a deafening whistle. The train backed out and stopped in the forest. Nobody had to tell us what to do next. We vanished into the woods.

Did you meet the conductor again during the war?

No, only in Łódź when I was working for Polpress and had gone to the LOT office to arrange a quick, early morning flight to Warsaw. An elegant, redhaired man was standing next to me. I looked at him carefully and asked whether he had worked as a conductor for the EKD during the war. 'I did', he replied. 'And I moved that train for you.'

What an amazing memory!

I was dumbfounded. I immediately asked him why he had done it. It turned out that he'd acted on a whim. He suddenly felt that he had to save that neat young man. He was pleased I was alive and we became friends. He was Henryk Szletyński, an actor, manager, professor and theatre director. Twenty years later, I sent him a basket of roses and a letter in memory of the rescue. Then, later on, I read in the press his reminiscences of Karol Irzykowski, entitled *Wspomnienie byłego konduktora* [Memoir of a Former Conductor]. It transpired that Henryk Szletyński had saved scores of people in a similar way during the Occupation, and that no one had thanked him except for Marianowicz, who not only remembered but sent roses. We can finish the story here, but I think it's a strange one. The moment at which someone looks at someone else and decides 'this one has to be saved' is strange.

Do you think that this story is, in a way, similar to that of the exchange of glances with the SS man who threw you a bottle of water? Do you think that sometimes, people understand each other better in a single glance than over years of superficial acquaintance?

I think that's true. Sometimes it's an imperative – I have to do something for that person. Perhaps it is the result of a kind of gathering tension, a terrible tension, a sharpening of all your senses, not only the normal but also the paranormal ones, in situations where something unusual, threatening, deeply abnormal is happening. Just think – the entire population of a city is being evacuated, you look at this mass exodus and suddenly feel that you have to do something within your own powers to oppose something, prevent something...

NINETEEN
Ninteenth Conversation

That was another 'metaphysical' adventure. I remember that we were going to take up the subject of the predictions on which occupied Poland fed. The earthly and heavenly signs which we interpret individually are one thing, but the general, widespread prophecies about happenings on a world scale are quite another. I've no doubt these interested you, if only as stylistic curiosities.

Of course. But first, I'm going to tell you about an encounter with a fortune-teller to whom I went, despite my own deep scepticism, at the suggestion of friends when I was in deep pain about my separation from Helenka. It happened in Brwinów and was my first and only visit to a fortune-teller.

It's good you didn't become addicted to it.

I'm not prone to addictions. This fortune-teller was an older woman, quite odd but without the conventional accessories of glass ball or black cat. The minute I walked in, wishing to impress me, she said, 'You're searching, searching for someone.'

That was hardly a great feat of clairvoyance, given that everyone was lost or displaced and constantly searching for someone.

But she didn't stop at that. She dealt her cards and said, 'The someone is an older man.' That brought me to my senses. I said goodbye, paid my bill and never tried anything like that again.

But you once mentioned a gypsy. I think you may have a predilection for magic.

During the Occupation, everybody was mystically inclined, to a greater or lesser extent. They believed in signs, omens, magic numbers. Some people were fascinated by prophecies. I also took each unusual occurrence as a sign. I remember the evening when I was leaving the apartment of a once-famous singer, Janina Korolewicz-Waydowa. My very nice professor,

Zdzisław Libin, lived there, and I had just had quite a depressing conversation with him. As I was walking out of the main entrance, a gypsy woman came up to me and said mysteriously, 'You are very low, but don't worry, you'll soon recover.' My mood improved enormously and my faith in myself was restored, particularly because she used the future tense. The faith that I would survive and achieve something was as necessary to me as the air I breathed.

As to the prophecies which were repeated during the Occupation, I read them. Not in the ghetto – I don't remember any prophecies there – but after I got out. The most popular ones were the Book of Revelation, the prophecies of Daniel, the prophecy of the Pyramids and, of course, Nostradamus. Endless copies of these texts circulated. Of the home-grown variety, the idiotic 'Mickiewiczowska' predictions and Wernyhora's prophecies enjoyed great popularity.

How were they interpreted?

All these prophecies are opaque, can be freely interpreted and can mean almost anything. During the war, they started to be applied to actual events, sometimes specific ones, although it was rather improbable that St John the Divine [in the Book of Revelation] was specifically referring, example, to the Battle of Tobruk. All these prophecies said that Poland would be reborn, and not just as a second-rate country, but as a world power. Another characteristic of these prophecies was the description of dreadful impending calamities. And there were more mundane things, such as some horses were going to drink water from some rivers.

But the pronouncements in these prophecies were unambiguously optimistic.

It was worth surviving because a reward awaited us from the heavenly powers, and a wonderful recompense for all harms: 'And I saw a beast coming up out of the sea, having seven heads and ten horns, and upon its horns ten diadems, and upon its heads blasphemous names.'

Do you think people really derived the will to survive from these enigmatic prophecies?

'He who has understanding, let him calculate the number of

the beast, for it is the number of a man; and its number is six hundred and sixty-six! People measured these words, added, subtracted, and in this way found solace. Towards the end of this part of the Apocalypse it is said that there will be resurrection.

Were the texts analysed collectively or individually?

Their actual interpretations circulated along with the prophecies 'to strengthen the hearts of the little ones'. The most popular were the prophecies of Nostradamus, a sixteenth-century prophet and counsellor to the king and queen of France, who wrote in verse. People have always been entranced by his predictions. He apparently predicted the League of Nations, claiming that 'the languages from near Lake Geneva will become boring in speech'.

That was pretty accurate.

He apparently also predicted Munich and Hitler, whom he called Hister and for whom only misery awaited.

And what did the 1893 'Mickiewiczowska' prophecy claim?

It was called 'Mickiewiczowska' because, during the seance, Mickiewicz's spirit was invoked. That same spirit described in bad verse what would happen to Poland in the future. In essence, he claimed: 'Poland will rise from sea to sea, wait for a half a century, God's grace will protect you always, so suffer and pray like a man'.

Prayer and suffering are our speciality. Were the prophecies uniformly popular throughout the entire period of the Occupation?

Their popularity grew in the worst times. The worse the general situation, the more people put their faith into prophecy and the power of prayer.

To finish, I will bring up one version of the prophecy of Wernyhora from the first half of the nineteenth century. It was published in 1834. It contains a realistic, suggestive vision of a pogrom and a great disaster:

Of houses only chimneys. Fields have been ploughed up by hooves, forests reduced to stumps, husbands like emaciated dogs, women like bitches, children like puppies. Sons lie hacked to pieces so that they won't rise and inherit the land of their fathers. Daughters pierced through their wombs so that they won't give birth to heirs. They drive them naked through the snow and the frost burns their feet. They walk through northerly winds...The Jews also curse their fate and howl in pain like cattle butchered in slaughter-houses. They have ropes around their necks.

He continues: 'Before me mountains of Polish skulls, a blackness of Jewish corpses, piles of Lithuanian bones, a sea of Polish blood.' After this apocalyptic vision comes a vision of resurrection, and then a completely incomprehensible fragment, which was learned by heart: 'First Turkish horses will drink water from the Vistula, then those from the two Indias, then Africans will come, and the Czech will sit with the Pole on Krepak.* The single-headed white eagle will swim across the water, spread its wings. Then mushrooms will fly down from the sky.' Interesting. The suggestion is that one must do penance, because the day of triumph is at hand. That, and wait for those terribly thirsty horses!

I hope you weren't just reading prophecies. I'm interested in what you did read, because I remember from the Occupation memoirs of others that people read Conrad, for example, avidly.

My reading was odd. Actually, throughout the Occupation, I filled in all kinds of gaps in my reading, and, also, the reading itself was undoubtedly a form of escapism. My most interesting reading was Proust. I also read all kinds of sagas. I systematically soaked up all of Balzac. Before the war, I had neither the time nor the patience for *La Comédie humaine*. I also read Stendhal, and I had access to books in English.

How?

People had books in their houses. It wasn't hard to get hold of them. I bought a mass of them in the ghetto. There was so much hunger and poverty that people sold everything. I remember a second-hand book dealer on Leszno Street from whom I was able to buy the Paris edition of Joyce's *Ulysses* in

---

* Former name for the Tatra and Carpathian mountains.

English for 50 złoty. It had to be the Paris edition because *Ulysses* was banned in England at that time.

You were already a bibliophile?

I was before the war. For example, I collected *The Pickwick Papers* in various languages. People of the older generation had a special relationship with that book, and I think that, even today, it would be possible to organize an army of followers who know *The Pickwick Papers* by heart. I also adored *Alice in Wonderland*, which I knew in the original, of course, because before the war, there was only one bad Polish translation, the work of a woman called Morawska.

And you yourself translated Alice?

Yes. I knew that *Alice* wasn't just any old children's book and decided to translate it for my own pleasure. That translation which I made in Brwinów during the Occupation disappeared, but I reconstructed it after the war and it came out in 1949.

Did you show your literary efforts to anyone?

I've already mentioned Leonid Fokszański, a talented poet some ten years older than me. He became interested in my poems in the ghetto and strongly urged me to write.

Apart from him, you had no other literary mentors?

No. After I left the ghetto, I didn't show what I was writing to anyone. Other than 'Ptak' [Bird], none of it seems interesting or worthwhile to me today.

At what point did you realize you had a 'calling', an awareness that you should take up literature?

It seems doubtful to me that I had a calling, as you put it, but I thought of myself as a littérateur only after the war, when I was living in Łódź with my wife.

TWENTY
Twentieth Conversation

Where did your mother end up after the Occupation?

I eventually brought her to Łódź, but after liberation, she spent some time in Brwinów. The story of how we settled in Brwinów after escaping the transport in Tworki is one of divine providence.

Just think – Tworki, a forest – it wasn't clear what to do. I had a notebook with me of addresses of people who were no use to me at all. And then it hit me! Among these addresses was that of an old French woman who had taught me before the war. I ran into her at the beginning of the Occupation, and she told me that she'd moved permanently to Brwinów, was giving lessons, and would I please visit her if I should find myself in the area. I had taken down her address.

That was it! How we got to Brwinów, I no longer remember. It was a completely different world. Sunshine, a bright little house, marshmallows in the garden – wonderfully idyllic. We rang the doorbell and asked whether Madame Durand was at home. The landlady said unfortunately not, Madame Durand was in Warsaw, amidst the uprising, and everyone was very concerned about her. She asked whether we were close friends. Of course, I said. Mutual lamentations about her fate ensued, and the result was that the landlady offered us the hospitality of Madame Durand's room. We expressed our gratitude, and so a few days went by in this little Eden. We were a bit concerned, however, about what would happen when our 'close friend' came back. And then, one day, came the sad news that Madame Durand was dead. The poor old woman had simply died of old age. For us, this was, in the full cynical sense of the phrase, a very happy coincidence. On top of that, we had something invaluable – a reference from the dead woman. It was known that we weren't just casual strangers, nor – Heaven forbid – Jews in hiding, but the closest friends of that Brwinów institution, Madame Durand. We lived in that house until liberation. Brwinów was one of our best wartime spots.

We had nothing of our own, but that was understandable. We were in the same situation as everybody else, if not rather better off.

The rest caught up with you. You were pioneers.

Of course. The landlady took pity on us and treated us with understanding. She gave Mother Madame Durand's famous cloak, which came all the way down to the ground. Mother wore it right until the end of the war.

Fate, it seems, wanted Madame, who had treated me so nicely in the street, to render one last, and by no means insignificant, service after death. The other old French teacher whom I had visited during the Occupation for no other reason than to ask how life was treating her had refused even to open the door. (I saw her shadow behind the curtains. She checked to see who it was and pretended not to be at home.) People reacted in various ways. Madame Durand was apparently programmed to help me even after death.

But surely that idyllic atmosphere didn't last up until the end of the war?

It started to be dangerous in Brwinów, even in Madame Durand's room. There were constant round-ups and young men were hunted down for labour camps. I didn't want to end up in the Reich under threat of Allied bombs, so I went to the god-forsaken village of Musuły, which lay some four kilometres from Grodzisk Mazowiecki.

Was that your idea?

I was directed there by the local office of R 90, the Chief Protective Council, where I worked for several months, partly to do something useful but mainly to send cards across the whole of the General Government looking for Helenka. I ran away when things started to get hot. I was told to go to landlord G. and warned that I would have to negotiate for myself the cost of basic food and lodging. So I went there, allowing myself one luxury – a case of toiletries. Washing myself at the well, I was able to retain some semblance of humanity.

Very many people went through Musuły. Migrations of people driven out of Warsaw were the order of the day. I felt dreadful because I kept on looking for the lost Helenka, and in Musuły I couldn't send cards or check the transports of wounded from the uprising. They were a terrible sight. My mother remained in Brwinów and knew exactly where I was, so that if need be, she could give me news of Helenka.

What do you remember of those weeks in Musuły?

There wasn't even a proper road into the village. Germans were a rare sight. The landlord slept in the shed, and in the room, there were beds made up to the ceiling with eiderdowns and pillows for the landlady and her daughter. We refugees from Warsaw slept in rows on the floor. Everyday, I ate soup made of pumpkins and milk. It was disgusting. (The one thing that was good there was the bread.) One day, the landlord said to me, 'You know, my daughter is by herself now without a man, wouldn't you like to...' (here he used a certain verb)_ her?' Imagine my fright! The grass widow resembled a haystack.

There were no other girls?

There were quite a lot of them, actually. The local girls were interested in me because I was 20 years old, clever and different: 'citified.' They would come to G.'s farmyard, sit in a ring and whisper. Sometimes I would pinch them. Such were our 'erotic' encounters. Two of them, the sisters F., daughters of the local rich man, were quite clever and clear in their expectations. They'd bring me food and good fruit (I picked little wild pears and plums for myself). And time passed, somehow, in this way.

And Helenka?

You'll laugh at me, but I really did think about Helenka obsessively. I went crazy, talked to God, blackmailed him, even: 'Dear God, give me my girl back or else I'll stop believing in you. You have to perform a miracle, otherwise I'm through with you.' During one such 'conversation', I saw a human silhouette on the road in the distance. It was Mother. I knew that she must have something important to tell me, otherwise she wouldn't have undertaken such a journey. It turned out that I had an appointment to meet one of our relations the following day.

What kind of relation was he and how did he manage to survive the war? You said everyone in the family had perished.

My mother mentioned the name Jan Rozental. A stereotypical Jew such as you'd see on the cover of *Stürmer* [Striker]. He lived in Germany before the war and married a blond Valkyrie, a gymnastics teacher. I remembered the very beautiful toys he used to bring me. In the late 1930s, he was deported to Poland with a group of Jews. His German wife went with him. My father helped them to get established. When I met him on the street in 1942, he was wearing a Tyrolean costume, and we greeted each other without enthusiasm. He asked how I was doing and said that because he was a German, he was working in a managerial position. He even gave me his telephone number. I called there and a voice answered in German, but when I asked for Rozental, there was total consternation. No one had heard of anyone by that name.

Another time, I saw him on the street in a cinema queue. A lot of people hid in the cinema then; it was safe there, thanks, no doubt, to the propaganda slogan, 'only pigs sit at the flicks'. Jews, in particular, often waited out round-ups in this fashion. He was pushing through the queue with that nose of his, his *Ausweis* and his Tyrolean hat. I couldn't understand any of it, any more than I could understand why he wanted to meet me in Grodzisk.

You probably weren't eager to see him?

I wasn't. However, I went, and there, in the market-square in Grodzisk, was Helenka. Mother had been afraid to tell me because she thought I'd go mad with joy.

What happened to her when you were separated by the uprising?

She went on living on Stępińska Street for quite a long time, and then, together with her parents and brother, went to Zalesie, where some peasant supported them in exchange for work in the fields. On a train, she met an acquaintance, who told her that all the stations were plastered with cards saying that some Marianowicz was looking for her, and gave the address as Brwinów. Without even telling her parents, she immediately got off, took down the address, and went on foot to Brwinów. She found her way to Mother's, and the following day, Mother came to me to arrange the meeting in Grodzisk.

That must have been some meeting.

It was really unusual because the moment we fell into each other's arms, the entire market-square was surrounded by Germans. We ran in panic into the nearest house and lay in the attic there until the round-up was over. I barely survived. The thought that I could lose this girl a few minutes after finding her nearly drove me mad. When it was possible to go out, we went on foot to my village, making love in ditches along the way. We never parted again for a single moment right until the end of the war. The Lord God reacted positively to my ultimatum.

TWENTY-ONE

Twenty-First Conversation

After you had found each other again, did you live with your mother?
(I believe that she didn't particularly like Helenka.)

Mother stayed in Madame Durand's room, and Helenka and I lived at the lawyer Łabęcki's. He owned a house in Brwinów and was a papal chamberlain, not just anybody. The chamberlain scowled at me and was a little terrified because I had been given the accommodation through the housing authority. First, he questioned whether we were a married couple, and reconciled himself, rather reluctantly, to the fact that we intended to marry only after the end of the war. Fortunately, my surname appealed to him, and he asked me where my family had its estates. In Podole, I said, which he accepted. Even more amusing, I discovered after the war that the Łabęcki's were a Frankist* family, from a Jewish mystic sect. That's probably why the chamberlain was so demanding.

We got quite a good room, but the neighbours were dreadful. They were small tradesmen, and the main subject of their conversation was the loss of all kinds of material goods – chairs of some sort played a major role, you'd think they were made of gold. The less somebody had, the greater the lamentation – which was understandable.

What did you actually do there?

Nothing. We loitered around, waiting for the end of the war. One day, I was lying in bed with Helenka, reading Stendahl's *The Charterhouse of Parma* to her out loud, when suddenly the door opened and several Germans burst in. They ordered me to get dressed. Helenka they ignored.

---

* The Frankists were a sect founded by Jacob Frank (1726–91). They bestowed Polish names and even aristocratic titles on Jewish families.

I can imagine how you must have felt, having got so far, to be trapped in such a way.

When they shoved me into a building in the centre of Brwinów with a group of other men, I hadn't the slightest doubt that they were going to take us to the Reich for hard labour. In those days, as I've already mentioned, that was potentially extremely dangerous.

Since we are here having this conversation, I presume you managed to escape somehow.

Yes. It's the story of how I became a pharmacist's assistant. The mayor of Brwinów at the time was a *Volksdeutsch*, one Mr Hoffman. An unbelievably elegant man who dressed as if he had stepped off the page of a fashion magazine: a lady's man. He had a weakness for the local pharmacist's wife, Mrs K., an attractive, though rather pudgy, woman. Their romance wasn't exactly a secret, as Mr Hoffman could often be seen out with her in an elegant two-wheeled carriage.

Did you know the mayor personally?

Well, yes, because as you know, I was doing community work for Brwinów's Chief Welfare Council committee. Mr Hoffman suddenly appeared in that crowd surrounded by Germans, shouting loudly, '*Der Apotheker! Der Apotheker!*' He wanted to find Mr K., whose wife was looking for him. Mr Hoffman explained to the German officer that the pharmacist was indispensable to Brwinów, and managed to persuade him of this. He called out his name and out of the crowd came an unprepossessing little man, pushing his way to the exit. I, in turn, started squeezing my way towards Hoffman. When I was close to him, I looked him straight in the eye and said, 'Mr Hoffman, I have to get out of here. Do you understand? I have to. It'll be worth it to you after the war. Say that I'm the pharmacist's assistant.' A hypnotized Hoffman said, '*Da ist noch der Apothekergehilfe!*,'* and the German nodded me out.

Did you have the opportunity to repay Hoffman for your release?

When the denazification trials were being held after the war, I testified, at Hoffman's request, that although I was not in a

---

* The pharmacist's assistant is here, too.

position to judge his behaviour as mayor, I could attest to the fact that, on such and such a day, he saved me from being transported to Germany. He did well for himself afterwards. I met him a few years later. He was still elegantly dressed, thanked me for my help, and told me that he was working in commerce and doing splendidly.

Since you were near the EKD rail-line, you must have met up with all manner of people you knew – masses of people went through there.

That's true, but you must remember that when the war broke out, I was not quite 16. I knew a lot of people, particularly by sight, and was not known to many myself. I recognized various writers and artists, but so what? Once I accompanied, at a safe distance, Iwaszkiewicz on his walk from the station to Stawisko. I was fascinated by the fact that this tall, middle-aged man was a great writer and that the house deep in the park was his residence. For a moment, I even thought of introducing myself as a relation of Słonimski, but I dismissed the idea.

You didn't really need anything from Iwaszkiewicz.

A good word would have helped, but it could have caused complications. One winter, standing on the station at Milanówek, I noticed that an ordinary-looking, oldish man was watching me from a distance. He was wearing a hat low over his forehead and was so smothered in scarves that I could hardly see his face. I paced up and down the empty platform and he never took his eyes off me. It was worrying. Was it a blackmailer? Maybe. But it could also be somebody taking me for somebody else, or someone who'd taken a fancy to me. I considered my options, which included running away or boxing the old man's ears with the bag of vegetables I was holding in my hand, when I saw him walking quickly in my direction. He was walking so fast that the scarf came off his nose, revealing the friendly face of doctor Maurycy German, our family dentist, whom we affectionately called 'Teuton'.

Was there an unwritten rule among people in hiding not to approach each other unless signalled in some way to do so?

Of course. I often passed people in the street whom I knew well, but would give no recognition of this. The other person might not have wanted to make contact, or might even have been in danger, and unexpected contact could have been mutually threatening. But Dr German was an experienced man and knew what he was doing when he approached me. We exchanged a few words and then he slipped a folded piece of paper into my hand and moved on. The paper turned out to be a ten-dollar bill, and from what he said, I figured out that he had been commissioned by the Joint* to help any Jews he came across. This is how I came across organized Jewish self-help. But the fact that German frightened me was just bad luck. I was even more terrified when I sat in his dentist's chair.

And what can you say about your work for the Chief Welfare Council?

Not much, really. It simply involved sending out thousands of cards about missing persons and receiving thousands of replies. The Council also organized a soup kitchen in Brwinów, which I made use of if only to be like everybody else. I stood, bowl in hand, by the cauldron from which the nuns were distributing soup. A beautiful girl was helping them. I looked at her and was struck by how much she looked like Zosia, whom I had known in the ghetto. I was overwhelmed with emotion when I realized there was no doubt about it – it was Zosia. She noticed me, and later we managed to arrange to talk.

You haven't mentioned Zosia until now.

I only became real friends with her at that time in Brwinów towards the end of the war. I met her first in the ghetto in the Provisioning Authority, whose office was located in two rooms rented from Mrs S., a tailor's widow. That attractive woman had a very beautiful daughter – Zosia – who lit a fire for us every day. I told you I worked with young men there, and her beauty evoked understandable feelings in us. Her well-meaning girlfriends told me that she was attracted to me and that maybe I could ask her out, but I was too shy to embark on an official romance.

You lost contact with her?

Totally, and I didn't believe that she had managed to survive, because she was quite a simple girl, didn't speak the best Polish

---

* The American–Jewish Joint Distribution Committee: international organization for Jewish welfare, active in eastern Europe.

and knew none of the Christian practices – all of which would have made it more difficult for her to hide.

Did she tell you how she stayed alive?

No, and I never asked. We greeted each other like long-lost friends. Walking with Zosia through that green, semi-rural Brwinów, I had brief moments of happiness, though the loss of Helenka depressed me. She told me that she and her mother had some savings and had been able to bribe a German officer to take them out of the ghetto. I repeat, I didn't ask her any questions. The survival of Jewish women was frequently a very delicate matter. I knew Jewish women who'd been rescued by Germans, and I would never presume either to say anything bad or make a moral judgement about them. No one who didn't experience these things himself should sit in judgement in these matters, as long, of course, as these women neither hurt nor denounced anyone. I want to believe that they survived thanks to people's decency and help.

You are as tolerant about this as you were about the people working for the Jewish community.

I always tried to adjust moral norms to reality. In any event, I established a real friendship with Zosia, and when Helenka and I were at lawyer Łabęcki's, she came running to us after several hours of bombing. The ground was rumbling, birds were wheeling overhead. Overcome with emotion, she shouted out that the Russians were entering Brwinów.

Even though you were expecting liberation, this must have come as a shock.

We ran out into the road and saw in the distance huge, clumsy, heavy tanks and, sitting on them, dirty, dishevelled figures. But it wasn't so much the Russians themselves that made an impression on us as the feeling that something had finally come to an end. I thought to myself: five years of nightmare are over and I'm alive. Alive! Everything is starting afresh. The Bolsheviks were a great question-mark, but who cared about that when, in order to feed the crematorium chimney, the Germans had taken away my right to live?

So the three of us, Helenka, Zosia and I, stood in the road, crying like children. You have to remember that that joy determined the attitude of very many people towards the new reality. It built hope. It was difficult to make a sober evaluation of the new situation.

How did your mother react?

Mother stayed in Brwinów for a long time, waiting to see what would happen. A dog called Toy kept her there as well. He'd attached himself to me in Mr Kropiwnicki's ironmongery shop. I walked out of there like an idiot with that fox-terrier, and then fobbed him off on my mother. Helenka and I were in Łódź by February 1945, and in the summer, we brought my mother there, too.

And Zosia?

I met her many times after the war when she was a married woman, and our friendship continued. In 1968, she left Poland to go to her mother, who was happily married and living in the United States. What happened to her after that, I don't know.

TWENTY-TWO
Twenty-second Conversation

You must be one of the few people who saw with their own eyes the ruined and empty post-uprising Warsaw.

Very few people actually know what happened to Warsaw between the collapse of the uprising and the entry of the Russians and of that Polish Army which, as was said, 'fought at the side of the Red Army'.

All the inhabitants were driven out of Warsaw, and the appropriate brigades burned and destroyed the city. Everywhere was rubble, except for those sections where the Germans lived. In the capital, there remained only single individuals hiding in the ruins. Every day, somebody was discovered and unceremoniously shot. My best guess at statistics, however, would be that, in fact, thousands of people were hiding in those ruins.

Do you know how those people managed?

I know these things only second-hand. The classic account is Wladyslaw Szpilman's *The Pianist*, which is fascinating reading.

While we are on the subject of deserted Warsaw, tell me how you got to be there.

After the uprising, as I've said, I was living in Brwinów and curious about what had happened to valuables which I had left at 83 Filtrowa Street when a shell hit our building, a tank rolled into the courtyard and we were ordered to leave our apartments. My mother and I automatically and unthinkingly hid certain things. The most precious things to me were not gold or dollars but mementos of my father. We put everything behind the pipe in the toilet, where we shoved a fair amount of paper dollars, a few gold pieces and our treasures – my father's fountain-pen, watch, cigarette case. Afterwards, in Brwinów, I tried to work out how to get there to retrieve these things.

It must have been very difficult to arrange.

At the edge of the city, on Wolska Street, stood the Räumungsstab, whose task it was to clear Warsaw, primarily of things of potential value to the Germans.

What system did the Germans use? Did they systematically clear empty buildings?

Yes, particularly factories, storehouses and warehouses. If, however, some important firm – Gerlach, for example – asked to be allowed to take something out of its holdings – and during the war, Gerlach worked for the Germans – there was no difficulty in getting permission to drive a truck into Warsaw. Because I knew young Gerlach, I asked him to take me along. I hung around the headquarters for quite a long time to make sure they didn't leave without me. I got there by EKD.

I can't quite picture the location of the Räumungsstab. Since it was on Wolska Street, was it in the city or on its borders? Were the city boundaries guarded?

Of course. A mouse couldn't have slipped through. The army formed a cordon around the city and there were barbed-wire fences all around. As I said, the headquarters of the Räumungsstab were located on the periphery, beyond the city limits. I was once there for a couple of days and met a lot of people. I saw the famous actress Ćwiklińska and several other well-known people there using various connections to try to retrieve some of their belongings. Not having connections myself, my only chance was Gerlach.

I arrived early one morning, but was told that the Gerlach truck had already left. I was disappointed, but luckily found a different means of transport: a horse-drawn wagon with a uniformed German as escort. About eight people had gathered around it, and for a fair amount of money, we had the right to stay in town until dusk. It didn't take me long to decide.

The roads were passable?

Yes – canyons amid the ruins. They made a terrible impression. The Germans weren't clearing anything. There were whole gangs of feral cats. Every so often, I could hear bullets whistling over our heads.

Who was shooting?

Probably the Russians on the Praga side, because who else could it have been? I can still hear that whistle.

Once I had driven into the city and saw armed Germans looking suspiciously at us, I suddenly became very afraid. I had had no hesitation about embarking on this escapade, but then my imagination started to work. I began to wonder why I had actually come: what was so important that I'd felt the need to leave the relative safety of Brwinów? But it was too late to turn back. Germans kept walking by with dogs. Periodically, the sounds of gunfire came from the ruins. I don't know who was being fired at. The effect was terrible. I drove across very familiar streets and saw only an enormous field of ruins. It was difficult to work out the town's topography.

What kind of agreement did you work out on that wagon? To drive to various addresses in turn?

The leader was the German, who decided that Filtrowa Street would be the last stop on the route. We stopped on Wilcza Street, and it was only then that I understood the precise nature of this expedition. These were not people coming to look for their own things, but hyenas searching for loot. They knew that wealthy people had lived on Wilcza Street and that they might find interesting things in the cellars. I realised that I was in very sordid company.

A woman was determined to go down into one of the cellars. At first, the German questioned this; an argument ensued, and, in the end, they both went down together. She returned dragging some kind of bundles, he, zipping himself up. I started to feel ill. I was paralysed with fear, not just physically but morally. We drove around and, of course, I never did get to Filtrowa Street. Eventually, the German looked at his watch and ordered us to turn around. The driver reined the horse and we went back.

Did you meet anyone else along the road? Any similar transport?

A truck from the National Museum, otherwise, not a living soul.

And you couldn't get off this wagon and find a Gerlach truck?

That would have meant death. To find oneself without protection in the shape of a German with safe conduct would have meant a bullet through the head. Had I walked down the street, any patrol man would have immediately shot me. I had to stay on that wagon.

We drove in the direction of Błonie; it was late and I was completely overwhelmed with despair. I decided to jump off the wagon outside Błonie. One of the participants in the expedition gave me a look of complete understanding and then threw me a bundle. 'Have it', he said, 'you got nothing, take it.' I put the bundle back on the wagon and ran, because I wanted to get back to Brwinów before curfew. The only thing I was left with was a beautiful cameo which I had picked up off the ground while the others were looting the cellar. Along the way, I took it out of my pocket and threw it into a cornfield so that I wouldn't be reminded of this experience. It is one of my most disgusting memories from the Occupation, and it revolts me. To this day, I don't know how I could have allowed myself to get into that situation.

There's nothing in it which puts you in a shameful light.

Objectively speaking, you're right, but it was horrible. Because, however, I sometimes cast myself in a favourable light in these recollections, there should also be a story which shows me in a different light.

You mentioned that you made it to Filtrowa Street later on. What happened to the mementos of your father?

On 18 January 1945, I again found myself in Warsaw, having gone there on foot from Brwinów. When I reached Wolska Street, soldiers stopped me and ordered me to take part in the operation to clear the city of rubble. It was quite amusing: throughout the entire Occupation, I hadn't allowed myself to get caught for any work, and now, a spade was being pressed into my hands and I was being told to join the rebuilding effort. I know it wasn't nice, but I didn't stay there a minute. Nobody knew how to escape as well as I did! I ran to Filtrowa Street, of course. The building was basically gone; only the staircase remained. An armed soldier stood downstairs. I said I had to go upstairs. At first, he didn't even want to talk, but then agreed, on condition that he'd go with me. We climbed the stairs to the third floor – my heart in my mouth. A dead woman lay on the stairs; books and toys were scattered everywhere. Instead of our front door, I saw some kind of burned furniture, but, marvel of marvels, the toilet was still there, as was the pipe. I put my hand inside and reached down deep to find a bundle of disintegrating paper – the dollars. The soldier watched without a word as I pulled them out carefully and laid then down on some blackened board. Then I pulled out a few gold 20-dollar pieces. The mementos of my father had unfortunately vanished. They had probably fallen out from under the pipe and people had chanced on them.

Did the soldier want anything from you?

His expression left no doubt about it. I laid the coins next to the paper money and pushed one of them towards him. He shook his head in an unhappy manner, so I placed a second coin there.

He wanted more?

On the contrary, less. He said irritably that he didn't know what that was, and asked, instead, for 200 złoty. I can't remember what you could buy for 200 złoty in those days – a few packs of cigarettes, perhaps. In any event, I didn't argue.

He could have taken everything and killed you as well. There would have been one more corpse on the stairs.

He could indeed have done that.

May I ask you something, out of sheer curiosity? What did you gain from recovering those crumbled dollars?

Well, the numbers on the bills had been preserved, and when I found myself in Belgium a year later, the Bank of England took 40 per cent and gave me 60 per cent of their value. That was quite a lot of money. With the złotys, we immediately bought ourselves warm clothing. At the market in Włochy near Warsaw, I bought myself an old-fashioned coat. I looked most elegant in it on the streets of Łódź. There's even a drawing by Zaruba which shows me strolling around Piotrowska Street in this 'Italian' creation.

You embarked on a new chapter of your life, and at this point, we must finish the first section of your memoirs.

Are you suggesting that there should be a sequel?

That's up to you.

The author and his 'bride', Nina Zoppot, 1931

My parents before I was born

The author as in the ghetto of Warsaw, 28 July, 1942

The author as an elegant in Wołomin, 1943

Helenka, my wife-to-be

Part 2
Family Recollections

TWENTY-THREE
Forefathers

I became seriously interested in my family history only after there was almost no one left to ask about it. My knowledge on the subject consists of remembered scraps of conversation and faded photographs, because everything else disappeared in the black hole of war. I remember portraits of my great-great-grandparents from the second half of the nineteenth century. They were founders and owners of a textile factory in Zawiercie and looked like typical German factory-owners of that time: both of them thin, with stern expressions and thin lips – he in a high starched collar and frock-coat, she in a severe black dress fastened with a brooch. Neither had any trace of Jewish features. Their name was Gincberg. From information I was able to gather, it appears that the photo is of one of the three Gincberg brothers: Adolf, Bernard or Wilhelm – I don't know which. In the 1870s, they built huge textile factories in Łódź and Zawiercie, and then, in 1880, amalgamated their enterprises. In this way, with the participation of the Warsaw banker Mieczysław Epstein, a joint stock company, 'Zawiercie', was created with initial capital of some 3.5 million roubles. My great-grandfather, Adolf Seideman, was the son-in-law of Adolf, Bernard or Wilhelm. I regarded him as my true ancestor. As a child, I liked to look at his photograph in the family album. He was portly, very elegantly dressed, and had a lush Karl Marx-style beard. He was sitting in a chair in Karlsbad, his legs crossed with some difficulty. I think that, in keeping with the fashion of the times, he went to the famous *Kurort* [health resort] every year in order to lose weight. Great-grandfather was head cashier at the Zawiercie factory, a position corresponding to that of financial director; nevertheless, I think that the

Seidemans were not very practical people. They had leanings towards absurd occupations (there were even artists among them). The traditions of the founders of the family would not be picked up again until my father came along. I somehow retained both traits: I have an absurd profession, but I don't lose sight of material gain.

Returning to my great-grandfather: he made an unquestionably good impression and so I wholeheartedly approved of him. However, I heard many less than complimentary words about him from my grandmother. He died towards the end of the nineteenth century, great-grandmother outliving him by a number of years. About her, I can say only that she came from a wealthy family and that she looked – judging from the photographs – just like a great-grandmother.

Right up until the outbreak of war, the family archives contained an interesting document: several dozen telegrams sent on the occasion of my great-grandparents' wedding – all of them in German. I think that the language spoken at home in Zawiercie was German, but I can't be sure of it. My great-grandparents' children – my grandmother, Uncle Herman and Aunt Róża, who lived in Warsaw, spoke beautiful, pure, literary Polish.

My grandmother, Henryka (also known as Henrieta and Jecia), was a person who inspired respect. I was 8 years old when she died. I retain an image of a person who was kindly but not given to intimacy. I used to visit her in the apartment on Koszykowa Street which she shared with her sister, also a widow, Aunt Róża Pańska. Of this apartment, I remember grandmother's old-fashioned desk, full of drawers and hidey-holes, which I was allowed to rummage through on condition that I left it tidy. I also remember a sewing table, and a little desk on which stood a crystal radio, and whenever I came, grandmother would remove her earphones. I would usually bring a wind-up film projector and show her films. These could be rented quite cheaply by the Pathé company shop owned by Juliusz Caboche on Jerozolimska Avenue. The catalogue included several hundred titles on various subjects. At that time, I was mainly interested in the comedies of Charlie Chaplin and Harold Lloyd. Later, when I had acquired an electric projector, I also borrowed films of concerts by famous virtuosi and boxing matches (Dempsey-Carpentier, for example, or Dempsey-Tunney). It surprised me that Grandmother, instead of staring at the sheet which did for a screen, would be staring almost exclusively at me. With her silver hair carefully pinned up, her dark clothes and somewhat formal air (despite her smile), she seemed beautiful.

I sometimes found guests at Grandmother's. They came at noon, but I used to arrive at different times. The food and drink was traditional and always the same: the elderly maid brought in coffee and a heaped plate of a steaming *matzi brei* (matzos which had been soaked in milk, mixed with eggs, then fried in butter and eaten either sweet or with salt). This – and only this – was evidence of Grandmother's attachment to Jewish tradition. For, in contrast to the rest of the family who had been baptized at the beginning of the century, she alone refused to break with Judaism and would not even allow any discussion on the subject. And she knew how to stand up for her beliefs.

Her nephew, Jerzy Pański, told me that Grandmother was an excellent cook, but always warned her guests that for one reason or another, the food hadn't turned out well. Under only one circumstance did Grandmother praise her own culinary creations – when a disaster had actually taken place. So the announcement, 'the cutlets are delicious today', was taken by experienced diners as a sure sign that they were burned. Although I only learned about this second-hand, I have, since childhood, distrusted anything which is extravagantly praised.

Grandmother had been widowed during the war when she was still quite a young woman. I don't know why she married my grandfather. Bernard Berman was a person the family rarely spoke about. My father spoke of him with a certain degree of pity, my uncle with amusement. (He once told a story about giving his father a gold watch during the war – he stared at it in amazement, not quite knowing what to do with it.) Grandfather was considerably older than Grandmother and probably not very well educated. Nor did he cut a fine figure. The marriage had come about as the result of some tragedy about which nobody spoke. I learned only recently from one of the last family members of the previous generation, Wacław Solski (Pański), about my grandmother's love affair with his father, Aleksander Pański, a doctor. Why it didn't lead to marriage, and why Uncle Pański later married my grandmother's younger sister, I don't know. But that's what happened, and the pretty, genteel 17-year-old girl married a random suitor. Poor Grandfather.

In his excellent book, *Moje wspomnienia* [My Recollections]* Wacław Solski devoted quite a lot of space to Grandfather. It is a totally unexpected posthumous tribute to a humble man who, during his lifetime, enjoyed little popularity. I quote a (considerably abbreviated) excerpt about the death of my grandfather in Moscow in 1916:

> Uncle Bernard was a shipping-agent in Warsaw. Before the First World War, he owned a shipping company on Zelazna Street in the vicinity of the freight station...I don't know why my aunt married him. Everyone in the family ignored him; no one asked his opinion about anything; he was treated as though he didn't exist at all, or only marginally...I was friends with Uncle Bernard. He often smiled knowingly at me behind my Aunt's back, or showed off his particular talent. This consisted of his laughing silently, then instantly turning serious. Aunt Henrieta did not like this. 'Stop the clowning,' she'd say dryly. She also did not like it when Bernard sang under his breath as he played chess. But in this case, Uncle refused to compromise. He regarded the singing as a privilege won after years of heavy fighting, one of his few rights and privileges.
>
> He was an excellent chess-player. He once took part in tournaments in Warsaw. He had no one to play with in Moscow, so sometimes he played with me, beating me with no difficulty...He did nothing in Moscow,

---

* Paris, 1977.

absolutely nothing...So I played chess almost daily with Uncle Bernard, because I, also, had nothing to do. The hotel was called Victoria, and stood on Twerska, the town's main street, now called Gorki Street...Uncle intoned 'Troika', in almost a soprano voice, raised the castle into the air and dropped it. The castle fell on the chess-board, knocking a few pieces over. Uncle Bernard fell back into his chair, and let out a single sound, like a surprised clearing of the throat. His head dropped onto his chest...That's how my uncle died. Not seriously, but like an insect rather than a person. The following day, his body was taken to the funeral parlour and, before evening, guests sat in the room drinking coffee. Aunt sat in an armchair at some distance from the table. The guests spoke in low voices, as if afraid of waking somebody up. They did not speak about Bernard at all.

I don't know why, but I think frequently and with affection about the grandfather whom I didn't know. He was apparently a good, pleasant, and not at all stupid, man who maintained his family at a reasonable standard of living. He managed to ensure an education for his three children. Surely it was appropriate that his shipping company was situated in the vicinity of the station. Where else should it have been – Castle Square, or one of Warsaw's fashionable streets? I feel sorry for Grandfather.

The story that Grandfather Bernard was the descendant of some particularly scholarly rabbi from the dim and distant past should probably be regarded as a family myth. I always thought of it as an attempt to cast glory on a common surname. Recently, however, in a reprint of a book by Matthias Bersohn, *Słownik biograficzny uczonych Żydow polskich* [Biographical Dictionary of Scholarly Polish Jews],* I found a note about a famous cabbalist, Isahar Berman, who lived in the second half of the sixteenth century and was a rabbi in Szczebrzeszyn. His works were translated into many languages and, Bersohn says, gained him

---

* Warsaw, 1983.

'everyone's high regard'. So, perhaps Grandmother's marriage wasn't so terribly unsuitable after all.

Grandmother died suddenly of a heart attack in 1932. My father was on the Riviera at the time, and the French police looked for him in order to inform him of his mother's death. He returned in time for the funeral. I remember him coming into the apartment, housekeeper Józef staggering behind him, as usual, with the cases. Father looked quizzically at us and dropped into an armchair. I remember his quiet words, 'She's dead', and his tears. Yes, tears –it was the one and only time in my life that I saw them fall across his normally stern face.

I didn't go to Grandmother's funeral – children weren't taken to funerals for fear it might upset their nervous system. I did, however, read the obituary in the *Kurier Warszawski* [The Warsaw Courier], where 'grandson' was featured last among the next-of-kin. I was very proud. Although not mentioned by name, I had appeared in print for the very first time.

TWENTY-FOUR
Herman and Hela

My grandmother's older brother was Uncle Herman Seideman. He was married to Aunt Helena, *née* Heiman. They had two children: Janina Konarska – later known as Słonimska – and Tadeusz. By the 1920s, Janina was already a very well-known graphic artist, and her social connections in aristocratic diplomatic circles necessitated a legalization of her pseudonym. My uncle's family had, in fact, been christened sometime at the turn of the century, but they had kept their not very Polish surname. Wanting to accommodate their daughter, they turned to the authorities in 1924, asking to be granted the name 'Konarski'. The name's legal owners, however, opposed this. In view of the Konarskis' opposition, my aunt and uncle had no alternative but to call themselves 'Konerski' – an unfortunate choice because it evoked the suspicion that they had once been called 'Kon'. This connection haunted Janina her whole life. The mildly anti-Semitic Maria Dabrowska notes in her *Dzienniki* [Diaries] for 1 January 1928: 'For New Year's Eve I went to the Wierzynskis'. Lechon, the Szererowski, the Breiters, Czarski, a young Sakowski (Seidenbeutel) were there...as well as a Mr Heyman, Miss Konarska – Kon – apparently a very talented painter, and Stanisław Balinski...Apart from the first and the last, all the others were – Jews'.

Uncle Herman (in later years, he went by the name Andrzej) was tall, handsome and blond, with a flaxen moustache. He looked like a farmer. As a young man from a good family, he had great hopes for himself. He studied engineering and played the alto violin. As a grown man, he married an attractive, very wealthy but not-so-young, lady. Aunt Hela was about 28 years old, daughter of the Łódź factory-owner and philanthropist

Edward Heiman. Thanks to this splendid match, my uncle soon became the director of his father-in-law's factory, and it was then that his complete inability to run anything, including my aunt, manifested itself. The disappointed Heiman made my uncle director of the factory orchestra, which was quickly dismantled under his baton. Uncle and Aunt moved to Warsaw, where they lived 'without gain and without loss' on Aunt Hela's money. Uncle did community work in schools, teaching children about music, and sometimes appearing with a chamber orchestra. His talent was mediocre, but he had another creative outlet: he was an inventor. He heard once that my father wanted to order a wardrobe for my room from Gembarzewski, a well-known cabinet-maker. That was a signal for him to join in the action. Having received permission from my father, who dreaded Uncle's protracted disquisitions more than anything, he made the drawings and a few weeks later the wardrobe was ready. Uncle presented it to us in the presence of a slightly embarrassed Gembarzewski. It was fairly shallow and, at the top, from pipes set perpendicular to the wall, other thin pipes stretched out into the room.

'What's the purpose of this arrangement?' my father asked, intrigued.

'Don't you see?' Uncle said in surprise. 'You can hang as many clothes as you want on these pipes.'

'Yes, but then the wardrobe won't close,' Father pointed out.

'So what? Who says it's always got to be closed?' Uncle replied sarcastically. The wardrobe cost only three times as much as a normal one, and made us leery of Uncle's innovative ideas. Less expensive was his idea for socks with removable heels (the uppers, he reasoned correctly, don't wear out). This idea demanded a purely technical solution, and my aunt puzzled over it of her own free will. It was like that with his invention of travel carts for transporting luggage. Uncle drew up an exact model, but because of the nonavailability of light metals at that time, it weighed more than the heaviest suitcases. Quite apart from that, stations teemed with porters, so Uncle's idea came into daily use only scores of years later, and the name of its inventor remained unknown. It is ever so with geniuses before their time!

As for me, Uncle – or, more accurately, Great-Uncle – Herman Andrzej rendered me the service of taking me to concerts at the Philharmonic, which gave rise to a habit of many years, unfortunately now long-abandoned. This taking me to concerts was in payment for their very frequent and – as used to be said – scrounging visits to our house. They were avid consumers, particularly of carp in aspic, and came, officially, to bite the heads off fish saved especially for them. I'm reminded here of a postwar Łódź barmaid's famous saying about fish-heads, 'the gentlemen Jews like them', but that would be inappropriate in the case of Uncle and Aunt Konerski (no one any longer remembered the problems with the name). Uncle Konerski regarded himself as an arch-Pole, while my aunt, when she was not eating fish, gave herself up to a variety of religious duties. Her most frequent activity was lying in church flat on her face with her arms spread out in the shape of the cross. Despite this, I was truly fond of Aunt Hela and was particularly impressed by her coarse language – somewhat surprising in one so devout. She'd say, for example, 'he doesn't need vaseline to get in her', or, 'she'd even let a dog do it to her'. After the war, she'd tell me about her life in the camp, complaining about the behaviour of the person on the bunk above hers: 'I couldn't sleep because she spent the whole night screwing'. The only mementos from my prewar home were at Aunt Konerski's, miraculously saved during the uprising. Aunt died in 1951, outliving my uncle by 15 years. Every day, right up to her death, she desparately awaited the return of her son, Tadeusz, who was last seen in the Starobielsk camp. She did, however, live to see the return to Poland of her daughter, Janina, and her son-in-law, Antoni Słonimski.

Aunt Hela's nephew, Aleksander Heiman-Jarecki, was a great industrial magnate, owner of 'Wola', (a textile factory), senator and landowner. (In the late 1930s, he acquired a splendid estate for around five million złoty, an enormous sum at that time.) In 1933, Aleksander married the actress Bronisława (Brysia) Koyallowicz, former wife of Kamierz Wierzyński (Wierzyński, in turn, married the former wife of the pianist Henryk Sztompka). Mr and Mrs Heiman-Jarecki were renowned for living it up, and their parties were a feature of the high life of that era. Premier Sławoj Składkowski, famous for his 'Economic Boycott – Why Not?' slogan, came to one of these parties. Apparently, the economic boycott of people of doubtful ancestry did not mean social boycott; nevertheless, the premier behaved in an unprecedented way: speaking in parliament some time later, he related his impressions of the party at the Jareckis' and said he doubted whether the taxes the senator paid actually corresponded to his real income. I promised myself then that if I ever invited some premier to my house, it would be for hot dogs.

The Jareckis found themselves in France in September 1939. He went on to England, where he remained for the duration of the war, before going on to Australia. She stayed with her family in Paris. When the Germans took over, she perished as a 'Jew-ridden' person in Auschwitz.

TWENTY-FIVE
Róża Pańska

Grandmother's younger sister, Róża, known as Runia, was a woman of regal bearing and unusual beauty. I remember that, in the late 1930s, the famous actor and eccentric Władysław Grabowski, on seeing her on the street, fell to his knees crying: 'You are still the most beautiful of women! You were, and remain, the single love of my life!' Grabowski was probably drunk, but, in fact, even in her 50s, my aunt made quite an impression. As a young girl, she married a well-known Łódź neurologist, Aleksander Pański. Before the Second World War, their house was the meeting-place for the town's cultural elite. My uncle, who specialized in detecting brain tumours, was not only an excellent doctor but also a social worker, head of the department of nervous diseases at the Poznański hospital. They had three sons: Antoni, Wacław and Jerzy, each one of whom distinguished himself in some way in Polish history, though they went their separate ways and were neither physically nor mentally alike. In the Łódź days, they were seen as monsters. Aunt told me about her little boys' many antics. Wearing Indian costumes, they'd attack their father's departing patients, waving tomahawks and threatening to scalp them.

At the beginning of the First World War, the Pańskis found themselves in Minsk, where Uncle practised medicine and was president of the Polish emigrants' association. When the Germans came in, all three sons, together with my father, left town, trying, in the midst of the prevailing chaos, to reach Poland. They were arrested by the German authorities in Kowno, and news of this reached Minsk. A little while afterwards, a patient came to see Dr Pański, offering her condolences over his sons' deaths – this, evidently, was what was being bruited about.

Uncle went into the other room, took a revolver out of a drawer, and shot himself in the head. He was 54 years old. Of course, his three sons were actually alive and well.

After the First World War, my aunt returned and lived a widow's existence with her sister, my grandmother. A few gentlemen tried for her hand, but, as she explained, after Uncle Pański, they seemed pitiful and comical to her. Love affairs were unthinkable in those circles – one older cousin, who had caught an unpleasant disease from her chauffeur, committed suicide. So, for the entire 20-year period between the wars, Aunt did nothing other than talk, talk, talk. She had no satisfaction from her sons – on the contrary, she agonized over the things being said about them – all three, rightly or wrongly, were regarded as communists. My father thought them simply idiots, and, as he was her beloved nephew, he helped to support her. We lived in the same apartment on Chłodna Street in the ghetto with her for a while. During the deportation, my aunt perished, along with her daughter-in-law, Antoni's last wife, Genia Markson, and her granddaughter – the unexpected joy of the last years of her life.

TWENTY-SIX
Zosia Flatau

Aunt Zosia Flatau, my grandmother's cousin, was a well-known figure in Warsaw. A small, garishly and eccentrically dressed older woman with a mop of grey hair, she looked so odd that passers-by would stare at her. In her youth, she was distinguished by her unusual grace and beauty, as well as by her considerable dowry. She married Józef Hosiasson, whose main claim to fame was being the head of the Polish branch of 'Bourjois', the famous French perfume. She had three children by him: two boys and a girl. The youngest of them was still an infant when she fell desperately and irrevocably in love with Edward Flatau.

'Edward Flatau was an archetypal figure amongst Polish neurologists, and at the same time, one of the founders of world neurology. His personal qualities and remarkable learning destined him for leadership, while his enormously rich, thoroughly original scholarly output and his social activities allow him to be included among the founders of medicine.' So ran the assessment of Flatau in Eugeniusz Herman's *Neurolodzy polscy* [Polish Neurologists].* But this is not all. Flatau was a man of culture, with a striking, almost demonic, appearance. His success with the fairer sex was on a par with his scholarly achievements. So what chance did poor Hosiasson have when, even in terms of his financial situation, Flatau – son of a great corporate merchant and an unusually dedicated doctor – could outdo any rival?

Aunt Zosia's abandonment of her husband and tiny children was one of the biggest scandals in metropolitan circles of the

---

* Warsaw, 1958.

Jewish plutocracy at the turn of the century. Her father was so shocked that he lost his sight, not to mention several tenements which he had to turn over to his former son-in-law in exchange for a divorce. Less affected by the affair was her mother, Aunt Leosia, from whom it would seem Zosia had inherited her rather flighty nature. My father used to say that, as a student, he'd supported himself for quite a while by playing cards daily with that very same, already widowed, great-aunt: he would seat the old lady in such a way as to be able to see her cards in the mirror. The poor old woman could never figure out why she always lost, and her desire to win back the money made her sit down to play again the following day. Father enjoyed this enormously and felt no guilt, because his aunt was the richest member of the family.

Zosia lived with Flatau for many years and had a daughter, Anka, by him. Unfortunately, Flatau, though by that time quite old, had an affair with a young actress who died in tragic circumstances. Later, he took up with a female doctor. Ironically, he left my aunt in much the same way as she had left her first husband. In 1932, Flatau died of a brain tumour, whose growth in his own brain he recorded day after day, very precisely and with the dispassionate interest of a scientist. His funeral was a real showpiece. The paper *Nasz Przegląd* [Our Review] ran an obituary which took up the entire front page. The text proclaimed: 'Edward Flatau, pride and glory of Polish Jewry'. A huge photograph of the deceased occupied the entire first page of the paper's illustrated supplement. The Jews treated him with enormous respect because he had refused to be baptized – a requirement, apparently, for a professorship. One of the French scholarly journals wrote at the time that it [Poland] was a strange country in which the great Flatau was denied the title of professor.

The phrase 'old age without dignity' perfectly describes Aunt Zosia's final years. Her eccentric dress was simply the outer manifestation of her existence. She squandered money and fell victim to all manner of swindlers and fraudsters. For example, she looked after some dubious refugee from Germany who was teaching her the latest dances. Another equally suspicious young man was teaching her to play bridge. Aunt was full of initiative and constantly tried to recommend her protégés to ladies of her acquaintance, much to their husbands' indignation.

I think that Aunt Zosia's abnormal behaviour was the result of her tragic isolation. Her daughter, Anka, was difficult and uncommunicative, while her sons from her first marriage – brought up by Hosiasson to hate their mother – did not maintain relations with her. While she was with Flatau, she tolerated this state of affairs, but in her old age, she developed a tremendous love for her grandchildren. She wandered around the parks where the little Hosiassons went, and bribed their nannies in order to be able to play with them. The sons, however, were unyielding. They both survived the war in Paris and died abroad, feeling that they had brought their vendetta to a successful conclusion. Aunt's daughter from her first marriage, Dr Janina Hosiasson (later Lindenbaum), maintained cool, formal relations with her mother. She was an outstanding philosopher, and fate connected her life in a particularly tragic way with that of her cousin, Antoni Pański.

During the Occupation, Aunt Zosia found herself in the Warsaw ghetto. We had only occasional contact with her. She apparently gave her entire fortune to swindlers in exchange for freedom and was utterly destitute by the time she was sent to a camp! But wealth was, by then, meaningless, because an end in the crematorium ovens was the same for the poor as it was for the rich.

TWENTY-SEVEN

Mother

Mother was born in the Latvian town of Dynaburg, supposedly in 1896. I say 'supposedly' because after much tampering with her date of birth, she probably lost track of it herself. My mother's family lived modestly, but they were not poor. Her father leased forests and traded in lumber, while her mother was no different from hundreds of thousands of Jewish mothers: eternally overworked and often irritable. My father's first meeting with her was when he paid his official engagement visit. He was offered half a glass of weak, dishwatery tea, of which he was prone to remind my equally miserly mother for the rest of his life. My mother was called Pola, but I suspect that her actual name was Perla. She was remarkable for her unusual beauty. She had six dark, typically Semitic, siblings, but was, herself, a golden-haired doll with blue eyes and a delicately shaped nose – a freak of nature giving the lie to racist theories.

Because of her beauty, my mother was sent to a first-rate boarding school where she studied with the daughters of generals. Generals! It was a source of unending pride to her. On leaving school, she found herself in Minsk, and applied for a job at the International Bank where my father was one of the managers at the time.

I know nothing, or next to nothing, about my mother's life before she went to the bank. I gathered, from my father's snide remarks, that there had been in her life a not–so–young admirer called Rabinowicz, and, from another quarter, that he was 'a very respectable man.' Mother kept his photograph, but in his case, respectability did not go hand-in-hand with looks. She also had a photograph of Boborykin, the principal of her famous boarding-school – a stern gentleman with pince-nez, whose picture she perused with awe for many years.

My mother must have been quite an enterprising lady at the time, since she got a job in the office of the bank's top director. The director, an older man, did nothing without consulting my father. Summoned by his superior, Father looked closely at the applicant, and on being asked, 'What do you think, Gustav Bernardovich, should we hire this young lady?' responded, 'We should, Director.' And that is how my genetic make-up was determined.

I don't know what happened next. From snatches of my parents' stories, I remember only that my father made a fortune in sugar factories in Russia, and that he and my mother fled by wagon to Wilno [Vilnius] across a nation in the grip of revolution. He took not only his own treasure but also some recently widowed countess with a whole lot of Russian gems sewn into various parts of her clothing. The journey was broken at many checkpoints. Both ladies stayed in the wagon, while Father apparently went up to the soldiers with a revolver in one hand and a 500 rouble bill in the other. They didn't make any difficulties for him. My parents married in Wilno, and that same evening – if my mother is to be believed – my father cheated on her with the countess. Perhaps it happened while they were unpicking the gems. I really don't know what to make of this shameful incident.

In Warsaw, my father's family received my mother extremely badly. My grandmother regarded her oldest son's unsuitable marriage as a curse. She had imagined that Father would marry a Rothschild at the very least. Father's sister and brother also didn't hide their disappointment, while friends and acquaintances, even though they paid Mother their compliments, couldn't get over the fact that a handsome, clever man from a good family – and very rich to boot – had taken up with some Latvian. I should add that my mother's daring spirit, which worked well in Russia, let her down all the way here. The poor woman couldn't ingratiate herself with the family and friends; and it is hard to avoid thinking that she would have done better to have stayed with Rabinowicz. She was desperately provincial, awkward and full of complexes. On top of this, tact wasn't exactly her strong point, and pretty soon, her relations with the entire circle of family and friends grew somewhat tense. That, of course, affected my father, and when my mother's successive pregnancies resulted in miscarriages, the situation became critical. It was then, when mother was approaching 30 and father 40, that, at the last moment, as it were, I appeared on the scene – her own most beloved son, and her security against a hostile environment. The situation now changed in a fundamental way. The impatiently awaited (only one in the whole clan!) healthy, fat and coddled infant – the hope for a future sure to be bright – had appeared. Grandma bestowed her approval on me, although on first viewing me, she criticized my hands – unfortunately, I didn't have my father's long, slender fingers but my mother's short, common ones. Despite this shortcoming, however, my mother acquired a longed-for legitimacy in nursing the scion.

And how she nursed! When I was a child, she wrapped me up, buttoned and unbuttoned me, took my temperature, put me to bed, rubbed me down, tucked me in, uncovered me, called in doctors. The illustrious paediatrician Władysław Szenajch came each time, examined me, pinched my tummy at the end of the examination, and mostly pronounced me as healthy, but sometimes he'd say, 'There's flu...streptococcal infection... measles...mump...scarlet fever. Give him raspberry tea to make him sweat and aspirin. Bring a urine sample for analysis – but don't send your own urine, Mummy! I know you'd do anything for your son, wouldn't you?'

When I started school, Mother suffered agonies because she couldn't come with me. When my whole class was going to Rejowka, a school colony near Warsaw to which we travelled by train, I noticed my mother peeping out from behind the coal by the station building to make sure that I managed to climb into the compartment. Another time, the face of our maid appeared at the window of the neighboring compartment, doubtless under orders to catch me in mid-flight if – God forbid – I should fall off the train. My irritation had no effect on Mother. I could throw tantrums, Father could back me up and call her an idiot, but she knew best.

Once, when I was in bed with some trivial cold, Mother asked what I'd like for dinner, and I said, 'Anything, except kasha'. An hour later, the maid appeared with a plate of steaming kasha. Without thinking, I picked up the plate and smashed it against the wall. It looked disgusting: the wallpaper covered with a white mush of globules which plopped onto the floor. Mother's shrieks brought my father into the room. He listened to my story completely calmly and said he understood. To give kasha to someone who asked for anything but kasha, in his estimation, amounted to provocation.

During the Occupation, my mother treated me like a valuable and very fragile possession. Although, at that time, her fear for her only son was understandable, she acted as though I was still an innocent little boy. She broke into my room in Wołomin once, and, on seeing the dishevelled bed, shouted in an accusatory manner: 'There was a woman here!'

'Who should there have been?' I asked, enraged. 'A man?'

She was at daggers with Helenka, but was very upset by her death in January 1952. Until the end of her life, she fought with my successive wives and non-wives, regarding all of them as glorified harlots lying in wait for my earnings, and ready, at any moment, to deliver me a fatal blow. She saw me as fragile and defenceless, mercilessly exploited by other people. My friends and acquaintances, unsuitable company for me as a rule, aroused her fear. She offended each and everyone in this way, and spoiled her relations with every living person who should have mattered to her, and yet she left this world feeling that she had fulfilled her maternal duty to the very end.

My mother had yet another trait: she was the most dreadful pessimist, poisoning every happy moment for herself and other people with her Cassandra-like prophecies. Before the war, when we were prosperous, she couldn't make the most our good fortune, saying that it was all going to come to a bad end. Things did, in fact, turn out badly, but others managed to enjoy the good times, while she wasted them worrying about the bad ones. She was always warning me about a thousand dangers, particularly illness and theft – illness and theft scared her more than anything else in the world. Since you can't safeguard against either – even I sometimes fell sick or was robbed – this confirmed her in her conviction that she was never wrong and that she understood life better than I, a na ve, beardless youth, did. The poor woman could never understand that being right takes no skill – that lies in establishing relationships with the rest of the always hopelessly benighted human race.

TWENTY-EIGHT
Antoni Pański

I didn't really know Antoni Pański very well. When I was small, he would make terrifying faces to scare me. That may be why I didn't seek him out later on.

Antoni (1895–1941) was the Pańskis' oldest son. He made a good impression – a brilliantly intelligent egoist with a tendency to eccentricity. He received his secondary school diploma in St Petersburg, his undergraduate degree at the Sorbonne, and studied for a doctorate at the University of Warsaw. During his early youth, he was connected with a leftist freedom movement. From 1918 to 1919 he served in the military, then joined the Union of Independent Socialist Youth.

In 1930, he went to England, where he moved in liberal left-wing intellectual circles. Bertrand Russell and Joseph Needham, for example, were among his close friends. Antoni Słonimski describes an amusing scene in his *Alfabet wspomien* [An Alphabet of Recollections]* when the famous biologist Needham admitted to him that he knew Polish quite well. It turned out that he had even translated some of Tuwim's poems into English, and his teacher and helper was none other than Antoni Pański.

After returning to Poland, Antoni was editor of *Przegląd Socjalistyczny* [The Socialist Review] for a few months. In 1932, he started work at the Central Statistics Office, from which he was fired in 1934, probably for his leftist convictions, although at that time, he belonged to no party. He subsequently devoted himself to translations from English, chiefly for the 'Roj' publishers (the later Roy publishers in the United States). The

---

* Warsaw, 1975.

most renowned authors Antoni translated were Bertrand
Russell, Lloyd George and Lytton Strachey.

He also wrote many professional papers in the 1930s which
are still cited today, mainly about Warsaw's demographic
problems. Antoni left Warsaw to go to Wilno [Vilnius] in 1939,
where he became director of Freedom, a conspiratorial socialist
organization. Its former director, Wacław Zagórski, in his book
Wolność w niewoli [Freedom in Servitude], says that as he was
leaving Wilno, he looked around for someone to take his place.
'I suggest Antoni Pański. An economist, highly educated and
very cultured... who took no part in political in-fighting before
the war... His candidacy... was unanimously accepted.'
Because of his excellent international contacts, particularly with
the British Labour Party, Antoni was shortly marked out to
become the representative of the Polish underground in Britain.
He received a British visa, but was arrested when the Germans
entered Poland and imprisoned in Lukiszki. He died in the
prison hospital in the autumn of that year, ostensibly of typhus.
That, at any rate, was the official German version. But,
according to *Poland Fights*, a bulletin published in New York,
Antoni was in fact tortured to death by the Gestapo.

Finally, a few words about Antoni's personal life. As a young
man, he fell in love with Janina Hosiasson, who was four years
younger than he, and who returned his affection. I think the
family was less than thrilled by this, and that Janina gave in to
pressure from her outraged aunts and uncles. As a result,
Antoni married Elza Aftergut, a pretty girl and a singer,
apparently, although there is no mention of her in professional
journals. They divorced in 1924, and Antoni, this time
overcoming all obstacles, took up again with Janina. They still
didn't marry, but lived together for quite a long time, though
they broke up again (for reasons that are not known) in the early
1930s. After that, Antoni had a string of love affairs. I remember,
for example, a story that Bella Gelbard told me in the 1950s:

'I lived with your cousin, Antoni, you know. He was a very
attractive man. Unfortunately, the only thing I remember is

---

*   London, 1971.

eternally standing in the kitchen frying cutlets'.

'Pull the other leg,' I thought to myself. 'You lived with all the most famous men of the time, including Einstein and Donald Duck!' But just to make sure, I said to Antoni's brother, Jerzy, 'Listen, was there some food that Antoni liked more than anything else?'

'Of course,' Jerzy answered, 'Antoni was crazy about cutlets!"

Just before the war, Antoni married Eugenia Markson, a student who was at least 20 years younger than he was and by whom he had a daughter. Janina, in the meantime, married Adolf Lindenbaum, an assistant professor of mathematics at the University of Warsaw. It seems that this was a marriage of convenience, as was Antoni's. Apparently, both of them, as mature people, had come to the conclusion that they were not meant to have a life together. This was to be decided under tragic circumstances. When war broke out, it turned out that they were irrevocably doomed to one another. They linked up again and showed up in Wilno (they were both politically active, legally and in the underground). A few days after Antoni's arrest, Janina was stopped in the street. She had two passports in her possession: one in the name of Lindenbaum, the other in the name of Pański – they were apparently planning to go to England together. Anna Jędrychowska writes in *Zygzagiem i po prostu* [In a Zigzag, and in a Straight Line] that an escape from prison had been planned for Janina, but because of her hesitation, it hadn't come off.

Janina was shot by the Germans shortly afterwards. I knew her, like Antoni, only a little. I remember an attractive young woman with luxuriant, greying hair – she had inherited her prematurely greying hair from her mother, Zosia Flatau. She was a very educated woman – a doctor of philosophy who had studied with Kotarbiński and Łukasiewicz. The philosopher Klemens Szaniawski, about whom I had questioned her, confirmed her status as a Polish logician.

I am sorry that I didn't know this splendid couple better. I feel as if I missed an important opportunity. I am also very sorry that Antoni's daughter perished. She would have been the only child, apart from my own offspring, who could have ensured the continuation of the family line.

TWENTY-NINE
Wacław Solski (Pański)

During my childhood, Wacław (1897–1990) was a terrifying, almost mythical, figure. 'Communist. Bolshevik,' my aunts said of him, though not, of course, in the presence of his mother, in front of whom no one mentioned Wacław. I knew him only from photographs, which confirmed his demonic character: a strange oval face, prominent nose, piercing eyes behind glasses, and mephistophelean beard – in a word, someone whose very appearance inspired fear. Wacław lived in Paris, where my father, who was somehow not afraid of him, met him every year and spent a lot fair amount of time in his company. He thought him an attractive eccentric – an outstanding Bohemian. Something in all this didn't add up.

My first encounter with Wacław took place towards the end of the 1950s in Warsaw. He couldn't come earlier because he was disgraced for having renounced communism. It took months, if not years, to get Gomułka's permission for him to come. But come he did, eventually – and here he was, sitting in the Bristol Café with Janina and Antoni. He certainly looked unconventional – very old-fashioned, like an actor playing an anarchist, but not in the least bit threatening. We shook hands and began to talk as though we had always known each other. It was hard to believe that wasn't case.

It is easy to write about Wacław's youth because he wrote about it in his autobiography, *Moje wspomnienia* [My Memoirs].* His 'unauthorized' book, which could not be published in the People's Republic of Poland, appeared, in 1977, in an issue of the Paris-based *Kultura*, and reached Poland 20 years later in a new edition by Aneks.

---

*   Paris, 1977.

Writing my own memoirs, I made use of extensive extracts from Wacław's memoirs many times. (This was completely acceptable to him.) In talking about the first three decades of his life (the *Sturm und Drang* period), although it is tempting to quote him over and over again, I will offer only a brief account. It seems that he became a revolutionary out of emotional need – he believed in a communist Utopia and that it would bring happiness to suffering humanity. His close friend, the poet Jan Lechon, considered him one of 'the high-minded people, humanitarian, witty – brutally so sometimes– but never angry'. This apparent brutality was part of Wacław's self-image. He probably saw himself as a cynical, even cruel, person (hence the na vely diabolical titles of his books: *Czarna spowiedz* [Black Confession] or *Opowiadania okrutne* [Cruel Stories].

I think another factor also played a part in the path he chose to follow: the very young Wacław thought of what he did as a great game, but then was drawn into a maelstorm of remarkable experiences. When he stopped being entertained by this, he bade a quiet farewell to his former image. Fanaticism was alien to him. And so, he joined the social democrats, because that's how he felt and it entertained him, and on top of that, he regarded other matters then as 'the occupation of idiots'. He changed his names in order not to cause his family problems by his political acts. When his family moved to Minsk in 1914, he worked as a driver and spent a year on the front line. Later on, as a 'professional revolutionary', he was involved at central committee level and took an active part in the October revolution. Arrested with his two brothers by the German authorities, he heard about his father's death. 'That was the worst moment of my life', he wrote in his memoirs. 'For many years, I was unable to think about, and am now unable to write about, my father's death'. This is probably understandable in light of the unusually tragic circumstances of that death.* It is characteristic, however, that Wacław does not explain the circumstances to his readers.

He spent the year 1918 in Warsaw, where, arrested by Polish

---

* See Chapter 25, Róża Pańska, this book.

authorities, he was put into the notorious Pavilion X. He was
due to be exchanged for Poles imprisoned in Soviet Russia, but
as a result of the outbreak of the Polish–Bolshevik war, the
exchange did not take place. Wacław escaped illegally to Minsk.
There, he edited the town newspaper – and then, as a member
of the Soviet delegation, acted as translator in the Polish–Soviet
negotiations in Riga. In 1922, he was in Berlin as Izvestia
correspondent, after which he became a diplomat in Paris. He
finally returned to Moscow, where he became a member of the
Union of Writers and was head of the screenwriters' division of
Sovkino.* He had the opportunity to meet with the top leaders:
Lenin, Trotsky, Stalin, Dzierżyński and he published many
articles and several books in Russian (among them, a volume of
journalistic pieces: *Współczesna Francja* [Contemporary France],
a collection of stories, and two novels: *Szklanka wody* [A Glass of
Water] and the satirical *Koła* [Wheels].

In 1928, he broke with communism. Interviewed by Renata
Gorczynska, together with Czesław Miłosz and Jan Kott,[†] he
said:

> Had you asked me why...I would have to think it
> over. In any case, I pondered the break for a long
> time...I thought about it so hard that I stopped
> talking to people. I was afraid that whatever anyone
> said to me would influence me...I thought I'd go mad
> that year. Finally, I rang up a man at the Soviet legation
> who was an old friend of mine and he came over. He
> talked to me for five hours, trying to persuade me not
> to do it. And then we both noticed a plainclothes
> policeman standing in front of my house. He was
> watching him, not me...Just one article about my case
> was published in Moscow: an announcement by the
> Writer's Union which consisted of a lie: on such and
> such a day, seeking a medical cure and receiving for
> that purpose money from the state, such and such –
> after which came all my titles and positions. It was a

---

*   Sovkino: Soviet film industry.
†   Aneks, 1987.

lie about the money. I had a lot of my own money because my books had come out, and on that money which I took out with me I supported myself for a whole year.

After the break, Wacław went on living in Berlin, where he published several books in German, and in Paris, where he published books in French and worked as a film-maker (with René Clair, among others). He moved to London during the war and there he made contact with the editor of *Wiadomosci* [News], Mieczysław Grydzewski, about whom he writes, in a book of memoirs:*

> I've forgotten how to write in Polish. I wrote in French and gave it to him, suggesting shyly that someone from the editorial staff translate it. He gave me an icy look: 'We don't translate Poles into Polish. Write it as best you can.' I wrote it. I asked Antoni Słonimski to correct it. He did so, but suggested that next time, I write in Chinese, because it would be less work. Later, I learned to write in Polish again.

In England, he published several books in his native language, among them, *Rękopis znaleziony pod dywanem* [Manuscript Found Beneath a Carpet], and *Pociag odchodzi po polnocy* [The Train Leaves at Midnight], a sensationalist novel about the struggles of the Polish underground during the Second World War. In addition to working on *Wiadomości*, he wrote for *Nowa Polska* [New Poland], edited by Słonimski. Together with Słonimski and Ksawery Pruszyński, he wrote a satirical issue for 1 April 1943 for *Wiadomości Polskie* [News of Poles]. This issue, which contained items about emigrant life, included some very amusing pieces. 'From the Polish *Ognisko* – [Hearth: a Polish club in London]':

> The Ognisko administration has asked us to announce that the premier has published a decree normalizing

---

*   London, 1971.

the rules for the game of bridge. According to this decree, Jews may take part in the Thursday bridge games at the club, but only Aryans may take honours and over–tricks. Finessing is forbidden to Jews.

I should explain that the parody was what would happen to emigrant relations if the right–wing Bielecki Nationalist Party came into power.

Of Wacław's life in London I know very little. Irena Tuwim told me that he was terribly afraid of air raids and was first in the race to the shelter. After the war, he moved to New York, where he lived for many years and was a prominent member of the Polish community. His life there was, at first, very humble. He was a lecturer in Ukrainian literature at some second-rate university; wrote articles for the Polish press (including the Paris *Kultura*); and took part, with Lechon, Wierzynski and Wittlin, in weekly radio programmes. Later, he had a dreadful car accident, underwent 14 operations and sued an insurance agency for damages. 'Friends recommended decent and respectable lawyers to me,' he said, 'but I hired two of the biggest thieves and crooks in New York.' Thanks to them, he found himself well-situated. He couldn't stand America, and ignored its existence in rather an amusing way. His modest apartment on West End Avenue constituted a kind of enclave, in time as well as place. Whosoever visited New York paid an obligatory visit to the old, but ever intellectually young, Solski, to hear not only his reminiscences but also his astonishingly accurate commentaries on contemporary politics. Wacław was one of a small number of people who foresaw, with remarkable accuracy, the inevitable collapse of the Soviet Moloch. We, of course, took this with a grain of salt. But it was yet another of that old original's paradoxes.

Wacław had two wives: the first in Russia – I don't know whether or not they were legally married (a tragic and slightly mysterious story); while the second he met in New York, a Polish woman, nearly 30 years his junior, who died shortly after him. One has to say that as a man of very considerable personal charm, he was totally unsuited to being a husband. I admired his wife, Lidka, for managing to live with him.

But perhaps, in spite of everything, it might have been worth it. And another thing: Wacław never denied his background, but at the same time, he didn't admit to it of his own free will. There's not a word about it in *Moje wspomnienia*; the autobiographical novel *Rysy twarzy* [Facial Features], in its description of the family house in Łódź, contains no allusion to his parents' Jewish background. After reading this novel, Słonimski said it was a falsification because of this suppression of Jewish roots – the Pańskis' domestic arrangements, despite the author's effort to portray them as such, are not those of a purely Polish family. Falsification is falsification – and that's all there is to it. Similarly, when Wacław ends his excellent autobiography with the observation, 'At the beginning of my memoirs, I promised the reader total sincerity. I can assure him that I wrote them with the thought of keeping that promise'. I, for one, take this with a grain of salt.

One of Wacław's most characteristic traits was his unusual, indeed unique, sense of the absurd. He had his own, very controversial, point of view on each and every subject. He expressed himself with ostentatious dismissiveness about universally acknowledged authorities. But it wasn't just the content of his statements that was shocking: the tone of his voice, the phrasing, the emphases, were all unique.

He obeyed no rules, not even those governing time, and was once an hour and a half late for dinner at the Słonimskis'. This considerably cooled his relations with Antoni, whose attitude to social engagements was one of formality. But Wacław was entirely above such tiresome conventions.

What kind of a writer was he? *Moje wspomnienia* reveals him as outstanding and highly individual, with a specific and easy-to-recognize Polish drift, 'a hammering home of the point, cutting to the quick', as Maria Danilewicz puts it. His stories are remarkable – I am not surprised that Tuwim called *Rekopis znaleziony pod dywanem* [Manuscript Found Beneath the Carpet] 'a magnificent work', and Kazimierz Brandys said *Szantażysta* [Extortionist] was 'a small jewel of Polish novelistic prose'. I rate Solski's novels, which are highly praised by Lechoń, less highly, and his poems (*Dym-Smoke*) least of all. In a word, his literary output is uneven: at its best, certainly worthy of attention, but (and may Wacław forgive me from the other world) it represents only a part of the unusual and inimitable individual who was my uncle.

THIRTY
Jerzy Pański

Aunt and Uncle Pański's youngest son, Jerzy (1900–79), was the stereotypical Jewish capitalist: he had a huge belly and unmistakably Semitic facial features. In the 1920s, he worked as an agent for one Szymon Turbowicz, a wealthy corn merchant, and at the same time, acted as tutor to his unruly son. In short, he had the right appearance and the right form of employment to serve as cover for the various tasks assigned him by the Polish Communist Party. (In 1939, for example, editing the bi-weekly paper *Przekroj* [The Review], Jerzy once found himself at the police station. The inspector scrutinized the enormous man in the expensive fur coat and apologized most graciously for the misunderstanding. A communist couldn't possibly look like this...

Jerzy studied philosophy at Warsaw University, but later worked at the Central Statistics Office, where many communist activists were to be found – Hilary Minc, later the economical guru of the communists, among them. His scholarly work, *Bezrobocie wśrod chlopow* [Unemployment Among the Peasants], written in collaboration with L. Landau and E. Strzelecki, undoubtedly contributed to the preservation of an accurate picture of the interwar period.

In the mid to late 1920s, Jerzy wrote reviews of works in translation and intelligent and interesting articles on the art of translation. Subsequently, he became a theatre critic. His writings were notable for their objectivity, culture, and discreet wit, but somehow they lacked a certain flair. Jerzy's chief occupation, however, was working as an editor for Roj publishers and translating, sometimes under his own name and sometimes under the collective pseudonym of Dr J.P. Zajęczkowski, books by Maurois, Duhamel and Benoist–Mechin.

There was not a trace of duplicity in Jerzy's nature. He was modest to a fault, reliable and honest. Because his mother was being supported by my father, he wanted to repay him in the only honourable way he knew – by tutoring me. I was a good student, particularly in the humanities. So these tutoring sessions tended to take the form of intellectual conversations about everything and nothing. I remember these meetings very fondly because I gained a lot from them, not least a love of books, first and foremost amongst which was the immortal *The Pickwick Papers*.

I should note that Jerzy didn't try to instill any kind of communist dogma in me, just a little scepticism towards established values. I am truly grateful to him for this. Unfortunately, after the war, when he returned from the Soviet Union and occupied many high positions, he revealed himself as a die-hard Stalinist. But even then, he was head-and-shoulders above the average party functionary. As director of state television, he was valued by his co-workers for his intelligence and sense of humour. Director Pański's anecdotes are repeated to this day. Once, for example, he fumed, 'It's disgraceful! They're saying that I hire only Jews! As if I don't hire Jewesses, too!'

Before the war, I was only ever once in Jerzy's modest apartment on Saska Kępa, and it was there that I met Romka, the woman he'd just married. She was tiny, and standing next to him, looked as though she wasn't of the same species. She was a woman of strong character though, with high principles. She changed in the last years of her life, and because of that, I remember her fondly. Jerzy also changed – after Romka's death – and in a very unlikely way, not only in terms of his world-view but also in his habits. He completely and utterly gave up all his political activities (which supports my theory that anyone who had received the Ziemiańska Café's liberal, cynical education couldn't, in the long-run, remain a communist). At the same, time he became a dedicated family man. He liked to spin amusing yarns – he was never at a loss for jokes – about his own past, and also oft-repeated ones about our various great-aunts and uncles. For example, one of our great-aunts was slightly mad. Once, at the station, she hit a Prussian gendarme with her umbrella. Heaven knows how the affair would have ended had it not been for Great-Uncle's quick thinking. He stood behind Great-Auntie, pointing at her with his left hand and, with his right one, drawing circles above his own head. Mercifully, the angry gendarme understood the signal, and said politely to her, '*Aber beruhigen sie sich doch, gnädige Frau!*'*

Yet another example of my coming from a quick-witted family.

---

* Please calm yourself, my good lady!

THIRTY-ONE
Janina and Antoni Słonimski

Antoni Słonimski was my favourite writer from the moment I stopped reading adolescent fiction. This happened in the 1930s, when political events started to cast a long shadow over my idyllic childhood. Słonimski, more than anyone else, was the perfect guide to the increasingly threatening world around me. In those days, his humanity, reason and humour seemed to me to embody the only acceptable outlook. And indeed, this still seems to hold good, since the history of the past century hasn't exactly provided arguments in favour of other, more radical, ideologies. I was impressed by the unique blend of wit and loftiness which informed every issue of *Kroniki tygodniowe* [Weekly Chronicles]. I don't need to add that I was enraptured by Antoni's poems and knew most of them by heart.

Antoni Słonimski became part of my family in 1934 through his marriage to my father's cousin, Janina Konarska – very exciting for a 10-year-old boy. I wasn't crazy about Janina, truth to tell, although I appreciated her talent and her beauty. ('Talent i uroda' [Talent and Beauty] was the title of the article written by the famous artist and teacher Tadeusz Pruszkowski about Konarska.) She was an excellent wood-engraver, the favourite student of Skoczylas, winner of many prizes at international graphics exhibitions and silver medallist at the international competition in Los Angeles in 1932. Her woodcuts were very popular, particularly those of saints and animals. She socialized with the elite circle of artists and literati known as the Skamander Group, but the real passion of her life was the company of young aristocrats, whom I always knew by their nicknames: 'Jaś', 'Tonio', 'Gucio', and so on. She also enjoyed the company of diplomats – Anglo-Saxon ones for preference, of course.

Janina was a gentle blonde with slanting blue eyes, beautiful but a little bland, attractive but not brilliant. Her marriage to Słonimski was a surprise not just to me. I had heard that she was attached to Wierzyński, and that Antoni was in love with her friend, the beautiful sculptress Irena Baruch. It never entered my head that my cousin could marry someone who wasn't, as used to be said, *pur sang*. A count, papal chamberlain, a chargé d'affaires, yes, but not somebody who ostentatiously admitted – even prided himself on the fact – that he was of non-Aryan background. For neophytes known for their bigotry, as the otherwise kind-hearted Seideman-Konarskis were, this well-publicized marriage of their daughter's must have been a bitter pill to swallow.

Before I became related to Słonimski through a happy stroke of luck, I sometimes saw him on the street, and was enormously impressed each time I did so. How could I not have run into him, since everyday, schoolbag on my back, I walked down Mazowiecka Street, where he lived at Number 10 when he was a bachelor. His house was near the Ziemiańska Café, a favourite haunt of the literarti. I first got to know Antoni on the occasion of a lecture he gave on the subject of the maiden voyage of the Polish ship *Piłsudski* to America. Truth to tell, I was disappointed by the lecture because it wasn't very witty. (I remember only his praising the ship's graphic art, and his joking lament that he hadn't found a woodcut by Janina Konarska in his cabin.) After the lecture, which took place somewhere on Kredytowa Street, the family crowded around the lecturer, who made a few conventional remarks and hurriedly moved off with Janina.

Antoni looked completely different at that time than in the postwar years, when he cut a thin, genteel *memsahib* figure. As a 40-year-old, he had a strong athletic figure and a chubby, somewhat arrogant, face. He was already bald. His entire beauty lay in his hands: he had long, elegant fingers, which Janina liked to emphasize in her later portraits of him. I would be lying if I said he created an agreeable impression. His sharp brown eyes peered maliciously from behind his glasses when he was talking to me – a small boy, shaking with emotion and gazing with almost religious awe at him. I recall that at about the same time, Słonimski paid us an official, rather troublesome, visit involving many elderly uncles and aunts. I think it was the result of some agreement: a visit to the head of the family, taking in all of Janina's relations at a single stroke. The great man behaved pleasantly, but said little. I felt he was bored to tears. He confessed to me later that at obligatory social functions he felt as though the walls were caving in on him. Despite my father's efforts, the atmosphere was awkward, and I experienced such mental anguish that I fled to the cinema without waiting for dessert.

Later, during the period of increasing anti-Semitism and furious incitements against Słonimski, I drank in, out of some kind of masochistic zeal, everything printed in the columns of various fascist papers, beginning with the *Falanga* [Phalanx]. The style of these attacks didn't vary: 'Let's shut the traps of the various Słonimskis once and for all.' 'If these three scoundrels [Słonimski, Tuwim, Wittlin] never wrote another word in their lives, these [here followed quotations] sentences would be sufficient for the noose to be their inevitable fate.' In 1938, *Wiadomości Literackie* [Literary News] printed Słonimski's poem 'Dwie Ojczyzny' [Two Fatherlands] which ended: 'Although this misty evening and starless night pleases you,/How will you chase me from my native land, when you don't know it yourself?'

The response was the arrival at the Ziemiańska Café of a fascist squad, whose leader, someone called Ipohorski, hit Antoni in the face, screaming, 'This is for "Two Fatherlands!"' The ensuing struggle was brought to an end with the arrival of General Wieniawa–Długoszowski. When news spread about the incident, the whole of civilized Poland was enraged. The Słonimskis' apartment couldn't accommodate all the flowers that were sent. I spent a large part of my savings on beautiful roses for Antoni, and was proud when Janina telephoned to thank me. I have to admit that her marriage to Antoni drew me closer to Janina. I now had something to talk to her about – Antoni, of course. Once, when she visited us in Konstancin, I asked her, for some reason, whether she was going to have children. To my great amazement she said, 'No, it's impossible. Antoni isn't a person you can have a son with.' I didn't quite understand her answer, but was embarrassed. Did it mean that you could only have a daughter with Antoni? One way or the other, Janina bestowed all her maternal instincts on her spoiled husband, and I remained the only child in the family – a favourable situation in some ways, perhaps, but one not without its difficulties.

In 1937, Przeworski published a fantasy novel by Słonimski: *Dwa końce swiata* [Two Ends of the Earth], first printed in serial form in *Wiadomosci Literackie*. Its hero, a humble bookshop assistant by the name of Szwalba, accidentally becomes one of a small number of people on earth granted the right to survive the extermination of humanity planned by a certain Retlich (an anagram of Hitler). Living beings fall victim to the rays sent down by Retlich; inanimate things stay untouched. So Szwalba roams around unpopulated, intact Warsaw, equips himself in shops, sleeps in the Europejski Hotel, and so on. The cover of *Dwa końce swiata*, the work of Lewitt and Him (two famous graphic artists of the period), was, in itself, a curiosity. It depicted Piłsudski Square, and in the centre of it, Szwalba, lying on a yellow couch (a conventional, graphic detail). In the background was the ruined facade of the Europejski Hotel, oddly realistic against a high blue sky, seen through burned-out windows. There were strange, unsettling trees in front of the hotel, and behind it, the ruins of the house at 40 Krakowskie Przedmiescie, where the offices of *Kurier Warszawski* [The Warsaw Courier] were located before the war. This photomontage, a totally different view of the destruction of the city from Słonimski's own, and astonishingly out of keeping with his writing, impressed itself with incredible force on my youthful imagination. It haunted me every time I went to Piłsudski Square, even just to see the changing of the guard. Years later, when this picture became a reality, I accepted it as something inevitable and matter-of-course which I had already known about for a long time. It is interesting that neither Antoni, nor Jerzy, with whom I became friendly after the war, could say anything to me on the subject which would have, in some measure, explained the meaning it had for me during the course of my psychological development. They simply acknowledged that the cover had been a misunderstanding to which they attached no importance.

About a year before the war, I gained the giddy heights of receiving an invitation to dinner at the Słonimskis! I was to go by myself, without my parents. I think this came about at the suggestion of Janina's mother, Aunt Helen Konarska. It could, however, have resulted from Antoni's meetings at bridge with my father and uncle. There were vague hints that Antoni had borrowed quite a significant sum of money from my father – most likely for 'that Szymon', as the Słonimskis' maid would say, referring to their favourite restaurant (Simon and Stecki's). It is not difficult to imagine what I went through over that invitation. I arrived too early at 2 Flora Street – my hosts were not even home yet. The maid showed me into Antoni's study, and went back to the kitchen. I was alone with his things, his books, his manuscripts, and it was then that I did the most shameful thing in my life – to this day, I break out in a sweat when I think about it. A modest little book, a kind of notebook, filled with jottings and drawings from the earliest period of Antoni's creative life, lay on a shelf among books and scraps of paper. It contained handwritten versions of his later, famous sonnets, and sketches by the poet who had begun his career as a painter. Despite my inner qualms, despite the Ten Commandments, I could not resist the temptation to have something like this for my own: to keep it as the holiest of relics; who knows, to guard it, even, from its author's carelessness. All a-flutter, I put the notebook in my pocket and forgot all about it when the Słonimskis came in. We ate dinner in a tastefully and unconventionally decorated room, sophisticatedly Bohemian in style. I don't recall any specific furnishings except for some very beautiful stools from central Africa – gift of the prolific traveller Janta-Połczyński. I was amused, recently, by a remark Maria Dąbrowska made in her *Dzienniki* [Diaries] for 1962: 'The Słonimskis have a beautiful and thoughtfully decorated apartment – a few antiques, yet modern. You find such apartments particularly among Poles of Jewish descent and 'unbohemian' artists'. The compliment was about the apartment at 6 Róż Alley, but it could also have been about 2 Flora Street, except that, although she was right about their background, their way of life was not 'unbohemian'.

The meal began with *barshcht*, a soup which I normally wouldn't have touched for any amount of money, but how could I be fussy at a dinner to which I had been invited by my beloved writer? So I ate the *barshcht* – an event that went down in family lore. The conversation was lively and not forced, my knowledge of literature, unusual for a schoolboy, amused my host. I remember that he said something positive about Czermański's recently published memoirs, but had forgotten the title. I immediately said, *W pluszowej ramie* [In a Plush Frame]. Antoni laughed, 'And it was I who thought that title up!' We spoke also about Gałczyński, who was writing filth in the 'nationalist' press while, at the same time, publishing wonderful poems in *Szpilki* [Pins]. 'Someone who writes poems like that can't be a ruffian,' I said, defending the poet, but it didn't redeem him in Antoni's eyes. 'A talented fellow,' he said, 'but totally irresponsible and shameless'. With this, he found in his library a copy of Gałczyński's *Utwory poetyckie* [Poetic Works], inscribed, 'To Antek, from Kostek'. 'Unbelievable!' he added with amusement. 'I barely know him'. We also talked about the anti-Nazi magazine *Gerechtigkeit* [Justice], to which my father subscribed, and which came out first in Vienna and later in Paris, I think, under the editorship of the well-known Austrian journalist Irene Harand. Antoni didn't know German, so he was interested in what I told him about this weekly devoted to battling the defamatory campaigns of various Rosenbergs and Streichers. 'Anti-anti-Semitism,' he said, 'is better than pro-Semitism, which I don't trust. Truth to tell, those who particularly adore Jews seem to me no less benighted than those who particularly hate them'.

After dinner, Antoni went to take a nap in his study, and I lost the chance to return the notebook, which was increasingly burning a hole in my pocket. I had committed a theft, of which I am ashamed, but not overly so, because history has blunted the effects of the crime. In September 1939, thanks to Aunt

Konarska, a large part of Słonimski's collection of books, with valuable dedications by contemporary Polish writers, came into my hands. As far as I know, Antoni took with him only two books, autographed by Stefan Żeromski and H.G. Wells: writers dear to him. The rest found their way into my library, because who would have taken better care of them? Among them were beautiful dedications by Pawlikowska, Kuncewiczowa, Lechon, Wierzyński, Iwaszkiewicz and Tuwim. I need not add that all these books, together with the ill-fated *corpus delicti*, Antoni's notebook, vanished without a trace in the maelstrom of war.

During the war, contact with Antoni was maintained through his poems. I heard his voice, 'thick with tears over Radio Paris, Radio Toulouse', when he recited 'Alarm', one of his most moving war poems. Later, printed in underground newspapers, or scribbled on slips of paper, his poems would reach us – little flashes of light amid the gloom of Occupation.

In the late summer of 1945, someone brought the news to Polpress, where I was working, that Słonimski and Pruszyński were among the group of English writers who had come to Warsaw and were conferring in the Polonia Hotel. I ran there, just as I was, and saw several foreigners sitting at a table in the restaurant. Among them was Antoni – thinner than before and more distinguished-looking. I waited until dinner had ended, and when people started getting up from the table, I plucked up courage, walked up to him and blurted out my name. 'Gustaw's son,' Antoni said, and drew me to himself in a warm embrace.

Since the publication of this reminiscence, several books have appeared which shed new (for me, at least) light on Janina's life before she was married. Irena Krzywicka, in Agata Tuszynska's *Wyznania gorszycielki* [Confessions of a Scandalous Woman], describes Janina as 'a very beautiful girl, extremely alluring, good, loyal, but not an intellectual type'. (Thank God!) She then says, 'Before she married, that attractive woman had one great, unhappy love which was hard to understand. She loved Karol Stryjeński, the husband of the painter Zofia.' Stryjeński was an architect, co-founder of the so-called Zakopane School. The worst was that he remained faithful to his eccentric – to say the least – wife. Then came the second chapter in my aunt's unhappy love-life:

> She nursed her friend, the actress (second-rate) Bronisława Kojałłowicz, Wierzyński's first wife, through a serious illness. And what happened was that Wierzyński fell in love with Janina. She, too, was not indifferent to him, he was handsome and attractive – but Janina was too good, too decent, to break up her friend's marriage. She decided to put an end to it and marry. She chose Antoni, which testifies to her good taste (good taste being one of her outstanding features).

Jarosław Iwaszkiewicz describes his first encounter with Janina in *Aleja Przyjaciol* [Avenue of Friends] (see the 'Tolek' chapter):

> I noticed, after a moment, a young person I didn't know sitting at a table nearby with a jolly group of people. Blonde, with a large head, beautiful blue eyes and gorgeous complexion, she seemed to me very beautiful. 'Who's that?' I asked, surprised. (Usually, one knew all the young ladies at the Ziemiańska.) 'How lovely she is! Lovelier than my wife!'...I didn't connect her with Tolek [Antoni]. And it went on for so long, more than ten years. Sometimes, I dropped in on Janina, who was living with her parents and brother on Warecka Street.

(This was actually not true, she was living on Zielna Street – but no matter!)

Later on, Iwaszkiewicz writes about the period in which he was in the diplomatic corps in Copenhagen: 'I did not know what was going on in the Literary world...About Antoni, I knew nothing...the telegram came as a surprise: "Janina and I are arriving on such and such a day in Copenhagen for three days. Best wishes, Antoni."' There follows an emotional description of three days which were 'the last memory of close contact with a dear and understanding friend. After that, it was all a catastrophe.'

When it comes to Janina's friend, the sculptress Irena Baruch, Iwaszkiewicz presents this romance of Antoni's in a somewhat different light: 'Irena Baruch was a very pretty, interesting young lady from a wealthy Jewish family (tea wholesalers). When Antoni was leaving to go to Brazil in 1925, my friend, Olek Landau, came with the news that sheets sodden with tears Irena had shed over Antoni's departure were drying in the courtyard of the house at 17 Foksal Street.'

Wacław Zbyszewski, three years younger than her and a devoted admirer, also writes about Janina in his *Ksiazka o Grydzewskim* [Book about Grydzewski]*: 'I got to know Grydz, as his friends called him, in 1930 in IPS or on the mezzanine of the Mała Ziemiańska. I was introduced to him by the beautiful Janina Konarska, later wife of Antoni Słonimski, who – together with the beautiful Stefania Tuwim – was the Egeria of the Skamander Group, lending them refinement and worldly charm.'

Her husband's individualism was so crushing, and his egocentrism so all-encompassing, that his wife had the choice of either submitting to his absolute domination or finding herself another life companion. Janina didn't hesitate for a moment: she chose marital happiness at the expense of her own career and fame which, in the postwar period, cried for vengeance. I never saw a better, more caring, more wonderful-in-every-way wife. I think she was happy. And that, in the end, is what matters the most.

---

*   London, 1971.

THIRTY-TWO
Tadeusz Konarski

Tadeusz ('Tadzio') – Uncle Herman's and Aunt Hela's son and Janina Konarska-Słonimska's brother – was perfectly beautiful. I identify him, in his youthful photographs, with Tadzio in Thomas Mann's *Death in Venice*. Tadzio's uncle, the factory owner Edward Heiman, sent him to study in England, where he got a diploma in textile engineering. He worked as technical director of 'Wola', a factory manufacturing cotton goods and owned by Heiman. In contrast to his father, he was good at his trade, although not particularly brilliant. But with beauty like his, he didn't really need to be brilliant. I think of Tadzio most of all in connection with a car. He was the first motorist in the family. He became fascinated with cars in the 1920s, and I must admit, he looked wonderful behind the wheel. I never remember Tadzio saying anything amusing or even noteworthy. Nevertheless, I genuinely liked him because he was a pleasant and harmless person.

Tadzio's marriage to Lucy caused a sensation. She was a young widow, born in Brussels, with a child from her previous marriage. Lucy's husband, an engineer called Dillon (a Pole, his name notwithstanding), lost his life during an innocent hike across a valley in the Tatra Mountains. He was stopped by a soldier who examined his papers, led him off somewhere and murdered him. The soldier was an army deserter who tried to cross to Czechoslovakia in Dillon's clothes and with his papers. Of course, he was captured and sentenced to death, which didn't return a husband to Lucy or a father to her child. Dillon was Tadzio's friend; the widow was young and alluring. Mrs Failly, her mother, came from Brussels for the wedding. Our whole family got together to receive her in such a way as to make clear to her the bridegroom's high social standing. When

I enquired about Mrs Failly's status, I was told she was the owner of a laundry. 'All this fuss for a washer-woman?' I asked. It turned out, however, that it wasn't a laundry, but a whole chain of laundries, and that Mrs Failly was a wealthy and distinguished person. The main feature of the occasion was the reception at our villa in Konstancin.

In 1939, Tadzio went to war and didn't return. In 'Przekleństwo' [Damnation], his poetic litany of German crimes, Słonimski writes, 'Because Tadeusz is a prisoner.' That prison, unfortunately, was Starobielsk. Lucy married for a third time after the war and went to America with her daughter. All that was left of the beautiful Tadzio were a few photographs and this cursory note instead of an obituary. Incongruously enough, it turned out that I was the only person who was able, recently, to provide the so-called Katyn family with information about Engineer Lieutenant Tadeusz Konarski, murdered in Starobielsk, together with his photograph. It has been worth living to a ripe old age, if only for this.

THIRTY-THREE
Anka Krause

Cousin Anka was the daughter of Aunt Zosia and Flatau. When she was still a young girl, she married a Krause, but the marriage was shortlived and unhappy – inevitably so because Anka was a lesbian. With age, this became more obvious from her appearance and psyche. Given prewar attitudes, it created tension. Anka lived in Flatau's beautiful house on Puławska Street. She had a degree in philosophy and was a talented violinist. When I was a child, I went to see her sometimes, and was allowed to choose a present from the hundreds of little objects kept in glass cupboards. I think this was Flatau's collection, comprised of everything in miniature. I remember the joy I derived from a beautiful mini pocket-knife with five blades – a real marvel of ingenious craftsmanship.

Anka was intelligent and talented. When the famous chocolatier Wedel announced a contest for the best memoir about his shop on Szpitalna Street, she was runner-up to Iwaszkiewicz. (The entries appeared in print in the book *Staroswiecki sklep* [An Old-Fashioned Shop].) With her considerable financial resources, she supported artists whose talents impressed her: she commissioned paintings from Witkacy and underwrote some of the ventures of Bruno Schulz, with whom she was in constant contact. Mainstream literature didn't interest her, but she'd talk with rapture to a youngster like me about the wonders of Gombrowicz's prose.

Anka was the only person I knew before the war who had seen the United States with her own eyes. (Later, Słonimski would also go there on the *Piłsudski's* maiden voyage.) Her trip was talked about for many months in advance – in those days, it seemed an expedition on a cosmic scale. My mother made her promise to visit her older brother, Morris Brin, who lived in New York. The brother and his family turned out to be cultured and pleasant people. Anka returned with a good impression of them. She brought back a dress from Uncle Morris's factory, which we gave to our cook, Mrs Boryńska. She also brought with her an offer from Uncle to set me up in New York if my parents wanted me to study overseas. Anka's account raised my mother's status in the family considerably (her *litvack* background was usually treated with open disdain). Mother made me write a letter to Uncle's older son, Marty. I did so in German (I didn't yet know English), but got no reply. Today, however, we are good friends with Professor Martin Brin and his family, and this may owe something to cousin Anka's travels in the 1930s.

Anka did not go into the ghetto during the Occupation. She lived somewhere in the country and apparently worked as a teacher. She perished at the hands of the Germans in Rabka, shot, together with her uncle and his family.

THIRTY-FOUR
Lutek and Janina

My father's uncle, Lutek Seideman, was a short, bald old man, incredibly active and filled with the best intentions. On one occasion, Father had lent him a few thousand złoty, and this made Uncle constantly bestow a number of unwanted gifts on us. Once, it was reindeer antlers, for which (with some difficulty) we found a spot in the villa Konstancin; another time, it was a painting – the head of a Jew. Uncle had a limitless supply of such pictures. If we had hung them on our walls, our apartment would have been turned into a gallery of Jewish heads. Since Uncle visited us quite often, we worked out a system of replacing our existing paintings with the Jewish heads during his presence under our roof. After he left, everything went back to normal, giving artists' models of slavic descent a chance, too.

I think Uncle died before the war, because I have no recollection of him during the Occupation. After the war, his daughter, Janina Krakowska, emerged from oblivion in the most unexpected way. She was the widow of Bolesław Krakowski, a lawyer, and she had a pretty daughter, Wanda. Twenty-five years ago, she telephoned me to say that she had come over from the United States and would like to see me. She had found herself in America together with her daughter, who had married in the camp, and all three had settled there. Wanda had two children and the family was comfortably off. But Janka was not happy because she felt more like a maid than a mother or grandmother: 'Jane do this; Jane do that'. In the end, she saved some of her pocket money and came to Warsaw. Here, the first place she went was to the Evangelical Reform cemetery, where her husband was buried. She was instantly recognized by the caretaker, Stanisław, who kissed her hand and addressed her as

'Dear Lady'. At that, 'Jane' burst into tears – her dreams had come true. She had travelled thousands of miles so that before she died she could feel like a 'lady' again. Just once.

THIRTY-FIVE
Professor Sterling

I got to know our relation Professor Sterling better during the memorable night of 25/26 September 1939, when my childhood ended. The house at 1 Boduen Street somehow survived destruction, and the Professor appeared quite normal against the backdrop of his study, but he was visibly shaken by what was happening all around. I thought he looked like an old walrus. He was huddled in an armchair, amazed that fate could have played such a rotten trick on a man like him who could not abide pandemonium and brute force. That same night, a shell exploded in the courtyard, wounding several people. The Professor immortalized himself by shouting, 'A doctor! Is there a doctor here?' Fortunately, my uncle was there, and he wasn't so great a medical celebrity as not to know how to dress a wound.

Living two floors higher (in an apartment belonging to the actress Irena Horwath-Groer, who was staying in Lvov), we grew very close to Władysław Sterling and his wife, Róża, sister of Professor Ludwik Hirszfeld. Władysław Sterling was an eminent neurologist, head of the hospital on Czystem Street, former student and close co-worker of Edward Flatau. His credentials included 200 scholarly works, some of which were ground-breaking (including, for example, the description of the so–called Sterling group). As a medical humanist, he became famous for his work on the subject of hysterical and mentally retarded children. Professor Eugeniusz Herman, in his *Neurolodzy polscy* [Polish Neurologists],* calls him 'the father of child neuropsychiatry.' Professor Sterling interested me mainly as a poet. He was famous only to a rather esoteric group of

---

* Warsaw, 1958.

readers – and for a single poem, at that. A. Bruckner states, 'Some poets are remembered for just one successful poem, Władysław Sterling (b. 1876), for example, by '*Hymn żałobny*' [Funeral Hymn]. While W. Feldman says, 'W. Sterling (*Poezye* [Poems], 1899) has been remembered by people of feeling for his deeply poetic 'Hymn żałobny'. It is a strange kind of fame to be remembered not as the writer of a single book, but of a single poem: 'Where do the dead go / Our dead?'

I have to say that the poem aroused – and continues to arouse – many feelings in me, in much the same way that symbolist art does, which can be looked at over and over again with increasing interest. I was curious as to what the author thought of his famous work 40 years later. It was a real pleasure to talk to the Professor. He was a man, in Professor Herman's words:

> of many talents, endowed with a simply phenomenal memory... remarkably observant, brilliant, witty, a raconteur and conversationalist of the best kind. He was the center of any social situation, even the ones he came upon by accident. His word in any discussion, whether strictly scientific, or literary... rivalled his no less sharp pen... nothing escaped his powers of observation, analysis, and synthesis.

A friend of my father's called Józef Langfier, who rightly or wrongly was also regarded as a man of letters (he turned several well-known works into radio scripts), took part in our conversation. When I asked him about 'Hymn żałobny', the Professor leant back in his armchair, stroked his walrus moustache and began to speak in a high, somewhat squeaky voice, underscoring his points by gesticulating with his beautiful, slender hand:

> *Hymn żałobny*? Well, yes, that poem made a great furore once, because it gave perfect expression to the aesthetic currents fashionable at the time. Unfortunately, gentlemen [one of these 'gentlemen' was me], in literature, only works of a ground-breaking, forward-looking nature have a chance of surviving. Take care,

young man [the Professor knew I was trying to write poetry], take care not to give in to the trends of the period, it's best to let them wash over you.

I got a lot out of my conversations with Sterling, although he could be dogmatic and unfair. For example, he completely underrated Słonimski's work and denied his talent. I tried to engage him in discussion, but to what purpose? He was 50 years older than me, so what chance would I have of persuading him to change his mind? Obese and not very attractive (the walrus association was not apposite), he nonetheless possessed enormous personal charm and was popular with the ladies. His wife took great personal satisfaction in his romantic successes. She bragged about them to her cronies, my aunt among them: 'I have to tell you about the great disappointment Władysław's just had,' she said. 'He had an affair in Nice with some little missy from Kraków, and bought her all kinds of expensive presents. When she came back to Poland, that low-class simpleton found out about Władysław's background and sent all the jewellery back to him. Look, this ring on my finger – he bought for her!' Mrs Sterling wasn't a woman who dazzled you with her intelligence (which was strange, given her brother's giant intellect). She had apparently been pretty and amusing in her youth, but under wartime conditions she became hard to take. Sometimes, the Professor reacted to her malapropisms and hysteria with amusement; more often, though, he reacted with irritation.

After moving to the ghetto, there were few opportunities to meet Professor Sterling. Sometimes we'd see him fleetingly on the street, but usually at a distance because he tended to move around by rickshaw. Social life was almost nonexistent in the ghetto, because who could even think about paying or receiving visits? The Professor apparently supported himself by treating a rich, hypochondriac rabbi.

When I left the ghetto, I knew that the Sterlings were alive – nothing more. Professor Henryk Makower, in *Pamiętnik z getta warszawskiego* [Dairy of the Warsaw Ghetto],* describes meeting the Sterlings in September 1942:

I was in my family's apartment on Gęsia Street...I dropped by the apartment next door, the Sterlings'. A few days earlier, I had rescued Mrs Sterling when some Ordnungsdienst was dragging her to the *Umschlag*...Sterling, who'd been given a respite number, looked bad. He had lost weight, his complexion was ashen, but he was keeping well... They were truly sorry to hear about the misfortune which had befallen their former neighbours, and they would like them to come over shortly.

Helena Szereszewska also writes about the Sterlings during this period. Shortly afterwards, the Professor and his wife were taken out of the ghetto and hidden on the Aryan side by Polish friends.

In *Historia jednego życia* [The Story of One Life],* Ludwik Hirszfeld describes the deaths of Róża and Władysław Sterling, and does so in a way which is unusual for him. His memoirs are remarkable for their clarity and precision, while this fragment gives the impression of having been cut and edited by another hand:

Periodically, I would hear about the tragic death of one of my friends...My brother-in-law, Sterling, Władysław [*sic*], and his wife, my sister, were killed at this time [i.e. spring 1944]. They were killed like this: at first, the neighbours started saying that Jews were hiding in the house, which threatened the house with danger. At a certain moment [*sic*], armed bandits arrived, looted the apartment and killed my sister and brother-in-law by shooting them in the back of the head. Seeing the looters, the neighbours immediately telephoned the German police. The gendarmes arrived, checked the bandits' papers and let them go. It turned out that these were bandits

---

*   Wrocław, 1987.
*   Warsaw, 1950.

who served the Gestapo and who later shared their loot with the German police.

I have severe doubts that this clumsy gibberish came from the hand of Professor Hirszfeld. Only the part which comes after this strikes me as authentic:

> Up until the very end, Professor Sterling was translating the poetry of Verlaine and Baudelaire... The Polish underground fought against spies and informers, and those whose guilt could be proved were sentenced to death. The case of Professor Sterling was also brought before the Polish underground court. This will not, however, give him or my sister back their lives.

Professor Hirszfeld undoubtedly wished to recount the true circumstances of the murders murders of Róża and Władysław Sterling. Acts which had as their goal the extermination of the Polish Jewish elite on the eve of the end of the war were performed by native fascists either with their own hands (as in the case of the Sterlings), or with the hands of others (in the case of Marceli Handelsman). These matters, which the publishers of *Historia jednego życia* apparently deemed too risky to be addressed, demand to be fully aired today, and without circumlocution ('the *alleged* plunder of the *alleged** property of unfortunate people who were in hiding for so many years') and half-truths. Perhaps the revelations on the subject of the so-called Sudeczki band will point in the right direction.

Professor Herman, in *Neurolodzy polscy*, writes that, in the presence of his murderers, Sterling 'retained an unusual calm.' And I, too, heard that he received them without fear, almost with irony. Perhaps he had even smiled beneath his moustache, feeling that he was already in 'the garden of mortal irony', as he wrote in his poem, in which all earthly passion and hatred seem endlessly insignificant and worthy of pity.

---

* Italics added.

THIRTY-SIX
Swiętokrzyska Street

We lived in a large apartment on the second floor of an old three-storey house in the heart of the city: 9 Swiętokrzyska Street. Fifty years later, the rooms and corridors – a lot of corridors – often appear in my dreams with astonishing accuracy. I remember each piece of furniture and each book in the library, each picture (my father particularly loved Noakowski), and each utensil in the kitchen ruled over by the irreplaceable Mrs Boryńska. The building was largely occupied by Jews. On the second floor lived Mr Mizne, owner of a well-known watch-maker's shop at 15 Swiętokrzyska Street. The apartment opposite ours belonged to an elderly gentleman called Mr Prywer, his wife and daughter.

Miss Czesława Prywer, an engineer and lecturer at the Free University, was a decidedly unlucky person. We knew in advance that whenever anything horrible happened – a row between my parents, my mother's ring getting lost, or my attack of 'flu turning into scarlet fever – Miss Prywer, smiling radiantly, would inevitably show up at the door on some completely unimportant and irritating mission. Mr Prywer's daily visits, by contrast, were quite different and non-threatening. He would bring his copy of the Jewish newspaper in Polish, *Nasz Przegląd* [Our Review], when he had finished with it, and receive in exchange *Kurier Warszawski* [the Warsaw Courier], with its wealth of obituaries.

Józef, the caretaker, ruled over the courtyard. Usually drunk, mustachiod, clad in a sheepskin coat and carrying a broom, he was a figure out of Kostrzewski's drawings. He was severe with all pedlars, haughty with servants and obsequious to the gentlefolk. I don't remember his wife, but I vividly remember his sons, particularly Franek – the biggest Don Juan on Świętokrzyska Street. He preyed on the so-called 'younger ones': those who had the most menial jobs, who were most often straight from the country and unaware of the ways of city life.

I remember two of the girls employed by us who were associated with Franek. Solid, squat Zosia gave in to her seducer's charms, but when she discovered he was also having an affair with Rózia from across the hall, she gave him such a hiding that he had to suspend his activities for quite a while. Zosia pulled herself together and eventually left us to take up a position which inspired great hopes – she became housekeeper to a priest. The case of shy, fragile Marysia ended in disaster. I was on holiday and heard from father some time later that the poor girl had gassed herself. Father had a lot of problems as a result of this, and for a long time, Franek was dragged through police stations.

Almost opposite our house, and somewhat set back from the road, was the headquarters of LOPP.* Behind this, in the morning, came an open red Packard taking the uniformed Premier Sławoj Składkowski to work. Despite his grim expression and his majestic beating of his hand against the door-frame of the car, this dignitary did not arouse my interest. A more interesting neighbour across the street was Mr Stefan Cesarski – I could see the inside of his apartment from the window. Mr Cesarski's little shop was in the same building: 'Zofia – Writing Materials and Tobacco Products'. In addition to cigarettes and notebooks, you could get things there which were not sold in other shops: little dolls, corks, pins, cheap jewellery – in a word, junk. Cesarski's most faithful customers were housemaids. He had them to thank, no doubt, for his sizeable (as it was rumoured) fortune. When the traffic in his shop had died down, the owner – an older, stocky gentleman with a web-eye – would stand in the doorway of his establishment, watching passers-by. His better half, Mrs Zofia, done up like some red-haired deity, sometimes took his place behind the counter with a regal expression on her face, so we called her 'Her Imperial

---

* The anti-aircraft league – a very popular organization before the war.

Majesty' ('Cesarski' means imperial). They had two nice-looking, rather reckless sons, one of whom contrived to kill himself riding a motorcycle to Wilanów, with a female passenger, through a famous bend called 'the death-trap'. The other son ended up in Paris after the war and had a Polish wife who became famous in the 1950s, apparently as a striptease artist. I think it is pointless to go on about the fate of this family, although the Cesarskis certainly enlivened Swiętokrzyska Street. It was not they, however, who determined the unique atmosphere of this street. Its distinguishing characteristic was the Jewish antiquarian bookshops scattered thickly between Nowy Swiat and Marszałkowska Streets. Almost all the known Warsaw antiquarians could be found here, often in adjoining houses – which didn't stop any of them from doing business. Similarly, the millinery shops were all on Żabia Street, right by the Saxon Garden. Żabia Street, has disappeared from the map of Warsaw, and today's Swiętokrzyska Street – a broad artery of no distinction – in no way resembles the former narrow, distinctive street of my childhood.

I often dream about the bookshops, and smell their unique odour. I go into Miller's to begin my stroll because this bookshop was the closest, at 13 Swiętokrzyska Street. Behind the counter stands Mr Ruwin Miller himself, superbly matter-of-fact and sedate. He is an elderly Jew without a beard, probably cross-eyed, because it is hard to look him straight in the eye. He is proud of himself and his shop, which, as the sign announced, had been there since 1897. He waits on me, a schoolboy, with respect, because customers like me represent a large part of the shop's profits. He names his price – and now comes the most interesting part of the dream – bargaining. I offer him half as much. Mr Miller shrugs – the transaction no longer interests him – and turns to the next customer. I go next to Kleinsinger's shop, at 19 Swiętokrzyska Street – maybe I'll get the book for less there. But bearded Kleinsinger is asking even more. At Baumkoller's, across the street at number 6, I deal with a salesman. He disappears into the depths of the shop – if I could only just once cross the threshold into that enchanted kingdom! – and returns a moment later without a word. A slight movement of his head means that the book isn't in stock. The great R. Kleinsinger (number 1 Swiętokrzyska Street) can have a copy for me the day after tomorrow but doesn't name a price. When the book's in, we'll talk. I go back to Miller's and say, 'So how much did you want?' Miller repeats the price in a bored tone of voice, I respond with my previous offer of 50 groszy, and we meet half-way. The book's mine. What book? Lesmian's *Łąka* [Meadow], perhaps, or Liebert's *Kołysanka jodłowa* [Fir Cradle]. Before I'm fully awake, I inhale the most wonderful smell of my childhood.

Miller was my father's purveyor. If I suggested that we should acquire some multivolumed work – such as Gutenberg's encyclopedia, *Wielka literatura powszechna* [Great Works of Literature], or the enormous edition, *Polska, jej dzieje i kultura* [Poland, Her History and Culture] – father would pick up the phone, agree a price with Miller, and a moment later, his assistant would bring the work in question upstairs. This was how I got most of the books in my library, but my most beloved books were the ones I bought myself during the course of my never-ending meanderings down Swiętokrzyska Street, with all their disappointments, indecisions, and glorious moments of fulfilment.

Just before war broke out, the normally quiet Swiętokrzyska Street began to resound with an ominous racket which was hard to endure. The Jewish antiquarians attracted swarms of fascist pickets. Sinister individuals in student caps and with canes in their hands blocked the way to customers who wanted to enter the shops. 'Don't buy from a Jew!' was the cry, and a leaflet, *Pod Pręgierz!* [To the Pillory], was distributed (or maybe sold for a few groszy) which included, in addition to journalistic gems, photographs of 'Aryans' (a term which was beginning to replace 'Polish-Catholic') compromising themselves by running errands in 'non-Aryan' shops. At first, these excesses didn't bother me – I even watched them with interest from the balcony. But then my German teacher, Mr Kaftal, got beaten up on his way to give me a lesson. His bleeding face was the first indication of the time that was to come.

THIRTY-SEVEN
The Death of My Father

When I read Malaparte's *Kaputt* immediately after the war, I was struck by the extraordinariness of his descriptions of the Warsaw ghetto. Describing the inferno of the ghetto streets, he mainly stressed the uncanny quietness, 'I went in ... and was immediately overwhelmed by the deathly silence which reigned on streets crammed with an impoverished, ragged and frightened mass. The silence was light, translucent', etc.

This was the complete opposite of my recollections, in which a terrifying roar dominated the ghetto. For many years, I thought that Malaparte, a writer not given to excessive truthfulness, was, even in this case, embroidering the facts – perhaps he had never actually crossed the border of Hell, on whose walls might have been written the words, 'Abandon all hope, ye who enter here'. I recently reread *Kaputt* and the matter was settled in Malaparte's favour. That latter-day Dante entered the ghetto with a companion: 'a tall, young, blonde man with a thin face and cold blue eyes'. That black-uniformed, non-commissioned officer of a special branch of the SS 'strode through the crowd of Jews like an angel of the God of Israel'. It was the sight of him which silenced the roar, and people were dying of fright, as though they'd seen Death himself. One rarely met uniformed Germans, especially those in black, in the ghetto, and to come across one certainly boded no good. A terrifying psychopath known as Frankenstein would come into the ghetto in order to kill perhaps 20 or so passers-by each time. Neither did the others come with good intentions. Because of epidemics, entry into the ghetto was on official business only, but the SS made the most of those occasions to vent their own murderous or sadistic instincts. Fortunately, there existed a kind of street wireless telegraph: passers-by warned each other by word of mouth. I can still hear the stifled whisper of an old woman: '*Me hapt auf die Panskie*'* – which saved me from walking into a round-up.

As a rule, I moved through the ghetto with great caution and, even without any warning, sensed when something extraordinary was happening by the behaviour of the crowd and the sudden eerie quiet. I don't know what threw me off my guard on Saturday 4 October 1941. Perhaps it was the feeling of disquiet in the ghetto. A threat of liquidation hung over the so-called 'small ghetto'. In truth, they had managed to set the limits of the deportations at Sienna Street, but everyone was wondering for how long. In his diary for that day, Czerniaków noted:

> Morning at Brandt's and Lewetzow's with Szeryński. At ten in the morning, a meeting at the governor's about the small ghetto. News is coming in that the small ghetto has been saved. Yesterday, Bischof said that Warsaw is a temporary refuge for Jews. The round–ups of street pedlars has yielded small results.

In taking a piece of the ghetto away from the Jews, the Germans had given nothing in exchange, so a population deprived of a roof over its head caused further overcrowding in the already appallingly overcrowded ghetto dwellings. As a result, the raging epidemic devoured even more people. In addition, the worst news possible was streaming in from the war front. The Germans were enjoying success after success and preparing for a decisive attack on Moscow. It appeared that nothing was able to stop their crushing onslaught.

The weather that day was also not conducive to optimism. It was rainy and unusually cold for October; the first snows were supposed to come in a few days. Because of the low temperature, I was wearing a hat. Had I only left the house that day without covering my head...

---

* They're seizing people on Pańska Street.

I must have been deaf and blind to everything going on around me, because, walking down Leszno Street after work, I neither noticed nor heard that something very unusual was happening. My distraction almost made me bump into a young uniformed German who was standing at the edge of the pavement to receive obeisances from passers-by. I wanted to take my hat off, but it was already too late. The German rushed up to me, knocked the hat off my head and hit me across the face two or three times, breaking my glasses. I was dazed, blinded and covered in blood. Luckily, his next victim appeared, and in this deplorable state I dragged myself home. I knew that nothing terrible had happened – I was alive, my eyes weren't affected, my teeth were still in place. It didn't make sense to see the situation as a loss of face, and yet I had never felt so abused and humiliated as I did now. It didn't improve matters that I wiped my face with a handkerchief. I should have gone in somewhere, washed and tidied myself up, but where? I can only say in my own defence that I was not quite 18 years old and, up until now, no one had hit me in the face. Sore, still bloody and unable to see much, I went home – where else could I have gone? Before I stepped into the hallway at 39 Chłodna Street, I burst into tears. In those days, the staircase was the favourite meeting-place for the residents of ghetto tenements. The apartments were too overcrowded for guests to be invited over, so conversations took place most frequently on staircases, where everyone could join in or leave at will. You could learn the latest news here – brought back most often by the community workers – and hear the commentaries of the more intellectual tenants. When I appeared on the stairs, Father was standing with a few neighbours, discussing the Sienna Street affair. Silence descended. In a voice choked with tears, I blurted out what had happened. Then my father looked at me strangely, and in a very quiet voice, as though talking to himself, said, 'I'm not going to survive this.'

I was taken into the apartment where I was washed and bandaged and, with a compress on my face, went to sleep. At around nine in the evening, Father came quietly into my room carrying a plate with a cake on it. He put the plate down beside me and tiptoed out. Immediately afterwards, I heard my mother scream. I didn't need to be told what had happened. Within seconds, the apartment was full of people. The doctor from across the hall was giving my father an injection straight into the heart. I knew it wouldn't help. A silence descended shortly, broken only by my mother's weeping. Father lay dead on his bed. Cigarettes lay on a bedside table. I took one and lit it. That was the first cigarette I had in my life. Then I went up to the mirror and looked carefully at my swollen face. I remember thinking, in a pathetically childish way:

> Remember this day – 4 October 1941. It is the most important date in your life. Your father is dead because of you. Your childhood has come to an irrevocable end. Terrible times are coming – you got a taste of them on the street today. You are alone in the world – your father will be making no decisions for you. Look at yourself at this pivotal moment in your life.

Was I surprised by what had happened? Oh, no. I had lived through this moment in my imagination dozens of times; I knew it had to happen. Father had not been feeling well, he looked ever worse, ever older, even though he was only 56. In addition to increasing heart trouble, he suffered from boils – a prevalent disease in the ghetto. Each evening, I rubbed him with creams of some kind and bandaged him. I felt like crying when I remembered the sturdy, athletic man of two years ago. A few weeks before the catastrophe, I had taken a photo of him on the balcony. (I took particular care that he wore his armband.) He looked like an old man. I thought that this saddest photograph of my father would be an everlasting memento for my children and grandchildren. Unfortunately, it vanished, together with all the keepsakes we deposited in the law courts on the day we fled.

For my father, the stay in the ghetto, despite our decent living conditions, was a true disaster. He had, during his whole life, been an unusually active man, always doing whatever he had wanted to. Here, for the most part, he had sat passively in an armchair. I liked to sit at his feet. I know he had dark thoughts, was always afraid for me, and wondered how long his financial resources would last. He once said, 'You must know that I am looking after 18 people,' and then added, 'When I'm no longer here, you absolutely must look after the family. Remember that.' Another time, he threw out, with feigned indifference, 'I'm already an old man and won't live for ever. If anything happens to me, be good to your mother. She's not an easy person, but that doesn't absolve you of the responsibility, understand?' I understood that he wanted to prepare me for his loss. Most often, though, he didn't say anything. We were capable of sitting immobile like that until something disturbed our silence.

Occasionally, he'd suddenly leap into action, organize something – the departure to the Weigl Institute in Lwów of a special emissary, for example – or a welfare activity such as adding vitamins to the rationed bread. He would engage in these things for a time – I even remember him helping to carry sacks of vegetables – and then his strength would fail and he would return to his armchair. Once – about ten days before his death – I had to go to the pharmacy for some medicine prescribed for him by Dr Jelenkiewicz. Sitting in the rickshaw, I played out my father's death in a remarkably realistic way, and when I came back, felt unspeakably happy that I hadn't yet lost him.

Our relationship hadn't always been easy. I made him angry, now and then, by going out and not returning until just before the curfew. Sometimes, we would reach breaking-point, but it was hard for me to live without people my own age. For his peace of mind, I should have given up my escapades, rare as they were. Now he lay dead on his bed ('It's lucky he died in his own bed,' Aunt Pański said) and Mother wept ceaselessly; I shed not a tear. His brother showed up shortly; he had been fetched by a policeman living in the area. Our neighbours left us alone and we sat in silence with Uncle and Aunt. (Mrs Boryńska was no longer with us. In September, her son had sneaked into the ghetto and taken his mother out almost by force.)

The day after his death, I delivered the sad news to our relations and friends. It's interesting that almost everyone was sceptical about the cause of the death. They reckoned it was another instance of undeclared typhus. (It seems that they associated the luxury of dying of a heart attack with normal times.) My mother, in the meantime, had contacted the Evangelical Reformed community by telephone, asking for their help in burying Father in the cemetery on Zytnia Street. It was an extremely difficult matter – almost impossible to arrange. The kind Pastor Zaunar, however, managed to intervene, via his community, with the Polish President of Warsaw, Julian Kulski. When we heard of the decision the following day, we saw it as bordering on the miraculous: we were permitted to bury Father in the Evangelical Reformed cemetery, and, furthermore, to take part in the funeral on the Aryan side. I know of no other such instances in the life of the ghetto, although I can't rule out that they may have happened. One way or another, it was an example of unusual kindness on the part of the Evangelical Reformed community and President Kulski – a kindness particularly worthy of being remembered against the background of our situation at that time.

The funeral rites took place on Tuesday, 7 October, in two stages: the first, in the ghetto, consisted of taking the mortal remains out of the apartment and accompanying them to the wall, or, more precisely, to the gate by Kercelak Square; the second, for my mother and me, was transporting the coffin to the Aryan side and taking part in the funeral proper at the cemetery.

Of Father's funeral, I have only disjointed memories of scenes and conversations: a throng of people, some we knew, some we didn't, moving through our apartment; the cortège wending its way down Chłodna Street; condolences, both routine and memorable. Among the latter, I include those offered by a man I never met before (or after), who introduced himself to me as a former colleague of Father's from the bank. This man told me a story about how, a few weeks before his death, Father had come to his house, out of the blue, and laid a substantial sum of money on the table, saying, 'I heard you are having problems,' and vanished as suddenly as he'd appeared. Another friend of my father's held my hand for a long time, whispering, 'He helped us. Now all our hope is in you!' I don't know what I said. I could think of nothing except what was happening around me.

I remember the crush in front of the house and the five of us behind the coffin: me escorting Mother, Uncle Stefan, Uncle Stefek and Aunt Franka. The cortège came to a halt by the wall and the coffin was loaded into a waiting car. After a lengthy checking of documents, Mother and I got into the car and left the ghetto for the first time in a year. The journey was short, the streets we passed strangely empty and quiet. At the cemetery, I was struck by the restful peace and the sight of vegetation. We so much missed greenery in the ghetto that the October landscape of the cemetery seemed like paradise to me, and the funeral to be Father's escape from a land of stony death to a land of eternal natural rebirth.

Although we had only told a few people, a fairly sizeable group of friends gathered at the burial, among them several who were taking no small risk by their presence. We were pleased to see Aunt Konarska, about whom we knew nothing other than that she was living somewhere on false papers, but under her own name. Maryla Roszkowska, the widow of a close friend of Father's, came up to us and asked whether or not we wanted to leave the ghetto this very moment. If so, her apartment on Marszałkowska Street was at our disposal. Remaining on the Aryan side didn't enter into our calculations for a variety of reasons, the first and most important of which was the community's pledge to President Kulski. Nevertheless, Mrs Roszkowska's offer constituted an essential part of our plans for the future. All these things together left me in a state of bewilderment – I remember not a single word of Pastor Zaunar's oration. I also don't remember the moment the coffin was lowered into the ground. It was all going on outside of me: I did not want to see anything, hear anything, understand anything.

When we returned to the car wearing our armbands, the children on Zytnia Street pointed their fingers at us and whispered, 'Look! Jews!' There was no hostility in this, merely curiosity aroused by the sight of the officially condemned. I think that for people who were setting the world on fire, we were pretty pitiful.

After this was published, I received the following letter from Professor Klemens Szaniawski:

Dear Kazik,

I read your account of your father's death in *Tygodnik Powszechny*.* I will refrain from commenting on it, because what is there to say? You might be interested, however, to know that this was not the only case of such a funeral. In the same year, 1941, I attended the funeral of a friend of my father's, Leo Belmont (Leopold Blumental), who had died in the ghetto. He was an unusual man from many points of view. Shortly afterwards, his wife was buried with him. Perhaps I'll have the opportunity to tell you all about this. In the meantime, sincerely... etc.

Klemens.

The letter is dated 23 April 1988. Unfortunately, there wasn't an opportunity to discuss this. All I can state is that I later heard about occasional burials of ghetto residents in Catholic cemeteries. I'm curious whether the Evangelical Augsburg cemetery (where the Belmonts are buried) and the Evangelical Reformed cemetery (where my father lies) were sites of other such burials at the time of the Occupation.

---

* The Popular Weekly: intellectual Catholic newspaper.

THIRTY-EIGHT
Uncle Stefan and Aunt Franka

Uncle Stefan Jermułowicz was the husband of my father's sister, Franka. He was of unprepossessing appearance: short, poorly built and, despite Aunt Franka's efforts, unkempt and slovenly. I once stood on the balcony of our apartment on Swiętokrzyska Street with Uncle Stefek. We saw a strange couple on the other side of the road – Stefan and Franka. Stefek let out a laugh: 'Look, a couple of shoemakers taking a Sunday stroll!' And indeed, Uncle looked like a petty tradesman while short, obese Aunt Franka looked like a little working-class woman. Their appearance, however, was completely deceptive. Uncle was an outstanding doctor and one of the most intelligent and wittiest men in his circle. Aunt, too, was a charming woman with enormous social skills and a sense of humour which I valued highly.

I adored both of them and was a frequent guest at their apartment at 16 Swiętokrzyska Street. These visits had a marked influence on my sexual knowledge. (No, please don't imagine that this was thanks to my aunt, or even to one of her two lively maids!) I was a small boy at the time and I attribute my – strictly theoretical – induction into the world of sex to the books in Uncle's surgery. Stefan was a doctor specializing in treating sexual dysfunction. I don't think he turned away patients suffering with dermatological and venereal diseases, but he was probably the first Warsaw doctor to call himself a sexologist. His advertisements (in his field of medicine, advertising did not constitute a *faux pas*) announced: 'Illnesses, disorders and irregularities in sexual functions. Eugenic consultation in sexual matters'. Uncle was a very successful doctor, and his surgery was visited by pre-war dignitaries whenever their achievements in erotic matters did not keep pace with their political successes.

Uncle wrote each case down in great detail in a huge book: patient's background; state of health; parents' state of health; when he'd had his first erection; when he'd begun masturbating and with what kind of frequency he continued to do so. First sexual relations; possible homosexual incidents; marriage; relations with wife (with all particulars about intensity and feelings of satisfaction); affairs on the side – their genesis and history; present situation within and outside the marriage. And, in particular, a precise detailing of failures in bed, written in a scientific manner but with most of the cases comprehensible to the young reader, who absorbed these handwritten notes of his uncle's with a beating heart and flushed cheeks. Each case was numbered and the key to personal particulars kept in Uncle's strongbox. But what did I care about surnames! I absorbed these stories of sexual disorders as though they were literature about the most intimate of matters, somewhat monotonous, perhaps, but how stimulating to the imagination!

In order to have free access to his study, I visited Aunt at the times my uncle was out and made the most of her great talkativeness over the telephone. At certain times, I could be quite free, because my aunt would be totally absorbed in conversations with her friends – and not just female ones! Because even though my aunt and uncle had the best and most loving of marriages I knew, Aunt had lovers from time to time. As a rule, they were tall, stout, mustachioed gentlemen in their 50s – married or single made no difference. Uncle took no interest in these matters until they became publicly and embarrassingly known. It was my father who most often intervened then. From later accounts, I know about one conversation he had with a certain Mr D., whose affair with my aunt became an open secret. Coming upon the romantic lover in the street, Father casually said, 'You look dreadful, Mr D., you are clearly exhausted ... I think you should take a prolonged rest-cure – starting tomorrow!' Father's concern, and his graciousness, in particular, apparently made an impression on Mr D., who did indeed leave Warsaw on the following day.

However, during his absence, the position of Aunt's lover was discreetly taken up in turn by Mr S.

Both of these gentlemen were far from being paragons of male beauty, but, as I have mentioned, Aunt's shape was closer to that of a ball than to that of a Venus de Milo. Applying my newly acquired knowledge from Uncle's books to imaginings about my aunt's romances, I was acquiring a point of view which would certainly have shaken my future sex life, had it not been for one of the maids, Jadzia, whose exclusive job it was to look after Uncle and his study. The sight of her was an effective antidote to the nightmares which oppressed me. I shortly came to understand why Uncle Stefan was so little upset by Mr D. and Mr S., especially since Aunt often went to take the cure in various Karlsbads, Ems and Kissingens. I have mentioned Uncle's first-rate intelligence, which was vastly above that of an average doctor of embarrassing ailments. He had had an interesting youth, spent partly in Russia, as well as many friends from the revolutionary period who were spoken of in hushed tones. In his *Wspomnienia* [Memoirs], Wacław Solski writes:

> In Piotrogrod, I lived [immediately after the Russian Revolution] with my cousin from Warsaw, Dr Stefan Jermułowicz, who had been mobilized at the beginning of the war. He worked in some army hospital and had a private practice in Piotrogrod, though this was not permitted. My cousin did not belong to any party and was not much drawn to politics. But one floor down in the same building lived Łapinski, with whom he was friendly. Before the revolution, Łapinski had a lucrative position with an insurance company and was very well off. He still had, from those good days, a cache of wines, about which he was knowledgeable. Bringing a bottle or two with him, he spent the evenings in Jermułowicz's apartment. Łapinski belonged to the left-wing Polish Socialist Party, which, in those days, held different views on many things to the Social Democratic Party of Poland and Lithuania.

Debates took place in my cousin's apartment in which Jakub Dolecki, Kazimierz, Cichowski, B. Wesołowski, Z. Fabierkiewicz and others took part. One day, Radek also came, accompanied by the most beautiful woman I have ever seen in my life. She was Larisa Reisner, daughter of a famous Russian professor, who later married Raskolnikov. Larisa Reisner was a journalist, and had published several remarkable books, articles and essays. She died of typhus in the 1920s.

I was aware that, despite his unprepossessing appearance, my uncle wasn't just anyone, but his ascendancy reached its zenith when the satirical *Cyrulik Warszawski* [The Warsaw Surgeon] placed one of his bridge jokes on its cover, making it into a catchphrase among bridge players. I also remember one of Stefan's jokes. To the patient who was surprised that the doctor didn't recognize him, he'd say, 'Your face tells me nothing, sir. Pull down your pants.'

The brunt of many of Stefan's jokes was my Uncle Stefek, and, in particular, what I would term his outstanding sexual attributes. I even recall the heroic poem that Stefan wrote about Stefek, which was read in Konstancin in front of the assembled family to the indescribable delight of the ladies. The title of the masterpiece was 'Pipek and Flipek.' Pipek was Stefek's nickname in the family, Flipek, the name of the dog in Konstancin which was particularly devoted to him. I liked and respected Uncle Stefan, because he had an artistic nature and was a multitalented person – in his spare time, he sculpted and played the piano quite well. One of his patients observed that he looked a bit like H.G. Wells.

Aunt Franka, I loved more than anybody else in the family – much more, I'm ashamed to say, than I did my own mother. Aunt had no children, and all her maternal instincts were focused on me. She hugged me, gave me presents, took me with her to cafés and all kinds of functions. She gave me a wall-clock with a horse which she'd bought in Karlsbad – the single thing which survived from my childhood days and which ended up with people it shouldn't have ended up with. Half of my toys, and later on my books, came from Aunt Franka. A trip into town with my aunt didn't just mean sitting in the Ziemiańska Café at a time when there was nobody interesting there, but also expeditions to the Bagatelle (the Dakowski garden where my aunts gathered), or to Philips on Mazowiecka Street, which was considerably closer. The outings to the Bagatelle (located, of course, on the street of the same name) involved a ride down the Aleja Jerozolimska in a *droshky*. This was a splendid experience, because Aunt would now and then bow ceremoniously to passers-by, and, following her example, I did, too. On one occasion, not being able to see in the crowd of pedestrians anyone bowing to her, I asked her to whom she was bowing so nicely. 'No one,' she replied. 'But it's more fun bowing while you take a drive, isn't it?' I had to admit she was right, and from then on, I always bowed to the street, even in a totally strange town. Thanks to this, the feeling of strangeness passed.

Aunt Franka detested my mother. Although she never talked about it, I knew full well that she considered her a hopeless person – a true scourge of God. I was completely on her side, and during my father's frequent absences, I valued the times I spent with his family as a wonderful break from the horrendously exhausting, ceaseless attentions of the woman who'd given birth to me. My father wasn't much bothered by the antagonism. He didn't take Franka very seriously, but he did adore Stefan. This found expression not only in frequent contacts with Uncle and Aunt, but also in financial matters. Uncle was well off, but he couldn't afford the investment which his idea for manufacturing a sensational anti-eczema cream demanded. So, just before the war, my father built and equipped a factory which was to start producing this medicine – let's call it 'Exemina' – but the project never took off. During the military operations in 1939, Uncle was mobilized as a reserve officer. I remember him going off, to Luck, I think, in his galoshes and with an umbrella, and Aunt winding an unusually long scarf around his neck. He returned, shortly, to live through the September gehenna with us. We, and Uncle and Aunt, lost our apartments at that time, and fled from 16 Świętokrzyska Street with Uncle Stefek to friends at 1 Boduen

Street, where we all lived until the forced move to the ghetto in October 1940.

In the ghetto, Stefan and Franka lived with Uncle Stefek on Sienna Street. Uncle worked as a doctor, not just in his specialty. He was very overworked and we saw little of him during this time. In the summer of 1941, both Stefan and Franka came down with Fleck fever. Aunt had a serious heart condition and Uncle also was not in particularly good health, so their chances of survival were reckoned as minimal. And yet, they both survived, thanks mainly to the efforts of Dr Jakub Penson, though it seems as if the ghetto's entire medical force had made it a point of honour to preserve their lives. Stefan and Franka emerged from this terrible illness looking old and emaciated. Aunt Franka's weight-loss was particularly frightening. Both were present at my father's funeral.

The change of boundaries in the Jewish quarter herded them into a strange little apartment in the courtyard of a through-building connecting Ogrodowa and Leszno Streets, through which swarms of ghetto residents passed every day. It was a single-storey house, a kind of gate-house, somewhat set back from the street. I visited them nearly every day. Uncle returned to his medical duties, and as he was leaving the house, Aunt wrapped a scarf around his neck. While he was out, she bustled around the house and, even though she was still not well, retained her optimistic outlook on the world, which for her was now reduced to an uninterrupted stream of human apparitions flowing past her window until curfew time. It was both visually and aurally intolerable, yet Uncle and Aunt lived in their terrible quarters until the first liquidation *Aktion* at the end of April 1942. They were driven out of their apartment at that time, and herded in a crowd, amid continuous shooting, to the *Umschlagplatz*. Those who fell were finished off on the spot. How Aunt Franka and Uncle Stefan managed to run from Leszno to Stawki Street, I do not know. I know only that Aunt died of a heart-attack at the *Umschlagplatz*, and her body was put on a truck together with the bodies of many other victims of the *Aktion*. Uncle was herded into a wagon, but at the last minute, someone recognized that he was a doctor and pulled him out of the crowd. Wearing an armband with a red cross on his shoulder, he returned to the ghetto, and from there, with the help of friends, got on to the Aryan side in a Jewish work brigade. A diamond ring that we gave to Uncle and Aunt just before leaving the ghetto made this escape possible.

For a while, Uncle concealed himself in some hideout, but then doctors whom he knew placed him in one of the Warsaw hospitals as a patient. He wasn't badly off there, because thanks to his so-called 'good' (i.e. reasonably Aryan) appearance, he could not only move freely around the hospital but also go out on to the street. It might seem that such a circumstance – a doctor hiding out in a hospital – would be dangerous, but one must remember that Uncle had never had anything to do with hospital medicine, and had not been active in medical circles. As a patient, he apparently enjoyed universal goodwill, and could regard his situation as advantageous.

During this period, probably in the early spring of 1943, I met him in one of Warsaw's less-frequented cafés. I no longer remember exactly where the meeting took place, but I think it might have been the café on Noakowski Street, which I regarded as fairly safe. It had two entrances: the kitchen door led into the courtyard of a through-building. Arranging to meet him there, I took a seat facing the front door (a habit which, as I have already said, has stayed with me to this day) and as close as possible to the door leading out to the back. I doubt if these precautions would have been of any real use in the event of actual danger, but I felt decidedly better for having an escape route. My appointment with Uncle had been initiated by him through a whole chain of trustworthy intermediaries. My nanny, Agnieszka Cieslak (known as Jagusia) had been the chief organizer. I remember the shock I got when Uncle Stefan appeared at the door of the café. I had waited for him quite a long time and imagined that he'd be the same as he was when I had seen him in the ghetto. As it was, his appearance appalled me: he was tiny, old and emaciated. He wore an over-sized coat which reached to the ground, which made him into a tragicomic figure, something like Charlie Chaplin. Fortunately, (I immediately thought to myself) he did not look like a Jew in hiding because no Jew in hiding would have dared go into town in such a bizarre outfit.

In order not to attract attention, we greeted each other without any sign of joy. The café was relatively empty, so we talked in an almost normal tone of voice. At first, Uncle appeared nervous, but my behaving normally had a calming affect on him. As for me, I felt better once I'd put his dreadful old man's coat into the cloakroom. He began by saying that he wanted to share some information with me about my father's estate. I was certain to survive the war – I must survive – so it was important that I knew about various matters known to him and which Father hadn't had time to discuss with me before he died. In fact, I no longer remember Uncle's instructions. I erased them from my memory when I realized, after the war, that our prewar existence was gone, like a lost Atlantis, and references to what had once been were met with shrugs of indifference. I expressed the hope that, with his help, I would see to everything after the war, but he smiled sadly, as if to say, that he didn't believe in his own survival. I questioned him about his living conditions in the hospital, which he said were satisfactory. He even bragged that he played bridge twice a week. 'You all thought I was useless,' he said, 'But there, I'm regarded as an expert.' I told him about myself, of course, my work in Wołomin, and even about Helenka. 'It's good you have a girl,' he said. 'Such matters, used in moderation, are good for the nervous system.'

'I know that from your books,' I said.

'How?' he asked.

I told him about my visits to his study when Aunt was talking on the phone. He seemed amused, 'Oh, that Franka!' he said. I sensed that he wanted to talk about her death and quickly cut him off, afraid that he'd fall to pieces. He asked whether I knew anything about what had happened to Stefek, but I hadn't heard anything about him after leaving the ghetto.

'He's a lucky devil,' he said. 'He always manages to squirm out of tight situations.' I offered to help him financially, but he turned me down, saying that he did not need any money. I argued that, with the sale of the villa, Mother and I were in an excellent situation. He was unmoved.

'Don't waste a penny on me', he said, 'I'm an old man, and all alone, at that.'

We were together for not quite an hour, and left the café separately. He looked me in the eyes when we parted, saying, 'Look after yourself. Who knows, perhaps we'll meet again.' Then he shuffled off, his long coat sweeping the floor. I stayed at the table for a while. I doubted that I would ever see him again.

Shortly afterwards, I was informed of Uncle Stefan's death. He had committed suicide by swallowing a whole phial of sleeping pills. The reason was depression. He had convinced himself that he had been recognized by someone on the staff. This may have been so, but I think really that he had had enough of the struggle – that he'd simply lost his strength. And that he didn't see the sense, even if he survived, of starting everything all over again by himself.

THIRTY-NINE
Uncle Stefek

My Uncle Stefek Berman was a very attractive man: tall, superbly built and slender, despite his years. He gave the impression of being athletic but, in fact, he never exercised, and was known for his huge appetite. So it is not surprising that he aroused enormous envy in his fat and eternally dieting family. To complete the physical portrait of Stefek, the dominant feature of his face was his prominent nose – not Semitic, but straight and even quite shapely, and exceeding the normal dimensions of human noses.

Stefek was always superbly dressed, though he didn't care about clothes in the way that my father did. Stefek's elegance was freer, less perfectionist, and because of that, more in keeping with his personality. To me, he seemed elegant in everything he wore – even his underwear.

Like Father, Stefek graduated from the Górski School. Both appeared on the list of graduates for 1903. (The fact that Stefek was two years younger doesn't speak well of my father's educational achievement!) After that, they both studied at technical institutions in Germany, with my father not finishing his studies and Stefek finishing them commendably with the title of Mechanical and Electrical Engineer.

The beginning of Stefek's professional career looked very promising. Following a practicuum in Germany, he got, despite his youth, a responsible and very well-paying position in St Petersburg. Wacław Solski, whose *Wspomnienia* [Memoirs] I frequently quote here, provides the following sketch of young Stefek in 1916. The occasion for the meeting was not a happy one: the *raison d'être* being a visit of condolence in a Moscow hotel after my Grandfather Bernard's death. Wacław writes:

Aunt [my own grandmother] was sitting in an armchair some distance from the table. The guests spoke little...not at all of Bernard. Among them was Dionizy, that distant uncle of mine, who was completely bald, said nothing, just smiled painfully. My cousin Stefek, Uncle Bernard's son, some 15 years older [10 years, in fact] than me was there, too. He had just come from Piotrogrod, where he was working as an engineer. When went through Piotrogrod on my way back to Pskov, he invited me to dinner at an elegant French restaurant on Nevski Prospekt. He said he ate there all the time. He was probably exaggerating – the restaurant was unbelievably expensive – but he was undoubtedly well-off...Miss Oleńka, who lived in the same hotel, made coffee on a primus in the bedroom and gave it to the guests. She didn't know a word of Polish and my Aunt didn't speak Russian, but they communicated somehow and were friends. 'Naturally,' Aunt told Dionizy once, 'you are quite right. In Warsaw I wouldn't be able to receive her, but here, abroad, where we are staying temporarily...' Uncle Dionizy didn't answer, but just smiled wanly as he was doing now. Oleńka, slightly too plump, with faded china-blue eyes, was the mistress of an officer of the Moscow garrison. My cousin had met her that very day. 'Please sit down,' he said to her. 'You keep running around with the coffee, rest a little, at least.' Oleńka smiled her thank. She had good manners and knew how to behave. She sat at the table, but didn't raise her eyes. She looked down the entire time. I was sitting next to her. She passed me a cup of coffee; I went to put some sugar in it and a cube fell on to the carpet. I bent down quickly to pick it up and saw that my cousin Stefek had his hand on Olenka's leg, slightly above the knee...

Exactly. Oleńka's leg serves here as a kind of metaphor for Stefek's later fortunes. It was all such a pity...He was an unusually intelligent, witty man of great personal charm. He could certainly have achieved a great deal, but he devoted himself solely and exclusively to the role of a Don Juan. Everything else he did was secondary to his primary goal: acquiring ever new, ever more (and later, ever less) attractive ladies.

The 30-year-old Stefek began working as an engineer in a good position in industry. At the same time, he published several books on popular science, which undoubtedly enhanced his social standing. I read (well let's say I leafed through) two of these works. The first of them, *Składniki powietrza oraz ich zastosowanie* [The Components of Air and their Properties],* appears to be a solid exposition of the subject. It closes with an interesting and forward–looking discussion of energy:

> The main goal today is to split the atom by artificial means and to release its enormous stock of energy... At the present time, work in this area is still only in a nascent state; nevertheless, scientists may, before too long, be forced of necessity to devote themselves entirely to this end. Ever-increasing mining may create shortages of coal in a few hundred years. It will take the earth thousands of years to replace the depleted ones. We are certain, however, that scientists of that time will succeed in tapping different sources of energy – energy, for example, which lies latent in metals waiting for scientific knowledge to release it.

I don't know to what degree these observations, made more than 70 years ago, can be seen as discoveries, but it seems to me that Uncle Stefek showed a deep understanding of what is today a key question. His second work, *Wstęp do teorii względności Einsteina* [Introduction to Einstein's Theory of Relativity],** is a reputable, popular exposition of the subject (as I was assured before the war by a trustworthy physics teacher). I know, too, that

---

* Warsaw, 1922.
** Warsaw, 1923.

there was a third book, on the subject of the scientific implications of aerial combat, but I know no details of it.

Uncle did not hold his position for long, unfortunately, because, as he maintained, he didn't share a common language with his boss, who was a complete idiot. (According to Stefek, the world was divided into very pleasant fellows and complete idiots.) His publications at Trepte's not only yielded no profits, but, I suspect, required him to underwrite them. It was a grim situation, but what was his loving brother Gustaw there for? He wouldn't refuse to save his very talented and underappreciated younger brother. From then on, the handsome, grown-up *Wunderkind* and acknowledged genius, Stefek, was totally maintained by my father. It was still said, from time to time, that he was doing something: giving lectures in physics to student nurses, for example, and acting as a director of my father's shipping company, Presto. But this occupation quickly came to an end, together with Presto, and Uncle's needs did not grow less. He lived in the family's former residence on Szkolna Street, where he employed domestic help in the shape of my former nanny, Jagusia, frequented the best restaurants and bars, and travelled abroad to fashionable resorts. In short, he led the life of a wealthy playboy. A lot of his time was taken up in playing bridge, at which he was a true master. I don't believe, however, that this was a source of income for him, because, to use his favourite expression, he played with a lot of good-for-nothings. Abroad, he entered dance competitions and won awards – in Pörtschach, for example. I remember this Austrian town because I saw Uncle's certificate there.

Stefek's chief occupation and greatest passion in life, as I've already mentioned, were his romances. He had many magnificent adventures, one of the ladies enamoured of him – a married woman – even committed suicide, lending thereby a touch of the macabre to his legend. A very wealthy woman drove him around Warsaw and its environs in her impressive cabriolet. He travelled to Krynica with one of his mistresses and to Abacja, that summer, with another one. The fact that he ruined our cousin Anielka B. (he deprived her of her virtue) became the source of serious family conflict. There was also no lack of romantic love – as represented by his involvement with Janina B., who was completely and utterly in love with him, and to whom he went back, from time to time, as to a safe harbour.

The well-known sexologist, Uncle Stefan, opined something like this: 'Stefek is, in his way, a male phenomenon. Not only is he very well endowed by nature, but he has achieved the highest degree of initiation in these matters.' I am sorry that I know relatively little about my uncle's achievements in this area – I mean about the most remarkable ones. I was simply too young to engage in any kind of exchanges on the subject with him. I just remember him making a passing remark to me about a party which he gave in his good days in St Petersburg: the gentlemen wore evening dress and the ladies, nothing at all except jewellery. I felt sorry for the ladies who must have been shivering with cold. On another occasion, in Konstancin, I suddenly noticed that his lower lip was swollen. I remember that he was sitting on my bed, talking about some bridge move (when they were one short, I was allowed to play bridge with the grown-ups). I commented on his lip, and he responded by saying that a certain lady had bitten him when they were kissing. This surprised and, indeed, seriously worried me. After that, I saw girls as vampires lying in wait for the chance to bite my lips to a bloody pulp. A few years were to pass before I realized that things weren't quite that bad.

Stefek was a frequent guest at our house, despite the violent and open hostility which existed between him and my mother. During the winter, he always came to Sunday lunch. Lunch was served at 3 p.m., but Stefek always arrived earlier and closeted himself with my father in his study. I don't know what the brothers discussed, but I am sure that Uncle moved from there to the dining-room better off to the tune of a week's worth of subsidy. According to my mother, this injection of money improved his already formidable appetite. When a last piece of meat remained on the platter, Stefek always enacted the same piece of pantomime. He looked round the table and then put the meat on his own plate, saying, 'Since you insist', and devoured it.

In the summer, Stefek came to Konstancin for weekends – a great source of pleasure to me, because I very much enjoyed his company. He impressed me with his slightly cynical attitude to life. He helped me to solve maths problems and brought up for discussion his rehearsed dislike of poetry. He regarded the writing of poetry as the height of stupidity. 'How can anyone write according to a set rhythm, and in rhyme, at that?' he would ask, partly in order to provoke me. He had respect for Słonimski, who, even though a poet, was redeeming himself with *Kronika tygodniowa* [the Weekly Chronicle]. He once showed me Zuzanna Ginczanka's collection, *O Centaurach* [Of Centaurs], dedicated 'To Mr Stefek because he doesn't like poetry'. 'A pretty girl,' he said, 'and not a stupid one. It's a shame that she spends her time on senseless things.'

Just before the war, I sensed that my uncle was going slightly downhill. He was no longer young and the period of his greatest conquests was behind him. Jagusia confided to Mrs Boryńska (our cook) that Stefek had picked up a very young girl in Zakopane, who had stayed and then made off with his wallet. Stefek no longer travelled abroad, he even bragged– and this I found hard to believe – that he ate lunches 'for white-collar workers' costing a złoty and a quarter. This may have meant that my father had reduced his allowance; or perhaps it was intended for my mother's ears (she was always annoyed that he was subsidised by my father).

A few weeks before the war broke out, Stefek presented my father with a plan for immediately liquidating his affairs, insuring the Warsaw apartments and moving right away to Zaleszczyki (a resort on the Romanian border) with the whole family, including Uncle Stefan and Aunt Franka. 'It's August,' he argued, 'we'll take off for the summer, no one will notice our leaving. If the situation improves, we'll return to Warsaw having lost nothing, in the event of war, we'll be in the ideal place from which to move off on further travels. What we need to do right away is buy or rent a house in Zaleszczyki, so as to avoid any surprises, and then hit the road!' The plan was ingenious, and I am surprised that my father didn't go along with it. There were, of course, many arguments against leaving, but few as compelling as the arguments in favour. Father would later say that staying in Warsaw was the stupidest decision he had ever made in his life.

When war broke out in 1939, we lived with Stefek at Uncle Jermułowicz's, and then at 1 Boduen Street. Stefek's good humour didn't leave him for a minute. He played bridge nearly every day, and when his female partners nervously asked, 'Tell me, how do I play bridge?' he would reply, 'You really play very nicely!' This was still paradise, after which came the hell of the ghetto. Stefek lived on Sienna Street with his sister and brother-in-law, and still came to our house in Chłodna Street for Sunday dinner prepared by Mrs Boryńska. I don't recall him ever working. I also know nothing about any of his sicknesses – in fact, I don't remember him having any except for frequent colds.

In late evening on 4 October when my father died, a specially assigned policeman brought Uncle Stefek to our apartment. He helped bravely with the complicated task of burying Father in the Evangelical Reformed cemetery. At difficult moments, he comforted me as well as my mother. It seemed to me that their traditional antagonism abated with Father's death. Uncle came to live near us in a beautiful house at either 20 or 22 Chłodna Street (we were living at number 16). He shared an apartment with an outstanding architect, Jerzy Gelbard, and his wife, Bela. Bela was, at the time, involved in a romance with her future husband, Władysław. Jerzy, too, had a lover. The apartment on Chłodna Street was, therefore, used one night by Bela and Władysław, and the next by Jerzy and his mistress. Their personal relations were excellent and Stefek also had no complaints about his housemates, other than the fact that Bela's eccentricities tired him a little. I remember his describing one particular scene: Bela's old dog suddenly lost consciousness – probably from too much to eat. Bela rushed into Stefek's room shouting, 'Mr Stefek, save my Fifi!' Stefek ran out of his room and poured water from a glass on the poor, fat (apparently lifeless) dog. The animal revived and Bela fell on her knees in front of Stefek, kissed his hands, and said, 'I will never forget you for this. You've given my Fifi her life back – you are a miracle-worker!' (I am telling this story exactly as Stefek told it, though I am not sure now what the dog's name was, or indeed, if it wasn't a male.)

All this took place against a backdrop of the most appalling human tragedy in the midst of a ghetto under sentence of death.

How could anyone care about a dog which had fainted, or, more to the point, joke about similarly trivial subjects? And yet one could – because no tragedy is entirely relentless – and even in the most desperate situations, a man is saved, if only for a moment, by his sense of humour. And my uncle wasn't used to talking about terrible things; he approached everything with a sort of ironic detachment. In this way, he was able to keep a healthy distance from the horror of the ghetto. He lived in it, yet, at the same time, apart from it. I understood him very well.

My relations with Stefek changed at the time of my father's death. I was no longer a little boy and, in addition, I had, in some sense, passed an important test. I managed not so badly with the immeasurable problems of ghetto existence and, more to the point, in accordance with my father's wishes, I helped the whole family. I noticed, then, Uncle's rather ostentatious tendency to respect my decisions, in particular about the absolute necessity of fleeing the ghetto without relying on jobs in German workshops and *Ausweise*. When we left through the law courts, we gave Stefek some valuable object – I don't remember what – which enabled him to organize his own escape. Contact between people was becoming increasingly difficult; there were constant round-ups and, as a consequence, Stefek lost touch with Aunt Franka and Uncle Stefan. I don't know the details of how he left the ghetto, only that, after a short stay in Warsaw, he went to Rzeszów because of his former lover, Janina B. I have no idea how he got to her. I know only that she was working as a teacher there and living with her mother in a room rented from strangers. Stefek settled near them and spent a lot of time with them. Apparently he was happy with his existence and had no cause for concern. I have no idea why the Gestapo showed up at the B.s' lodgings. Nor do I know why they took Stefek without taking down any of his credentials. As he was being taken away, he paused in the doorway for a moment and said to both women, 'Thank you for everything.' Janina's mother later confided to her landlords that she was worried that Stefek's parting words might cast suspicion on her and her daughter. She may have been right, as the following day, the Gestapo came back and took both women away as well.

After the war, Janina's brother, Professor B., returned from England to Poland. Apparently, he held not the Gestapo but my uncle responsible for the death of his mother and sister. He regarded the comment, 'Thank you for everything', as evidence of criminal carelessness. He, the newly-arrived-from-England Professor B., knew for certain that had it been he who was being led to his death, he would have behaved differently. He also tried to convince one of my acquaintances that Stefek was the curse of Janina's entire life. Had it not been for him, she would have survived the war in peace. That there might have been other things no less important to her than surviving the war never even occurred to him, despite the fact that his area of medical specialty entailed some knowledge of psychology.

FORTY

Konstancin

I dreamed again about our villa in Konstancin. Dilapidated and black with age, it looked incomparably worse than it looks in reality today. I was going to live in it, it appeared from the dream, but unfortunately circumstances didn't allow it. The war was in progress and I was a hunted man threatened with exposure. I went to a house which stood next door – it looked like Attorney Domański's villa, a ruin you pass on the way to Obory. Some people were living there, as lights flickered from burning candles. I went inside. The interior was grim. Nobody took any notice of me. A woman with a child at her breast said in a half-whisper (not to me) that there was a room for rent on the second floor. Her voice seemed strangely familiar – perhaps it was the voice of my first wife. Someone shone a candle up stairs so narrow that I couldn't squeeze up them. The stuffy air gripped me by the throat. I gave up on renting the room and went outside. The woman with the child didn't even look at me. And again, I was gazing at our villa, which now looked completely different...

One doesn't have to be a Freudian to work out the fairly obvious symbolism of this dream: a desire to return to a former home best symbolizing the family's prewar situation; an attempt to settle down in a neighbouring hovel, and the impossibility of finding the means to feel at home under such conditions. Could this be a continuing war-syndrome, a subconscious, deepseated threat of a return to the time of Occupation which had been my lot in life, while all that came later seems precarious, granted to me only as a temporary reprieve? It is amazing the hold which that period still has over my subconscious, dominating it completely. Some 40 postwar years lived in 'normal' (were they normal?) times have been unable to redress the effect of that five-year period. It still impinges on me, blackmails me and always threatens to return. Everything which came later and which constitutes the real substance of my life – my work, women, apartments, travels, friends – seems temporary, fleeting, and subject to annihilation at a stroke. And deeper down still, the old prewar life is rendered completely unreal, mythologized, closest to the heart.

Konstancin – the symbol of our prewar life, and so tragically neglected today – represents a world of memories not just for me but for many people. I came here as a small child, long before my father thought of buying the villa. I lived with my mother in a villa called 'Moja' on Sienkiewicz Street. The front of the castle was occupied by Senator Stefan Laurysiewicz, business tycoon and one-time colourful figure of bohemian Paris and lover of Zapolska. We occupied two rooms on the first floor in the centre of the building. The really interesting things, however, took place on the ground floor. That's why every morning, I would call out, 'Cocoa down', which meant that I wanted my breakfast downstairs in the passageway. I fell down the stairs once and bumped my forehead. My father was expected, and so my mother and nanny pulled my hat down low to cover the bump. Unfortunately, Father's first words were 'Why did you pull his hat down over his forehead?' and the ensuing row was all the worse.

'Moja' came back to life recently in the blind poet Jadwiga Stańczak's beautiful reminiscences. She was the daughter of the prewar owner of this villa with whom we were very friendly. She gave Miron Białoszewski a fascination for Konstancin, and he devoted a considerable part of his remarkable prose to singing its praises.

As a small boy, before the purchase of our villa, 'Promyk', I had visited the famous boarding-house 'Leliwa'. I remember a popular writer of the time, Alfred Konar (*Siostry Malinowskie* [The Malinowska Sisters]), sitting in an armchair and exchanging light banter with Mrs Karwosiecka, the owner of the hotel. Mrs Karwosiecka, choking with laughter, was saying through her tears, 'Oh, that Mr Konar, that Mr Konar, he grows wittier by the year' – the wit in question looking as if he was long past 80. I also met the head of the Konstancin village, the popular writer Wacław Gąsiorowski(author of the novel *Mrs Walewski*, which was adapted for a famous film starring Greta Garbo). On on occasion, Father and I paid him a visit on some matter – I think about the poor state of Przebieg Street.

At that time, Konstancin was a very appealing place ('And what harm did that do to anyone?' as one of my friends would say.) The stream which fed Lake Jeziorka was crystal clear; we bathed in it and lounged on Konstancin's beach. There was a beautifully maintained park with tennis courts, splendid restaurants and cafés and little kiosks where we bought sodas and drinks of all kinds, not to mention caramels and 'Anglas' – thin chocolates. These were poor on taste, but they came with cards which we would collect and paste into special albums. Anyone who collected a whole set of cards got an album, and something else, as well. (I don't remember what, but to us little ones it was all enormously interesting). Finally, there was the railway station – the trysting-place for the youth of the area. My God! I waited there for hours just to catch a glimpse of a certain Marysia, who would ride by on a silvery bicycle, not even deigning to look at me.

Słonimski revealed his deep attachment for old Konstancin ten years before he died. I knew that he went there (his early poem 'Letnisko' [Summer Resort], written in 1916, testifies to this, but it is hard to find any particular sentiment in it). But in 1966, writing *Jak to bylo naprawde* [How It Really Was], Słonimski revealed what may have been, up to that point, an unconscious nostalgia: 'You see, how can I say it, there's something very soothing there, something like Konstancin in 1912.' And he starts to speak about green foliage and butterfly-nets; about how the air smelled and how green it was; and about sausages from before the First World War. And about rolls you can't find any more and cold milk and fish and braided bread, and everybody going to the station after dinner to wait for the Warsaw train. And how you hear the engine-driver, old Charon, give a long, drawn-out whistle and the train arrives, and we all look to see who's arrived, because the passengers are our dear dead. And that when he, Rajzeman, arrives, his daddy and N. and old friends will wait for him on the wooden platform where there are gas-lamps, and they'll ask him about everything and talk by lamplight in their former home long into the night about films, books and jokes which appeared after they had died. And then, he said:

> I'll go with them to the station and wait on the platform for passengers from the other side of life, and if it is someone who was pleasant and had friends he'll have someone to wait for and talk to. If it is someone who wasn't liked, he'll stand jealously on the side. And we'll all be young again and kiss girls from the Leliwa boarding-house, and stroll around the garden holding a girl by her small warm hand just after it has rained and everything is fragrant, and you can take long, deep breaths such as I've not been able to for a long time.

If I have never thought seriously about leaving Poland it is probably because of Konstancin – that odd place, unlike any other, where even despite abandonment and neglect, a beauty looks down on us which can be recaptured, if only in memory.

It is a beautiful summer morning sometime in the 1930s. I am sitting in a deckchair by the porch at our villa in Konstancin reading Edgar Wallace. At my feet lies old, fat Nelka (who performs the duties of ratter), breathing heavily. She is ugly and noisy, but unbelievably intelligent. A little further off, Father and his brother are playing rummy under an umbrella. All is quiet. Not a word is spoken. Now and then from the kitchen come the voices of women preparing lunch. Birds rustle at the top of the spreading oak tree which is giving me shade. Everything is idyllic, when suddenly, little Nelka leaps up and runs to the gate, barking. (She is too fat to react to passers-by; she puts herself out only for visitors.)

'Who the devil is it?' Father asks crossly, glancing at the gate.

'Bloody hell! There's never any peace in this house!' Uncle complains.

'Damn!' I say, without looking up from my book.

Mr and Mrs W. appear at the gate. They walk up the avenue towards us, smiling broadly, certain that their visit will bring pleasure to their hosts.

'That's all we need!' hisses Father, throwing his cards down in fury.

'Goddamn those bores!' adds Uncle.

'Damn!' I repeat, leaving *The Three Just Men* at the most interesting part.

Both gentlemen get up to go to meet the guests.

'What a pleasant surprise!' Father shouts from a distance, beaming with pleasure.

'How nice of you to think of us!' Uncle says. Nelka barks furiously, giving true vent to her feelings. There are endless hugs and I, too, try to assume a joyous facial expression.

This is my introductory lesson in elementary hypocrisy.

I learned from somebody who specializes in Konstancin history that 'Promyk' belonged, from 1911, to Maria Białkowska, from 1923 to the wealthy cement-works owners, Maria and Antoni Eiger, and then to the Choromańskis. Mrs Silberstein bought it in 1928. She was the widow of the well-known Łódź factory owner Stanisław Silberstein, and liked to live in the style of a lady. Her Konstancin residence, 'Nowina', occupied a large area, with a second, smaller house in the style of a Polish manor-house, probably originally intended for the servants. It was this house (what used to be called the 'dependency'), together with a considerable piece of land, that my father bought from Mrs Silberstein, entrusting the eminent architect Maksymilian Goldberg with its reconstruction.

I remember the exact moment the deal was struck with Mrs Silberstein. The conversation took place on the terrace at 'Nowina'. I was served hot chocolate, and then driven around Konstancin in a black Chenard-Walker limousine driven by a uniformed chauffeur. When I came back, we were *de facto* owners of 'Promyk'. Our property was in a prime location: in the heart of Konstancin at the intersection of Przebieg and Mostowa streets, right by the River Jeziorka. We went kayaking on the river. It was my father's favourite occupation. I often dream about the bamboo-covered banks of the lake which we would cut through to pick waterlilies and watch frogs sunning themselves. I adored those moments, because I never had my father so much to myself as I did then, in the summer, on the river.

Before the war, Konstancin was a beautifully maintained place, enjoyed especially by the Warsaw plutocracy. The Society for the Improvement of Summer Resorts, which, in 1890, undertook the creation of 'a new resort by the name of Konstancia' (after the owner of the parcel of land, Countess Potulicka from Obór), wanted to establish 'a model suburban resort for the wealthy population of Warsaw, the need for which has been felt for a long time'. The lay-out and building of it was completed very quickly and in accordance with official plans. The dominant style was Viennese Secession,* and Konstancin had several large houses shaped like little castles. Each house was different – the only one of its kind. What a pleasure it is, in this age of standardized architectural ugliness, to look at the remaining gems of Secessionary building! To own a villa in Konstancin was a form of ennoblement, but, at the same time, it brought with it the obligation of caring for one's house and the whole area. In summer, one could meet '*tout Varsovie*' (anyone who was anyone in Warsaw, that is) on the avenues in the park. Houses belonging to Polish and Jewish tycoons stood close to each other, for instance, those of Jan Wedel, Gustaw Wertheim, Józef Landau and the brothers Pfeiffer. Then there were the villas of eminent lawyers: Marian Niedzielski, Franciszek Paschalski and Ludwik Domański. But the glory of Konstancin was the famous writer Stefan Żeromski's house, in which Anna and Monika Żeromska lived after his death. The writer Zenon Przesmycki-Miriam also lived there, as did the aforementioned Wacław Gąsiorowski. Add to these the composer Ludomir Różycki, the mathematician Kazimierz Kuratowski, the journalist Witold Gielzynski and, finally, the editor of *Mucha* [Fly], Władysław Buchner, and you will have some sense of the uniqueness of this place.

---

* An architectural style popular in the late nineteenth and very early twentieth centuries.

Our 'Promyk' was a fairly modest villa, but nonetheless stylish (it was, after all, a Polish manor-house), and extremely well-suited to our family's needs. My room on the first floor overlooked the drive, which was flanked with lilac trees. Beneath me lived our gardener, Antoni S., and his wife, Eleonora. There's no question that Antoni was an excellent craftsman and performed his various duties to our complete satisfaction (as we used to say in letters of recommendation for servants). Despite his advanced age (he was well over 70), he was remarkably energetic and managed our garden and orchard extremely well, in addition to taking care of the livestock (dogs, hens, ducks, geese) and seeing to everything in the house and surroundings that needed to be preserved or repaired. Antoni had a wife who was a few years older than him and who helped with the lighter household chores. It appeared, from his rather boastful stories, that his wife had once been a great beauty and that their oldest child was actually not his, but the daughter of some 'Mr Director' of a sugar factory, or maybe a brick-works. Despite this, he regarded his marriage as a great success, and I never remember him treating his wife with anything other than love and respect. Antoni had no vices: he didn't drink or smoke and was unusually industrious. He worked in the garden all day, and in the evening, after supper, he'd don a pair of steel-rimmed glasses and read to his wife a 'five-penny special' (in other words, the *Mały Dziennik* [Small Daily] – the cheapest and most unenlightened of newspapers). He sounded the words out with difficulty, in a monotone which remained the same whatever he was reading. I don't know whether his wife listened, or whether she dozed off, but Antoni didn't stop until he'd read the paper from cover to cover and got his money's worth. Antoni and Eleonora had long ago moved off the land, but they retained many peasant traits, the most burdensome of which was kissing the hand of everyone who, in their estimation, was 'gentry'. Me they called 'Young Master', and only after a very long time of my begging them, with my father's support, did they start to call me by my first name, making up for this by referring to me in the third person: 'Has Kazik seen the neighbour's kittens?' for example, or 'Someone's come to see Kazik.'

Antoni and his wife brought to our Konstancin establishment a dowry in the shape of two wonderful mutts: Nelka and Ciapek. Like them, both dogs were well advanced in years, and both were jewels of the species. From the very first, the terrier-cross, Nelka, assumed the role of cuddly plaything. We adored this pudgy crosspatch for her almost unbelievable intelligence. Once, towards evening, she disappeared in a completely mysterious fashion, and a long search of house and garden yielded no results. Was it an amorous escapade on the part of a sworn spinster? There was nothing we could do, so we went to bed with heavy hearts, and Antoni, as usual, locked the gate for the night. In the morning, Nelka was found by the frontdoor of our villa. She was completely exhausted, her claws bloody and torn. It turned out that, not having returned for the night, she had dug her way in, which must have taken her many hours of onerous work. What moved us most about her was her sense of guilt – she apologized to everyone in turn, and seemed amazed that, instead of being severely punished, she was caressed.

Ciapek was a ginger mongrel with no aspirations to the genteel life. Even though no one would have given two cents for the foxy Romeo, he enjoyed great renown. Antoni recounted to me a story told by the local dog-warden. The man decided to capture that Nestor of Konstancin mongrels. Two or three times he almost had him, and each time, Ciapek managed to escape. His trick was simple and effective: instead of running away, as any ordinary dog would have done, he ran straight at the dog-warden and swerved off just as he reached him. The dog-warden congratulated Antoni wholeheartedly for owning such a master of subterfuge.

From May to October each year, our villa was vibrant with life, particularly on Sundays, when the entire family and a whole mass of friends descended. At two in the afternoon, a traditional country dinner was served in the garden: sour milk and potatoes, stuffed chicken *ą la polonaise* with cucumber salad and fruit of the season. (I might add that in those days, chicken tasted like chicken, and milk smelled like milk.) The gardener and his wife were traditionally invited to Sunday dinner. On weekdays, they cooked for themselves. Once, when we arrived in Konstancin unexpectedly, Eleonora offered me potato soup. All the other culinary extravagances of my later life pale into insignificance beside the memory of this soup.

We had a very cordial relationship with Antoni. To me, he was the authority on the practical knowledge of nature. I sometimes rose at dawn to listen to birdsong as I helped him with gardening chores. I liked his wife, too, and gladly listened to her prattling on about what things had been like 50 years ago in manor-houses and farmhands' cottages. We regarded these people almost as family, and so were particularly upset when they let us down right at the beginning of the Occupation.

Shortly after the military *Aktion* finished in 1939, our neighbours in Konstancin informed us of the things that were happening in our villa. Out of the blue, Antoni had become politically active, and had begun proclaiming how good and just Hitler was. Under the new government, he assured his listeners, there would be no masters, people would finally be equal and unbelievably well-off, while Jews would get the punishment they deserved for their transgressions (echoes of the *Maly Dziennik* [Small Journal]?).* Strangest of all, the hoary agitator gave the impression of not being quite sober. It transpired that just after we'd left, when detonations and sinister lights in the sky were bearing witness to Warsaw's fate, Antoni settled himself in for good in our well-stocked cellar. In the course of a week or two, he had downed several dozen bottles of fine wines set aside for my wedding by my father. Thus bolstered by aged Burgundy or Tokay, he suddenly felt like the owner of the villa, freed by the ruins of Warsaw of all the rights and duties by which, up until now, he had been bound. What could he do in this situation except spread the news about the good Hitler?

It is hardly surprising that we broke off all contact with the gardener, and took care that he knew as little as possible about our whereabouts. At a later date, we found out that our villa was occupied by Fritz Schultz, one of the biggest tycoons of the General Government and the owner of the largest workshop in the Warsaw ghetto apart from Többens'.

---

* Reactionary, anti-Semetic journal, published before the war by Catholic clergy.

Schultz was a tradesman from Gdańsk who realized, in time, that exploiting slave labour in Occupied territories was a golden opportunity for growing rich. When he moved through his fur workshops, the Jews working there could have greeted him with the words: '*Ave Fritz, morituri te salutant!*'* A cripple who could barely move on his crutches, he wasn't a criminal type, but a cynic indifferent to the moral aspects of his own situation and prone to humane gestures, especially when they didn't cost him a pfenning. This cheerful beneficiary of crime had a devoted slave in Antoni. I think of this with sadness, as I do about our dogs, Nelka and Ciapek, fawning on the new occupant.

Had we been interested in preserving our house in the best possible state for the postwar period, Schultz's presence would have had its advantages. (Houses lived in by so-called 'wild' tenants were most often discovered in ruins after liberation.) Unfortunately, 'Promyk' no longer belonged to us, as, driven by financial necessity, we had decided to sell our villa to Mrs L.

Mrs L. was the widow of some forester or farmer who was vice-minister of some insignificant resort in some insignificant administration – some fly-by-night of the 1920s (it could be checked, but why bother?) She was still not bad looking and, it was said, had a Jewish lover with whom she did excellent business in works of art taken out of the Warsaw ghetto with the cooperation of the Germans. Her lover, it was thought, was the antiquarian Alfred Schulberg, who was later murdered in the ghetto. Mrs L. did well out of the Occupation. She had pots of money and happily spent it on Jewish real estate – apparently, she liked anything Jewish. Trading 'non-Aryan' property was forbidden, so she acquired houses and villas for less than half their worth. Because there was some risk that it wouldn't be easy to prove possession after the war (for example, as a result of the physical extermination of the contractors), she protected herself with a mass of pre- and postdated purchase-and-sales agreements, in order to take the property over in the most expedient way possible when the Occupation bonanza came to an end. We made contact with her through the lawyer Pilecki,

---

* Those who are about to die salute thee, Fritz.

and the transaction was concluded with the assistance of the (indispensable) lawyer Ploska.

I remember very clearly the drawing-room in which she received us in a seductively see-through peignoir, among beautiful furniture and items the origins of which I preferred not to think about. Even though we were outside the law, I have to admit that she treated us well. I have associated the moment of relinquishing our villa with the moment of acquiring it and the visit to Mrs Silberstein, although this time, no one offered me hot chocolate or took me for a ride in a Chenard-Walker limousine. My mother and I signed dozens of documents, and then came into possession of what was then a large sum of money (the property was actually worth about three times as much). Because we were sad about Konstancin, we soon shared this money with our friends who owned 'Moja'. It became, for a while, (selling 'Moja' was a mutual decision), 50 per cent ours.

We didn't let Mrs L. down and survived the war. Immediately, in January 1945, I went to Konstancin with my future wife, Helenka. We went on foot. (Our own legs were the only possible means of locomotion.) We found the villa in excellent shape, but completely cleared of our furniture and belongings. Antoni and his wife greeted us with low bows and a tearful account of how the Germans had taken everything away. I learned later from our neighbours that Schultz and his entire household had cleared out overnight, taking none of the villa's fixtures or fittings with him. (Why should he have taken anything?) Clearing the house of every last thing was obviously the doing of Antoni and his family, who lived in Klarysew. The only things left were his own primitive implements. When we were invited in to tea (a guest in the house is God in the house) and I walked into Antoni and his wife's room with Helenka, I noticed the sole surviving object from my prewar existence – a child's wall-clock with a boy on a horse, brought back years ago by Aunt Franka from Karlsbad. I wanted to take it right away, but Antoni begged me to leave it until my next visit, when his own clock would be back from repair. When, a few weeks later, I appeared in Konstancin again, there was no sign of either Antoni or the clock. I could, of course, have gone to the S. family in Klarysew and extracted the stolen goods with the help of the militia, but I thought to myself, why begin a new life by making claims which the local population would construe in a certain way, i.e., they have returned and are looting Polish property? The war was only just over for me; why start it up again – and against whom? Against a couple of illiterates, 80-year-old Antoni and 85-year-old Eleonora? I gave up on our possessions, and if I have any regrets, it is just for the clock – the little base-metal souvenir of my chilhood and its memories.

In the 50 years since the end of the war, I have been nostalgic for strolls down Konstancin's Przebieg and Mostowa Streets, to look at 'Promyk', hidden in the depths of the garden – the sole surviving landscape of my childhood. A few months ago, I went there again with friends, and couldn't believe my eyes . . . No, it wasn't a ghastly dream: my 'Promyk' had vanished. The new owner had razed it to the ground in order to replace it with his own, no doubt impressive, residence.

Bertrand Russell once wrote that for old people, the past becomes a greater burden by the day. If it really is so, then I should not regret the disappearance of 'Promyk'; indeed, perhaps I shouls rejoice in its loss. The pity is that so far, I have not been able to do so . . .

FORTY-ONE
My Parents and Brother

My parents lived together like cat and dog. When I was little, they still slept together in their marital bed and from time to time, father took mother on long journeys abroad. Afterwards, he moved onto the couch in his study, and went abroad, apparently, on his own. But was he really alone? I once unlocked a drawer in his desk with a key I selected with great effort and found a passport application for a woman I didn't know, with her photograph pinned to the documents. At that moment, unfortunately, I heard sounds. I shut the drawer in a panic and didn't dare open it again. I had only time to catch a glimpse of the young woman's photo. Shortly afterwards, my father went to France on business, and stayed there rather longer than usual. He sent cards first from Paris and then from Le Havre, where he was to receive a large shipment of tobacco, but oddly enough, the postmarks were from Nice. It would have been beyond my mother's powers of observation to notice this discrepancy, but as for me... To this day, I don't know whether he underrated me, or whether he (quite correctly) depended on my male solidarity.

The relations between my parents grew worse each year. Father spent more and more time out of the house, and when he was at home was so uncommunicative it was almost as if he weren't there. I saw him most often at dinner-time, which was a sort of ceremonial ritual. After dinner, he went to bed. He often spent evenings in town with overseas guests or Polish contractors, of whom there were many to entertain. Sometimes, he would come home with friends and play bridge or some other game until late. Despite the fact the doors were closed, shouts and laughter came from his study, together with the acrid smell of tobacco. Mother preferred father's absences to these card-games, which burdened her with having to feed the guests. She referred to them as a lot of freeloaders and con-artists. 'I saw Wanda L. on the street today wearing a new fur coat,' she berated father, 'I wonder how that poor man of hers found the money to buy Persian lamb?' Father took no notice of the obvious innuendo in these comments, but who knows if she wasn't right? After all, he was famous for his largesse, and when he walked out of the house in the morning, 'clients' were already standing at the gate with sob-stories about their lives. Father would interrupt them by getting straight to the point – 'How much?' – and rarely refused to help. Sometimes, he distributed these gratuities from his *droshky*, which drove up very smartly from the stand on Czackiego Street. I was proud of Father's openhandedness, and in Mrs Wanda L's case, happy that she wouldn't have to suffer from the winter's cold. I liked her because, when I was little, she would sit me on her lap, smothering me with kisses and saying that I smelled of milk. She smelled good, too, and it was so nice to snuggle up to her that I certainly wouldn't have denied her that Persian lamb.

My parents' quarrels and rows became more frequent. When they thought I was asleep, their stifled, far-from-friendly whispers reached me from the adjoining room. This should have had a terrible effect on my psyche, but it didn't. I have to confess, with some embarrassment, that not only was I not upset by the bad relations between my parents but I was entirely indifferent to them. I adored Father and took his side in every marital dispute. I regarded my mother as an impossibly quarrelsome person and was convinced that right could not be on her side. I am somewhat embarrassed today by my rigid certainty in this matter.

Did I suspect that my father's overseas guests were the products of his imagination? Probably, although from time to time, I saw them for myself. For example, once I was with Father in Konstancin and a certain Mr Amancic came round, who, in keeping with his name, looked just like a screen lover. Amancic was, if I am not mistaken, the owner of a tobacco plantation of which my father was representative for Western Europe. The gentlemen were pondering the text of a letter in German, and even though both knew the language very well, were having trouble with a particular word. It never occurred to either of them, of course, to consult me in the matter. I let Father and Mr Amancic struggle for a while, and then asked what they would give me were I to make a suggestion and should it prove acceptable. They assured me that I could have whatever I liked. So I said casually, 'kompensieren'. They received this enthusiastically, and, in addition to general acclaim, I got a wonderful bonus in the shape of a fountain-pen. It was a Parker Vacuumatic – a transparent miracle with horizontal veins. It must have cost about 40 złoty, and was bought at Mary Mill's shop on Marszałkowska Street, which had the most beautiful pens in the world. Just crossing the threshold of that establishment as a customer was an unforgettable experience.

Let us assume, then, that the guests really did exist, and that Father devoted one evening a week to them and the Polish contractors. They probably went to the 'Adria' nightclub, or some other establishment. Another evening was devoted to playing cards, while the end of the week was usually given over to family and friends in our villa in Konstancin. (We rarely entertained on Swiętokrzyska Street; Konstancin served as the centre of our social life.) That would account for four evenings. So to whom, and to what, did father devote three evenings a week? I was almost certain that father 'had someone', but I never thought it was as serious as, in fact, it was. I don't think my mother quite understood the situation, either. On top of that, in 1938, my father's health problems started, and a sinister box of nitroglycerine appeared among those personal objects of his which I so much liked. The Occupation pushed marital misunderstandings and complications of an emotional nature far into the background. Father died in the Warsaw ghetto on 4 October 1941, and it seemed as if his death would put an end to those conflicts once and for all. It didn't. Directly after the war, my father's lover, though still unseen, made her presence known in a very singular way. The next scene of the drama was enacted in the cemetery.

The Evangelical Reformed cemetery on the corner of Zytnia and Mlynarska Street played, and continues to play, an important role in my life. I spent a lot of time there after I left the ghetto because I felt very safe there, although that feeling was based on the illusion that the Germans wanted to leave the dead in peace. I no longer had a home; Father's grave was the only place which linked me to the city. After the war, I didn't immediately go back to Warsaw. Mother, too, spent the first postwar period in Łódź, and so it wasn't until towards the end of 1945 that we were able to put up a gravestone. During the time that we lived outside of Warsaw, we paid numerous visits to Father's grave, and on several occasions, found fresh flowers there which hadn't come from anyone we knew. Stanisław, the cemetery's gardener and caretaker with whom I was friendly, told me in confidence that a young woman with a little boy was bringing the flowers. This set my imagination working. I wanted to learn everything I could about this mysterious woman. I even offered Stanisław a substantial sum of money in exchange for putting me in touch with her. Unfortunately, my efforts were fruitless. My father's mistress apparently wanted no contact with me, because that might entail encountering my mother. My mother, in turn, managed to extract from Stanisław the details of the visits, even though I had asked him to keep quiet. She reacted in a surprisingly tragic way. I assumed that, since she had reconciled herself to the existence of a rival when Father was alive, it would have been all the more easy for her to accept the situation after he had gone. As it turned out, however, Mother was happier in the role of widow than wife, making full use of her legal rights to Father's grave and of highly embellished memories. The fact that another woman had shattered her illusions drove her to the point of a nervous breakdown. In addition, that hussy had had the nerve to come to the grave with her bastard and express surprise that we – the widow and son of the deceased – still hadn't bothered to erect a stone for him! I don't know what my mother said to Stanisław, but if he had repeated even a part of it to that other woman, it is hardly surprising that we never got to meet. Mother expended an enormous amount of energy on this matter, and prohibited me from making any contact with 'that whore', making it clear that if I did so, she would, at the very least, kill herself.

It is hard for me to say now to what degree this blackmail weakened my efforts to trace Father's mistress and her son. I probably did what I could, but I was too busy to visit the cemetery every day. Despite frequent visits to Father's grave, and even despite a letter sent through Stanisław to the unknown woman, I wasn't able to establish contact with her or my brother. Yes, brother, because there is no way she would have visited the grave of a man she had been close to with a boy who was not his son. She eventually stopped coming. When I pressed Stanisław about her, he swore that he had given her the letter and that he hadn't seen her recently. I think he was telling the truth and that she probably went overseas with the child.

Who was she? Who is she? I am still certain that she wasn't in the ghetto. Was she hiding on the Aryan side by herself, or with somebody who gave her son a name? Perhaps she didn't need to hide at all. I often think of her, and particularly of him – my brother. Does he exist in reality or just in my imagination? Did his mother tell him who he was, or did he, against her best intentions, remember the modest plaque in the cemetery in Warsaw? Perhaps we have passed each other on one of this world's many streets. Perhaps we will find each other thanks to this book.